.

Building Inclusive Elections

Elections around the world are plagued with the problem of unequal levels of participation. This can have profound consequences for election results, representation and policies. This book focuses on the interventions that can be used to redress the turnout gap and other inequalities within the electoral process.

The book defines the concept of *inclusive voting practices* to refer to policy instruments which can reduce turnout inequality between groups and mitigate other inequalities within the electoral process. Studies from around the world then examine how policies can affect inclusivity on election day. This includes research on enfranchising felons and migrant communities; compulsory voting; voter ID requirements; voter registration practices; investment in electoral management; gendered electoral violence; accessible voting practices; and overseas voting. As a result, this book will be of interest to scholars of democracy, democratic theory and elections, as well as having major policy implications worldwide.

The chapters in this book were originally published as a special issue of the journal *Policy Studies*.

Toby S. James is Professor of Politics and Public Policy at the University of East Anglia, Norwich, UK. He has published widely on electoral integrity, political leadership and the policy process. His books include *Elite Statecraft and Election Administration* (2012) and *Comparative Electoral Management* (2020). He is a co-convener of the global Electoral Management Network.

Holly Ann Garnett is Assistant Professor of Political Science at the Royal Military College of Canada and cross-appointed at Queen's University, in Kingston, Ontario, Canada. Her research examines how electoral integrity can be strengthened throughout the electoral cycle, including electoral management, registration and voting procedures, election technology, civic literacy and campaign finance. She is a co-convener of the global Electoral Management Network.

Building Inclusive Elections

Edited by
Toby S. James and Holly Ann Garnett

Routledge
Taylor & Francis Group

LONDON AND NEW YORK

First published 2021
by Routledge
2 Park Square, Milton Park, Abingdon, Oxon, OX14 4RN

and by Routledge
52 Vanderbilt Avenue, New York, NY 10017

Routledge is an imprint of the Taylor & Francis Group, an informa business

British Library Cataloguing in Publication Data
A catalogue record for this book is available from the British Library

ISBN13: 978-0-367-50950-7

Typeset in Minion Pro
by Newgen Publishing UK

Publisher's Note
The publisher accepts responsibility for any inconsistencies that may have arisen during
the conversion of this book from journal articles to book chapters, namely the inclusion
of journal terminology.

Disclaimer
Every effort has been made to contact copyright holders for their permission to reprint material
in this book. The publishers would be grateful to hear from any copyright holder who is not here
acknowledged and will undertake to rectify any errors or omissions in future editions of this book.

Contents

Citation Information

The chapters in this book were originally published in *Policy Studies*, volume 41, issue 2–3 (2020). When citing this material, please use the original page numbering for each article, as follows:

Chapter 1
Introduction: the case for inclusive voting practices
Toby S. James and Holly Ann Garnett
Policy Studies, volume 41, issue 2–3 (2020), pp. 113–130

Chapter 2
Restoring voting rights: evidence that reversing felony disenfranchisement increases political efficacy
Victoria Shineman
Policy Studies, volume 41, issue 2–3 (2020), pp. 131–150

Chapter 3
Are inequalities in representation lower under compulsory voting?
Eric Guntermann, Ruth Dassonneville and Peter Miller
Policy Studies, volume 41, issue 2–3 (2020), pp. 151–171

Chapter 4
Conceptualizing more inclusive elections: violence against women in elections and gendered electoral violence
Paige Schneider and David Carroll
Policy Studies, volume 41, issue 2–3 (2020), pp. 172–189

Chapter 5
Electoral integrity, voter fraud and voter ID in polling stations: lessons from English local elections
Toby S. James and Alistair Clark
Policy Studies, volume 41, issue 2–3 (2020), pp. 190–209

For any permission-related enquiries please visit:
www.tandfonline.com/page/help/permissions

Notes on Contributors

Joseph Anthony, Department of Political Science, Oklahoma State University, OK, USA

David Carroll, The Carter Center, Atlanta, GA, USA

Alistair Clark, School of Geography, Politics and Sociology, Newcastle University, Newcastle upon Tyne, UK

Ruth Dassonneville, Department of Political Science, University of Montreal, Montreal, QC, Canada

Holly Ann Garnett, Department of Political Science and Economics, Royal Military College of Canada, Kingston, ON, Canada

Eric Guntermann, Department of Political Science, University of California, Berkeley, CA, USA

Toby S. James, School of Politics, Philosophy, Language and Communication Studies, University of East Anglia, Norwich, UK

April A. Johnson, School of Government and International Affairs, Kennesaw State University, Kennesaw, GA, USA

David C. Kimball, Department of Political Science, University of Missouri–St. Louis, St. Louis, MO, USA

Bridgett A. King, Department of Political Science, Auburn University, Auburn, AL, USA

Peter Miller, Brennan Center for Justice, New York, NY, USA

Kevin Pallister, Department of History and Political Science, Bridgewater College, Bridgewater, VA, USA

Sierra Powell, Department of Political Science, Mount San Antonio College, Walnut, CA, USA

Paige Schneider, Department of Politics and Department of Women's and Gender Studies, The University of the South, Sewanee, TN, USA

Victoria Shineman, Department of Political Science, University of Pittsburgh, Pittsburgh, PA, USA

Introduction: the case for inclusive voting practices

Toby S. James ● and Holly Ann Garnett ●

ABSTRACT
The voter turnout gap has plagued many elections around the world, with differential levels of participation between groups having the potential to effect election results and policy outcomes. Despite this, there has been little empirical or normative theorization of the interventions that can be used redress the turnout gap and other inequalities within the electoral process. This article defines the concept of inclusive voting practices to refer to policy instruments which can reduce turnout inequality between groups and mitigate other inequalities within the electoral process. This is anchored in a strategic-relational theory of structure, agency and political change. Different state responses are conceptualized and the normative case for an interventionist rather than repressive or laissez-faire approaches is set out. A research agenda is set out which is taken up in subsequent articles in this special issue.

Introduction

Writing in 1960, Schattschneider (1960, 98–111) noted how only approximately 60 out of 100 million eligible voters in America cast their ballot. Considering the possible effects of universal turnout he suggested that:

> The whole balance of power in the political system could be overturned by a massive invasion of the political system … the unused political potential is sufficient to blow the United States off the face of the earth. (98)

Fast forward into the twenty-first century and the consequences of voter turnout – or non-turnout are felt in the US and in other countries around the world. Whether it is the US Presidential election, landmark referendums such as the UK Brexit referendum, or the contest for the Nigerian Presidency: voting matters. The effects of the ballots cast at the polls have decisive impacts on national politics, public policy and even the broader international system. However, the votes that are *not* cast make a profound difference too. Turnout levels are often low, uneven and the results of many elections may have been different with fuller participation. This has a renewed importance in established democracies where new electoral cleavages have arisen. It is commonly thought, for example, that these cleavages are based around age (Norris and Inglehart 2018), but since young people are much less likely to vote, electoral outcomes are less likely to be in their favour. Meanwhile, variations in turnout have a continued importance in electoral autocracies which are struggling to make the full transition to liberal democracy because, amongst other reasons, turnout is reduced by threats of electoral violence, keeping autocrats in power.

Voter turnout is affected by many factors, but the machinery of the electoral process plays a crucial role. America has a long history of the political elite using racially-based discriminatory practices to deter citizens from voting (James 2012). The passage of the 1965 Voting Rights Act was designed to eliminate this, but concerns remain today as restrictive voter ID requirements have been rolled out across many states (Hasen 2012). The US experience, however, is too infrequently situated into broader international experience. Threats to inclusive voting practices are emerging elsewhere, as the UK and Canada have introduced, and revised their voter identification requirements. In Africa, biometric technologies have required citizens to have their fingerprints taken before registering and voting. Poor provisions for overseas voters have prevented diaspora populations from voting in central America and elsewhere. Violence against voters remains a fundamental problem which deters many groups from going to the polls.

The academic literature in this area remains underdeveloped. Democratic theory rightly preaches that elections should be "free and fair" (Dahl 1971), but rarely makes reference to the importance of inclusive and convenient polling practices. There are "best practices" in the international community (Carter Center 2014), which argue for inclusive procedures, but these remain unconnected to political theory. Work by political scientists in the US on American democracy does not necessarily capture the nature of the threats in other parts of the world, or propose workable solutions to them. A broader reconceptualization of the concept of "inclusive voting procedures" is required to unify these literatures and enable a global approach to promoting fuller turnout.

This introduction to the special issue on inclusive voting practices will begin by considering the nature of group-level inequality in voter turnout worldwide. It will then review existing work on how institutional procedures can shape voter turnout. Next, it will define the concept of inclusive voting processes through a strategic-relational approach. Different state responses to voting inequality are considered and the case for an interventionalist approach is laid out. Finally, the special issue ahead is briefly summarized, which takes on the agenda for considering inclusive voting practices.

The global turnout gap

Literature on voter turnout has long demonstrated that the characteristics of people who turn out to vote, and the characteristics of those who stay away are not the same. Some of the most important socio-demographic variables considered in this literature include age, income, education, gender, ethnicity and disability, as well as attitudinal variables such as political interest (Smets and van Ham 2013). It is important to note, however, that much of this literature rests on the study of established democracies.

First, studies have broadly demonstrated that voter turnout increases from youth to middle age, and then experiences a slight decline for the oldest age groups. The reasons for lower voter turnout among the youngest voters stem from a variety of factors including lower levels of political interest, civic duty, social pressure and the perceived importance of voting (Jankowski and Strate 1995; Smets and van Ham 2013; Strate et al. 1989). Literature on voter turnout has also suggested a slight decline in turnout among seniors, possibly due to health issues or difficulties in getting to the polls (Cutler and Bengtson 1974; Norris 2002; Smets and van Ham 2013). These studies suggest that turnout levels among groups of voters, and perhaps even generations of voters, are rarely equal.

The socioeconomic model of voter turnout (Brady, Verba, and Schlozman 1982; Verba and Nie 1972) posits that an individual's social status, including the type of job, level of education and income, is an important predictor of voter turnout. These studies suggest that education influences a variety of factors that directly influence the choice of whether to vote or not, including civic skills, political attitudes and feelings of efficacy, and the social networks that instil a duty to vote (Burden 2009; Emler and Frazer 1999). It is worth mentioning that the scholarly community is increasingly sceptical of the argument that education actually causes higher voter turnout, with some arguing that education level serves as a proxy for other factors relating to social status, family background and other early life influences (Burden 2009; Kam and Palmer 2008; Persson 2015). Nonetheless, the relationship between education and turnout has been demonstrated both in the American context and cross-nationally, though it is important to note that some scholars have found that the predictive power of education is lower, or even non-significant, in some Western European countries (Gallego 2010; Norris 2002).

The relationship between gender and voter turnout has also been well-studied. Firstly, lower levels of turnout among women may, unsurprisingly, exist in places where women's civil rights are less secure (Desposato and Norrander 2009). Additionally, some research has also suggested that gaps in political knowledge and interest between men and women may also relate to unequal levels of turnout (Carpini and Keeter 1996; Lizotte and Sidman 2009; Mondak and Anderson 2004; Verba, Burns, and Schlozman 1997). These gaps in turnout could be due to a number of reasons, including differential educational attainment, the availability of time to devote to amassing political knowledge, or gendered patterns of employment.

Voters from ethnic minorities have also been demonstrated to have lower levels of turnout than other voters. A variety of reasons for this phenomenon have been studied. Most scholars acknowledge some potential influence of lower socioeconomic status among some minority voting groups. Other studies focus on structural barriers to voting, suggesting that lower turnout among minorities may be related to voter suppression, or cases of electoral laws that unfairly disadvantage minority groups (Hajnal, Lajevardi, and Nielson 2017). Other research suggests it is more of a matter of mobilization or empowerment (Banducci, Donovan, and Karp 2004). In the American context, for example, Fraga (2018) finds that ethnic and racial minorities turn out to vote at lower rates largely because they are not mobilized to be engaged with politics.

Finally, research has demonstrated a sizable turnout gap between citizens with and without disabilities. Research from the United States, for example, has suggested about a 20-point turnout gap between those with and without disabilities (Schur et al. 2002). This may be related to a variety of reasons: including polling place accessibility and lower registration rates (Schur 2013; Schur, Ameri, and Adya 2017). Additionally, citizens with disabilities may have lower levels of social capital (Schur et al. 2002), a phenomenon also found for populations with low levels of health (Mattila et al. 2013). These voters may also not be part of the networks that would encourage them to vote, characterized by higher levels of income and education. Finally, citizens with disabilities may have a lower sense of efficacy to participate in politics, especially if they are not part of the afore-mentioned social networks that encourage civic engagement.

According to psychological models of voting, political interest is key to explaining whether a voter will turn out or not (Blais 2000). Citizens with higher levels of political interest will pay more attention to politics and election campaigns. Importantly, that inter-est may translate into greater political knowledge, which may decrease the information costs of voting, such as forming political preferences, researching candidates and deter-mining where and when to vote (Carpini and Keeter 1996; Popkin and Dimock 1998; Zaller 1990).

To demonstrate the significance of the variables mentioned above, Table 1 presents a multi-level logistic regression model of the predictors of an individual's responses that they "vote always", with data from the 6th wave of the World Value Survey. Unfortunately, disability and being a member of an ethnic or racial minority are difficult to measure at a cross-national level and are therefore not included in the analysis. It also includes two important control variables related to the electoral laws in a country: whether voting is com-pulsory and the type of electoral system (Blais and Aarts 2006; Blais and Carty 1990; Blais and Dobrzynska 1998). The results support the previous discussion regarding the relation-ship between gender, age, education, income and political interest and voter turnout.

See Appendix 1 for more details about data.

In sum, there exist clear turnout gaps based on a variety of individual characteristics, from age and gender to disability and health. The question now remains: how can these gaps be closed?

Table 1. Predictors of "Vote Always"

	0. (1) "Vote Always"
Female	−0.04**
	(0.02)
Age (linear)	0.03***
	(0.00)
High School Education	0.14***
	(0.02)
Post-Secondary Education	0.36***
	(0.02)
Income Steps	0.01***
	(0.00)
Interested in Politics	0.58***
	(0.02)
Compulsory Voting	1.11***
	(0.26)
Mixed Electoral System	0.26
	(0.29)
Proportional Representation Electoral System	0.22
	(0.25)
Constant	−1.51***
	(0.21)
Rho	0.16
	(0.03)
N (Individuals)	77,813
N (Countries)	55

Note: Multi-level models. Standard errors in parentheses *** $p < 0.01$, ** $p < 0.05$, *$p < 0.1$.

Existing work on inclusive voting practices

Inclusive voting practices are defined in this article as policy instruments which reduce inequality in the electoral process for citizens, including, but not limited to the voter turnout and registration gap.[1] There are many other aspects of the electoral process which can do this, such as the electoral system design. Here, we focus on how citizens to register to vote and cast their ballot.

The idea that voting processes can affect turnout, inclusivity, and by extension, democratic outcomes, is not new. It has been conceptually underdeveloped, however, and remains absent in many definitions or discussions of democracy and electoral integrity. The traditional pillars of democratic theory were silent on the issue, for example. Minimalist approaches to defining democracy, such as those set out by Dahl (1971) and Przeworski (1999) identify many features of elections that are prerequisites for a state to be defined as democratic – but these include little about how voting takes place other than that it should be done in secret. In contrast, substantive theorists define democracy as the realization of certain principles. For Beetham (1994), for example, this is political equality and popular control of government – but there is no detailed mapping of the electoral institutions that can help to realize this.

Detailed policies for realizing this goal of equal turnout is more prevalent amongst the international community. The third wave of democratization and globalization led to the development of global networks of international actors who sought to define standards for how elections should be run, which were sketched into international treaties, political agreements, interpretative documents and other sources (Carothers 2003; James 2020, 160–196). Such agreements have been consolidated into assessment manuals so that they can be used by observers to evaluate elections. As the Center (2014) manual details, this includes a commitment to a variety of practices that seek to ensure inclusively and political equality. To take one example, the United Nations Convention on the Rights of Persons with Disabilities, adopted in December 2006, calls on states to:

> ensure that persons with disabilities can effectively and fully participate in political and public life on an equal basis with others, directly or through freely chosen representatives, including the right and opportunity for persons with disabilities to vote and be elected. (United Nations 2007, 21)

These agreements are landmark moments towards the realization of inclusive voting practices. In fact, these statements are often taken as the definition of electoral integrity itself (Norris 2013). They remain unconnected to political theory, however. Allowing political actors to define what inclusive practices work removes the role of the academic research to assess, refine and change "best practices".

Modern political science largely overlooked electoral practices as an area of study, instead focussing on voter behaviour and the effects of electoral system, until Wolfinger and Rosenstone's seminal (1980) work responding to the question *Who Votes?*. They produced some of the early empirical work on why voting practices can make a difference. Over time, many more studies followed. These were mostly based on evidence from the US, many triggered by the politics of the National Voter Registration Act (for a review see, James 2012). Studies gradually have expanded to other established democracies, however (see, for example, Garnett 2019a, 2019b; Germann and Serdült 2017;

Goodman and Stokes 2018; James 2011). Outside of Western democracies, work has been less frequently published with exceptions including Virendrakumar et al. (2018), who charted the (non) availability of inclusive practices for disabled voters in Africa.

Additionally, existing research has for the most part been framed within a rational choice (institutionalist) framework, but this has been a subject of criticism. Wolfinger and Rosenstone explicitly started with a rational choice conception when they explained that " ... we find it useful to think in terms of the benefits and costs of voting to the individual ... The easier it is for a person to cast a ballot, the more likely he is to vote," (Wolfinger and Rosenstone 1980, 6–8). Rational choice theory has been much criticized, however (Aldrich 1993). Given the marginal difference that a single vote can have – voting is an entirely irrational act anyway. It is therefore important to understand the cultural and normative context in which voting takes place. As Galicki (2018, 41) argues, "voting can be viewed as an act of belonging or acceptance of the "system"". She therefore sets out sociological institutionalism as an alternative approach. This includes a focus on the wider set of informal norms and the cultural context in which individuals vote – rather than just the formal-legal institutions and how they structure incentives.

There has been some work to conceptualize different types of practices to promote equal turnout. For example, James uses the concepts of expansive and restrictive forms of electoral administration according to whether they increased or lowered turnout in a meta-analysis of earlier studies, and places procedures onto an 11 point ordinal continuum (James 2010). Similarly, Pallister uses the term election administration inclusiveness to refer to "the degree to which the administration of the electoral process facilitates or hinders the ability of eligible citizens to vote" (Pallister 2017, 3). Procedures were then ranked on a three-point scale.

Other work has considered the political and policy consequences of inclusive voting practices. Do they favour the parties or candidates from an ideological position? What are the policy consequences? Are some procedures, for example, capable of redressing the severe economic inequalities that are present in most societies? Some scholarship has sought to use the questions to argue that electoral practices have consequences for the theorization of the state. Theories of the state are meta theories about the nature of the state, it's relationship with citizens and in whose interests it serves (Dunleavy and O'Leary 1987). The liberal democratic model of the state saw it as a neutral arbiter between competing interests. Elite theory instead argued that the state can be shaped by the incumbents to suit its own interests. James therefore argued that governing elites would be tempted to choose voting procedures that maximized their chances of winning seats. Meanwhile, in their earlier writing, Piven and Cloward (1983) claimed that the battle for inclusive voting procedures involved attempts to redress racial and class struggles.

There have been several advances, but there are also notable gaps. It seems to be widely recognized that normative theory is important for justifying elections as a method of rule, but says nothing about the details of how elections should be run. There is evidence that voting and registration procedures matter, but they tend to draw on empirical studies of the US. There are some theoretical works conceptualizing the causal effects on institutions and citizens, but these are not always developed in full.

What are the basic requirements for underlying theory? First, it must include both the effects of calculus as suggested by rational choice theorists and the role of cultural context set out by sociological institutionalists. It is not an either/or. Individuals are more likely to vote when it is more convenient for them to do so – but cultural context should matter as well (Peters 2005).

Second, it requires a theory of causation that is sensitive to context. The same voting practices in one country may have different meanings in different setting. It might not be possible to neatly transport and implant a policy from one jurisdiction to another.

Thirdly, it must acknowledge that knowledge about the likely effects of reforms among the agents of practices can cause counter-effects. The introduction of voter identification requirements might, ceteris paribus, cause voting levels to decline because some voters will not have access to the required ID. However, a counter-mobilization against "voter suppression" may indirectly cause voter ID to have a positive effect on turnout. The lines of causality are therefore complex.

A strategic-relational framework

The effect that voting practices might have on voters can be conceived through a structure and agency relationship. There is a rich scholarship from the social sciences on the relationship between structure and agency (for example, see: Hay 2002, 89–134). Agents are the political actors under study – in this case voters at an aggregate and individual level. Structure refers to the contextual factors that might shape the behaviour of the actors. There are a variety of perspectives, ranging from an *intentionalist* position that emphasises the freedom of the individual to act without constraint, to the polar opposite *structuralist* position in which individuals are simply the bearers of their social context. An intepretivist approach provides the exemplar of the former approach in which individual are given autonomy to act within their beliefs (Bevir 2010; Bevir and Rhodes 2002). Conversely, and paradoxically, rational choice theory gives agents no autonomy – they are assumed to be driven by a logic of calculated interests which are shaped by their contextual environment (Hay 2002, 103–104).

The *strategic relational approach* to structure and agency that is used in this article was developed by Bob Jessop (2001, 2005). This has not been used to conceptualize the relationship between the citizen and electoral institutions until to now, since the common position is to use rational choice theory. The strategic relational approach, however, has been used in other areas of study on political institutions such as the study of prime ministers (Byrne and Theakston 2019; James 2018a).

This approach conceptualizes agents as strategic actors who are capable of free-thinking. However, they are situated within a strategically selective environment which might shape their preferences, incentives and beliefs. It involves studying how agents might find themselves in situations that might "privilege some actors, some identities, some strategies, some spatial and temporal horizons, some actions over others; and the ways, if any, in which actors (individual and/or collective) take account of this differentiated privileging … when choosing a course of action" (Jessop 2001, 1224). Strategically selective environments therefore do not determine outcomes because agents are reflexive actors capable of strategic learning.

Importantly, the approach begins from a critical realist ontological and epistemological position conceptualizes the world as having a stratified social reality. There are therefore many deep structural causes which might not be immediately observable to the researcher using purely behaviouralist techniques. These structures often include gender or class-based politics. In the field of elections, this sensitizes us to how individuals might be more subtly persuaded to vote or not vote.

It is also important to note that this approach is often linked to a realist conception of knowledge. Rather than seeing the world as an object that can be studied in a hermetically sealed environment, the accumulated knowledge about the world is shared with it. As a result, those under study can change their strategic behaviour, armed with this knowledge (James 2018b; James 2020, 18–30). For example, one research finding might be that voter identification requirements lead to lower levels of turnout amongst some groups. The documentation and dissemination of this knowledge to political parties, activists and voters, however, might change their future behaviour.

Causation is therefore context-specific. The use of quantitative methods can help to identify how institutions have shaped behaviour in the past, but it is no guarantee that these causal effects will reoccur in the future. Actors have the ability for strategic learning from past experiences. Meanwhile, the same institutional practices may have different effects in different situations where cultural meanings and practices are different (James 2020, 27–28; Pawson 2006, 21).

The strategic-relational approach has been applied to a few empirical avenues of research, so the structures that might affect the agents under study have not yet been sketched out. We therefore set out the following propositions about those which will shape individual behaviour:

- Most obviously, *electoral laws and institutions* will shape whether individuals vote by providing the institutional environment. At the most obvious level, legal enfranchisement is a prerequisite for participation. Requirements to provide different forms of identification, for example, will affect the calculus of whether to vote by making it more burdensome.
- The technical, managerial and financial *resources* available to electoral officials will matter too. A lack of polling staff might mean that queues will develop which could discourage voters. Poor or faulty equipment, lack of accessibility features for disabled voters, or reduced funding for voter outreach activities could be the result of financial austerity policies (James and Jervier 2017). Policy instruments such as voter registration reforms can have "back-office" effects on the running of elections, such as increased costs (James 2020, 199–220).
- *Cultural practices* might also be exclusionary. The act of casting a vote is not a robotic act – but one which takes place in locations with embedded social meanings (Bertrand, Briquet, and Pels 2007; Coleman 2013; Orr 2016). But such cultural practices and meanings are never neutral – they can have exclusionary dynamics. Rituals and norms can shape expectations about the "proper" role of individuals. It might become "normalized", for example, for women to vote as instructed by men in polling stations as part of a set of patriarchal power relations (Bardall 2011).
- *Strategic action* of others will be important. In a world of necessity, actors will take strategic action to coerce or shape the behaviour of others. In the context of elections, these tactics might involve campaigning behaviour around the poll which are intimidating or threatening, or might explicitly threaten or undertake violence against others in order to win an election (Birch and Muchlinski 2018).

- *Informational resources* about how to register to vote and cast a ballot can shape whether citizens participate on Election Day. The state may not, for example, provide clear websites detailing the process (Garnett 2017). There can also be concerted disinformation campaigns by parties and other agents to deter some blocs of voters from participating, by claiming that polling stations are closed, voting hours are different to what they are or falsely suggesting voter identification requirements are needed (Pal 2017).
- More deeply rooted *educational resources*, meanwhile, provide citizens with knowledge about citizenship and how they can be active in the political system. These could be widely distributed, held by a minority, or widely absent in a political system (Verba, Scholzman, and Brady 1995).

The generative mechanisms therefore include both culture and calculus, transcending the traditional institutionalist accounts of human behaviour (Peters 1999).

A strategically selective environment will shape individual behaviour, but the environment can also be shaped over time by the actors situated within it. As Jessop remarks, actors:

> orient their strategies and tactics in the light of their understanding of the current conjuncture and their 'feel for the game.' (Jessop 2001, 1224)

It in the context of elections, citizens, activists and parties might seek to alter the laws and cultural practices through which elections are run to generate a new strategically selective environment. There is therefore an interactive and iterative relationship with agents that can change structures through advocacy, as Figure 1 illustrates.

State response: electoral policy and machinery

If there is a strategically selective environment in which there are uneven levels of turnout amongst groups, how could the state respond? We categorize state responses to the challenge of ensuring inclusive elections:

- *Repressive.* Rulers will often shape the apparatus of the state in order to maximize their electoral interests. This might involve *deliberate* attempts at voter intimidation, instructions to stuff ballot boxes, or placing polling stations in areas far away from the voter. Repressive policies are therefore deliberate and partisan attempts to restrict the participation of particular groups with a view to gaining political advantage. This is not

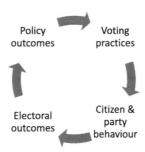

Figure 1. The cyclical relationship between voting practices, elections and reform.

limited to autocracies. Governing elites may instead seek to deploy strategies to suppress voter turnout amongst key groups through policies such as onerous voter identification requirements, etc.

- *Laissez-faire.* Political inequality does not always come about through such active repression. In fact, elections could be nominally "free and fair" by international standards and the criteria set out by minimalist democratic theorists such as Robert Dahl, but the outcomes of the electoral process could be marked by high levels of political inequality. This is because the state might, borrowing language from economic policy, take a minimalist, laissez-faire approach to running elections where the most basic polling provisions are provided. Elections are hypothetically implemented to a high standard in so far as the rules, however the onus has been left to the individual to educate themselves, register and vote. Typical policies might include the absence of proactive efforts to tackle underlying uneven levels of voter education or turnout. Responsibility to register to vote might lie with the citizen.
- *Interventionist.* Lastly, an interventionist approach is where the state is proactive at identifying cultural and material inequalities in voting practices in a given socio-political context and develops policies to address these. These policies will be context-specific to the nature of the problem. However, they might include proactive or automatic registration systems, election violence mitigation or social media regulation.

The case for inclusive voting procedures

If there is a strategically selective environment in which there are uneven levels of turnout amongst groups, how *should* the state respond?

As the review above makes clear, there has rarely been a detailed, explicit link between the study of voting procedures and normative political theory. An important decision has to be made for how to define democracy. There are, of course, a variety of different ways of doing this. One common approach is to take a minimalist approach in which a polity can be considered "democratic" if we are able to witness the presence of certain institutional arrangements. Robert Dahl's *Polyarchy* provides the classic exemplar of such an approach (Dahl 1971). Robert Dahl claimed that democracy was characterized by the "continuing responsiveness of the government to the preferences of its citizens, considered as equal weights" (Dahl 1971, 1). Unpacking this, Dahl thought that there were eight institutional guarantees that would be needed for a polity to be considered a polyarchy, the ideal system of government. These included the "right to vote", "free and fair elections" and "freedom of expression" (Dahl 1971, 3).

Meanwhile, substantive normative theorists criticized the idea of evaluating institutions according to whether they match a pre-determined list of procedures. David Beetham, for example, argued that doing so provides no rationale for why these institutions should be considered "democratic" (Beetham 1994, 26). Most worryingly, basing assessments on a pre-defined list offers no way of considering how that list could be improved over time (Beetham 1994, 26–27). He therefore encourages us to evaluate democratic institutions by the outcomes that they produce. In particular, a polity can be considered democratic where it realizes the goals of political equality and popular control of government.

While these approaches have many differences, one theme that it is common to theme both is political equality remains central. The world may is likely to involve varying levels of social and economic equality, but democratic institutions should neither privilege or disadvantage any citizen. They should be "considered as an equal weight" as Dahl claims or collectively considered as equal's as Beetham suggests.

Repressive electoral procedures, as sketched out above, would clearly be a violation of these normative goals. It is also the case that laissez-faire policies, however, are insufficient for realizing the ideals of political equality in a democracy. If citizens are in strategically selective environments in which their propensity to vote is affected by factors outside of their control, then realizing political equality requires intervention. If there is electoral violence then the state response cannot be laissez-faire – intervention is required to ensure that everyone is able to vote without intimidation. If there are lower levels of electoral registration amongst young people then interventions are required to address to bring balance. If voters with disabilities are less likely to vote because the polling stations are designed for those without disabilities, then interventions are required.

In the sphere of economic policy, laissez-faire policies have often been grounded with a moral defence. The role of government should be minimal to create free market conditions, in which businesses and entrepreneurs can prosper, generate profit and economic wealth. The argument of monetarists and free-marketeers is that mutual benefit is gained as wealth "trickles down". But there is no mutual gain in electoral integrity or democratic politics with state non-intervention. Those who benefit are the parties, candidates and voters who are already winners; those who lose are those who do not participate. Democratic states must therefore seek out and implement interventionist, inclusive voting practices.

A further critical argument of intervention is that voting is an individual responsibility and the state should not play a proactive role in shaping individual behaviour. These arguments are intuitively compatible with liberal democracy, which sprang from a defence of the rights of the individual. The absence of inclusive voting practices in a strategically selective environment, however, immediately sees the power and equality of many individuals and groups being undermined. Without such interventions, individuals might find themselves with formal voting rights, but situated within a legal, cultural, administrative, informational and educational environment in which they are unequal to their peers and much more unlikely to vote than a peer. Moreover, *group* inequality can be generated from the absence of inclusive voting practices. Societies are not collections of identical individuals. Social patterns, class structures, political cleavages emerge which brings divergences amongst group's interests. Allowing a turnout gap, without intervention is therefore a direct breach of the principles of democracy.

Special issue ahead

This introductory article has set out the concept of inclusive voting practices and given it a normative grounding. What constitutes an inclusive voting practice, however, is partially contextually specific because it depends on the level of turnout inequality between groups in a given scenario – and how different policy instruments interact in different spatial–temporal environments. This special issue therefore pushes open a new research agenda to consider: [2]

- What are the different causal pathways for causing exclusion at the ballot box? Who tends to be excluded or negatively affected by voting processes?
- Which electoral processes are effective at ensuring inclusion? Which are not? What proactive state action and regulation is required?
- Beyond introducing political equality, what are the wider effects of inclusive voting practices?
- Given their importance, when and why are such policies instruments not undertaken by the state?

Subsequent articles take the agenda forward, beginning with Victoria Shineman who focusses attention on how many would-be electors are excluded from the franchise. The move towards becoming a full democracy involved the franchise being extended to women, non-property owners and all ethnicities, but some groups remain legally unable to vote. Felons are amongst many groups in democracies who are acutely affected by the outcome of elections but who in some jurisdictions have their right to vote removed because of their prior criminal record. Shineman considers the effects of restoring voting rights to felons on their attitudes and behaviours, using experimental treatments to help make the normative case for inclusive voting practices.

Eric Guntermann, Ruth Dassonneville and Peter Miller look at the effects of compulsory voting. This is potentially one of the most important inclusive practices because in theory it eradicates inequalities in turnout by ensuring everyone votes, thereby reducing the difference between rich and poor. They consider whether this then also has effects on the nature of representation within legislatures.

Paige Schneider and David Carroll consider the problem of electoral violence. Violence and perceived threats of violence are an obvious impediment for citizens voting. Although there has been considerable literature on the topic, the authors argue that the gendered nature of electoral violence needs to be built into any future research on the topic and has so far been overlooked. They illustrate this using their ethnographic fieldwork in Uganda.

Voter ID requirements have often been at the heart of contemporary political debate about voting practices. They have been incited to be modern "Jim Crow laws" because they reduce turn out amongst some groups, more than others. Joseph Anthony and David C. Kimball look at the implementation of photo ID implementation in Missouri. Meanwhile, Toby S. James and Alistair Clark consider the uneven experiences of voters in English local elections. The effects of the introduction of a set of voter ID pilots, the first ever in British elections is then charted.

Citizens are often left in long lines to wait to cast their vote. Bridgett King identifies how these wait times and other administrative irregularities are experienced differently across different groups in the American electorate. The effects of these problems on voter confidence in the electoral process are then mapped.

The experience of citizens with disabilities as considered by Powell and Johnson, who note how they are considerably less likely to vote. They assess the ways in which people with disabilities are disenfranchised by election administration barriers such as voter registration, voter identification regulation and methods of ballot submission, using survey data from the US.

Another community to be legally disenfranchised are non-resident citizens, who might wish to vote abroad. Kevin Pallister notes that many countries have reformed policies to enable them to vote. Pallister identifies the drivers for these reforms in the cases of El Salvador and Guatemala to help to identify generalizations about when and why moves to inclusive practices might occur.

The coverage of the articles is therefore geographically extensive and cover many voting practices. The articles collectively help to establish which practices constitute inclusive voting practices, what their effects are, and what the drivers might be. In the concluding article, we draw out the lessons from the special issue as a whole for the study of democracy and electoral institutions. We think that a profound rethinking of the concept is needed so that it includes the provision of inclusive electoral practices. We also set out the policy lessons for the international community and governments worldwide, upon whom the burden lies to respond to the research and introduce inclusive electoral practices.

Notes

1. We should of course also be mindful of other forms on inequality in the electoral process. For example, if citizens are given an unequal experience at the polling stations because of their ethnicity, age or geographical location then this too violates the principal of inequality. An inclusive voting practice would seek to address this too, even though it was not directly related to turnout.
2. Papers were primarily drawn from leading academics and policymakers from the pre-APSA workshop on "Building Better Elections: New Challenges in Electoral Management", held at MIT in Boston in 2018, convened by the editors. This workshop was supported by a Connection Grant from the Social Sciences and Humanities Research Council of Canada.

Disclosure statement

No potential conflict of interest was reported by the authors.

ORCID

Toby S. James http://orcid.org/0000-0002-5826-5461
Holly Ann Garnett http://orcid.org/0000-0002-2119-4399

References

Aldrich, John H. 1993. "Rational Choice and Turnout." *American Journal of Political Science* 37 (1): 246–278.

Banducci, Susan A., Todd Donovan, and Jeffrey A. Karp. 2004. "Minority Representation, Empowerment, and Participation." *The Journal of Politics* 66 (2): 534–556.

Bardall, G. 2011. *Breaking the Mold: Understanding Gender and Electoral Violence.* Washington, DC: IFES.

Beetham, David. 1994. "Key Principles and Indices for a Democratic Audit." In *Defining Democracy*, edited by David Beetham, 25–43. London: Sage.

Bertrand, Romain, Jean-Louis Briquet, and Peter Pels. 2007. *Cultures of Voting: The Hidden History of the Secret Ballot.* London: C.Hurst & Co.

Bevir, Mark. 2010. *Democratic Governance.* Princeton, NJ: Princeton University Press.

Bevir, M., and R. A. W. Rhodes. 2002. "Interpretive Theory." In *Theory and Methods in Political Science*, edited by D. Marsh and G. Stoker, 131–152. London: Palgrave.

Birch, Sarah, and David Muchlinski. 2018. "Electoral Violence: Patterns and Trends." In *Electoral Integrity and Political Regimes: Actors, Strategies and Consequences*, edited by Holly Ann Garnett and Margarita Zavadskaya, 100–112. Abingdon: Routledge.

Blais, André. 2000. *To Vote or Not to Vote?: The Merits and Limits of Rational Choice Theory.* Pittsburgh: University of Pittsburgh Press.

Blais, André, and Kees Aarts. 2006. "Electoral Systems and Turnout." *Acta Politica* 41 (2): 180–196.

Blais, André, and R. K. Carty. 1990. "Does Proportional Representation Foster Voter Turnout?" *European Journal of Political Research* 18 (2): 167–181.

Blais, André, and Agnieszka Dobrzynska. 1998. "Turnout in Electoral Democracies." *European Journal of Political Research* 33 (2): 239–261.

Brady, Henry E., Sidney Verba, and Kay Kehman Schlozman. 1982. "Beyond SES: A Resource Model of Participation." *American Political Science Review* 89 (2): 271–274.

Burden, Barry. 2009. "The Dynamic Effects of Education on Voter Turnout." *Electoral Studies* 28 (4): 540–549.

Byrne, Christopher, and Kevin Theakston. 2019. "Understanding the Power of the Prime Minister: Structure and Agency in Models of Prime Ministerial Power." *British Politics* 14 (4): 329–346.

Carothers, Thomas. 2003. *Aiding Democracy Abroad.* Washington, DC: Brookings Institution Press.

Carpini, Michael X. Delli, and Scott Keeter. 1996. *What Americans Know About Politics and Why It Matters.* New Haven, CT: Yale University Press.

Center, Carter. 2014. *Election Observations and Standards: A Carter Centre Assessment Manual.* Atlanta: Carter Center.

Coleman, Stephen. 2013. *How Voters Feel.* Cambridge: Cambridge University Press.

Cutler, Neal E., and Vern L. Bengtson. 1974. "Age and Political Alienation: Maturation, Generation and Period Effects." *The ANNALS of the American Academy of Political and Social Science* 415 (1): 160–175.

Dahl, R. 1971. *Polyarchy: Participation and Opposition.* New Haven, CT: Yale University Press.

Desposato, Scott, and Barbara Norrander. 2009. "The Gender Gap in Latin America: Contextual and Individual Influences on Gender and Political Participation." *British Journal of Political Science* 39 (1): 141–162.

Dunleavy, P., and B. O'Leary. 1987. *Theories of the State: The Politics of Liberal Democracy.* Basingstoke: Macmillan.

Emler, Nicholas, and Elizabeth Frazer. 1999. "Politics: The Education Effect." *Oxford Review of Education* 25 (1/2): 251–273.

Fraga, Bernard L. 2018. *The Turnout Gap: Race, Ethnicity, and Political Inequality in a Diversifying America.* Cambridge: Cambridge University Press.

Galicki, Celestyna. 2018. "Barriers to Voting and the Cost of Voting among Low Socioeconomic, Young and Migrant Voters in New Zealand." *Political Science* 70 (1): 41–57.

Gallego, Aina. 2010. "Understanding Unequal Turnout: Education and Voting in Comparative Perspective." *Electoral Studies* 29 (2): 239–248.

Garnett, Holly Ann. 2017. "Open Election Management Bodies." In *Election Watchdogs*, edited by Pippa Norris and Alessandro Nai, 117–126. New York: Oxford University Press.

Garnett, Holly Ann. 2019a. "Early Voting: Comparing Canada, Finland, Germany, and Switzerland." *Election Law Journal: Rules, Politics, and Policy* 18 (2): 116–131.

Garnett, Holly Ann. 2019b. "Evaluating Online Registration: The Canadian Case." *Election Law Journal: Rules, Politics, and Policy* 18 (1): 78–92.

Germann, Micha, and Uwe Serdült. 2017. "Internet Voting and Turnout: Evidence from Switzerland." *Electoral Studies* 47 (June 2017): 1–12.

Goodman, Nicole, and Leah C. Stokes. 2018. "Reducing the Cost of Voting: An Evaluation of Internet Voting's Effect on Turnout." *British Journal of Political Science*. doi:10.1017/S0007123417000849.

Hajnal, Zoltan, Nazita Lajevardi, and Lindsay Nielson. 2017. "Voter Identification Laws and the Suppression of Minority Votes." *The Journal of Politics* 79 (2): 363–379.

Hasen, Richard L. 2012. *The Voting Wars: From Florida 2000 to the Next Election Meltdown*. Grand Rapids, MI: Yale University Press.

Hay, C. 2002. *Political Analysis*. Basingstoke: Palgrave Macmillan.

James, Toby S. 2010. "Electoral Administration and Voter Turnout: Towards an International Public Policy Continuum." *Representation* 45 (4): 369–389.

James, Toby S. 2011. "Fewer 'Costs,' More Votes? UK Innovations in Electoral Administration 2000-2007 and Their Effect on Voter Turnout." *Election Law Journal* 10 (1): 37–52.

James, Toby S. 2012. *Elite Statecraft and Election Administration: Bending the Rules of the Game*. Basingstoke: Palgrave Macmillan.

James, Toby S. 2018a. "Political Leadership as Statecraft? Aligning Theory with Praxis in Conversation with British Party Leaders." *The British Journal of Politics and International Relations* 20 (3): 555–572.

James, Toby S. 2018b. "The Higher Education Impact Agenda, Scientific Realism and Policy Change: The Case of Electoral Integrity in Britain." *British Politics* 13 (3): 312–331.

James, Toby S. 2020. *Comparative Electoral Management: Performance, Networks and Instruments*. New York: Routledge.

James, Toby S., and Tyrone Jervier. 2017. "The Cost of Elections: The Effects of Public Sector Austerity on Electoral Integrity and Voter Engagement." *Public Money & Management* 37 (7): 461–468.

Jankowski, Thomas B., and John M. Strate. 1995. "Modes of Participation Over the Adult Life Span." *Political Behavior* 17 (1): 89–106.

Jessop, Bob. 2001. "Institutional re(Turns) and the Strategic – Relational Approach." *Environment and Planning A* 33: 1213–1235.

Jessop, Bob. 2005. "Critical Realism and the Strategic-Relational Approach." *New Formations* 56: 40–53.

Kam, Cindy D., and Carl L. Palmer. 2008. "Reconsidering the Effects of Education on Political Participation." *The Journal of Politics* 70 (3): 612–631.

Lizotte, Mary-Kate, and Andrew H. Sidman. 2009. "Explaining the Gender Gap in Political Knowledge." *Politics & Gender* 5: 127–151.

Mattila, Mikko, Peter Söderlund, Hanna Wass, and Lauri Rapeli. 2013. "Healthy Voting: The Effect of Self-Reported Health on Turnout in 30 Countries." *Electoral Studies* 32 (4): 886–891.

Mondak, Jeffery J., and Mary R. Anderson. 2004. "The Knowledge Gap: A Reexamination of Gender-based Differences in Political Knowledge." *The Journal of Politics* 66 (2): 492–512.

Nations, United. 2007. *United Nations Convention on the Rights of Persons with Disabilities*. New York: United Nations.

Norris, Pippa. 2002. *Democratic Phoenix: Reinventing Political Activism*. New York: Cambridge University Press.

Norris, Pippa. 2013. "The New Research Agenda Studying Electoral Integrity." *Electoral Studies* 32 (4): 563–575.

Norris, Pippa, and Ronald Inglehart. 2018. *Cultural Backlash: the Rise of Authoritarianism-Populism*. New York: Cambridge University Press.

Orr, Graeme. 2016. *Ritual and Rhythm in Electoral Systems: A Comparative Legal Account*. Abingdon: Routledge.

Pal, Michael. 2017. "Canadian Election Administration on Trial: 'Robocalls', Opitz and Disputed Elections in the Courts." *King's Law Journal* 28 (2): 324–342.

Pallister, Kevin. 2017. *Election Administration and the Politics of Voter Access*. New York: Routledge.

Pawson, Ray. 2006. *Evidence-based Policy*. London: Sage.

Persson, Mikael. 2015. "Education and Political Participation." *British Journal of Political Science* 45 (3): 689–703.

Peters, G. 1999. *Institutional Theory in Political Science: The 'New Institutionalism'*. London: Pinter.

Peters, G. 2005. *Institutional Theory in Political Science: The 'New Institutionalism'. Second Edition ed*. London: Continuum.

Piven, F. F., and R. A. Cloward. 1983. "Towards a Class-Based Realignment of American Politics." *Social Policy* 13 (3): 3–14.

Popkin, Samuel L., and Michael A. Dimock. 1998. "Political Knowledge and Citizen Competence." In *Citizen Competence and Democratic Institutions*, edited by Stephen L. Elkin and Karol Soltan, 117–146. University Park: Penn State University Press.

Przeworski, Adam. 1999. "Minimalist Conception of Democracy: A Defence." In *Democracy's Value*, edited by Ian Shapiro and Casiano Hacker-Cordon, 23–55. Cambridge: Cambridge University Press. [Reprinted in Robert A. Dahl et al (eds) The Democracy Sourcebook].

Schattschneider, Elmer Eric. 1960. *The Semi-Sovereign People: A Realist's View of Democracy in America*. New York: Holt, Rhinehart & Winston.

Schur, Lisa. 2013. *Reducing Obstacles to Voting for People with Disabilities, Presidential Commission on Election Administration*.

Schur, Lisa, Mason Ameri, and Meera Adya. 2017. "Disability, Voter Turnout, and Polling Place Accessibility." *Social Science Quarterly* 98 (5): 1374–1390.

Schur, Lisa, Todd Shields, Douglas Kruse, and Kay Schriner. 2002. "Enabling Democracy: Disability and Voter Turnout." *Political Research Quarterly* 55 (1): 167–190.

Smets, Kaat, and Carolien van Ham. 2013. "The Embarrassment of Riches? A Meta-Analysis of Individual-Level Research on Voter Turnout." *Electoral Studies* 32 (2): 344–359.

Strate, John M., Charles J. Parrish, Charles D. Elder, and Coit Ford. 1989. "Life Span Civic Development and Voting Participation." *American Political Science Review* 83 (2): 443–464.

Verba, Sidney, Nancy Burns, and Kay Lehman Schlozman. 1997. "Knowing and Caring About Politics: Gender and Political Engagement." *The Journal of Politics* 59 (4): 1051–1072.

Verba, Sidney, and Norman H. Nie. 1972. *Participation in America: Political Democracy and Social Equality*. New York: Harper & Row.

Verba, Sidney, Kay Lehman Scholzman, and Henry E. Brady. 1995. *Voice and Equality: Civic Volunteerism in American Politics*. Cambridge: Harvard University Press.

Virendrakumar, Bhavisha, Emma Jolley, Eric Badu, and Elena Schmidt. 2018. "Disability Inclusive Elections in Africa: A Systematic Review of Published and Unpublished Literature." *Disability & Society* 33 (4): 509–538.

Wolfinger, Raymond E., and Steven J. Rosenstone. 1980. *Who Votes?* New Haven, CT: Yale University Press.

Zaller, John. 1990. "Political Awareness, Elite Opinion Leadership, and the Mass Survey Response." *Social Cognition* 8: 125–153.

Appendix 1. Variables and data sources for Table 1

Variable	Details
Individual Level	
Gender	0 Male
	1 Female
Age	Continuous Variable (16–99)
Education	What is the highest educational level that you have attained?
	0. No formal education
	1. Incomplete primary school
	2. Complete primary school
	3. Incomplete secondary school: technical/vocational
	4. Complete secondary school: technical/vocational
	5. Incomplete secondary school: university preparatory
	6. Complete secondary school: university- preparatory
	7. Some university-level education, without completion
	8. University – level education, with degree
	Reduced to three categories:
	0. Did not complete, or less than secondary education (reference)
	1. Completed secondary education
	2. Some or completed university-level education
Income	On this card is an income scale on which 1 indicates the lowest income group and 10 the highest income group in your country. We would like to know in what group your household is. Please, specify the appropriate number, counting all wages, salaries, pensions and other incomes that come in.
	0. Lower step
	1. Second step
	… etc.
	9. Tenth step
Voting	When elections take place, do you vote always, usually or never?: National level
	1. Always
	2. Usually
	3. Never
	Reduced to two categories:
	0. Usually or never (combined since there is often a bias towards stating that one usually votes)
	1. Always
Political Interest	How interested would you say you are in politics?
	0. Very interested
	1. Somewhat interested
	2. Not very interested
	3. Not at all interested
	Reduced to two categories:
	0. Not at all or not very interested.
	1. Somewhat or very interested
Country-Level	
Compulsory Voting	0. Not compulsory
	1. Compulsory
Electoral System	0. Plurality/Majoritarian
	1. Mixed
	2. Proportional Representation
	(Categorical variable with plurality/majoritarian as reference category)

Datasets

- WORLD VALUES SURVEY Wave 6 2010–2014 OFFICIAL AGGREGATE v.20150418. For more details, see: http://www.worldvaluessurvey.org/wvs.jsp
- International IDEA. Data & Tools. https://www.idea.int/data-tools

Countries Included:

Taiwan	Yemen
Georgia	Algeria
Palestine	Argentina
Germany	Armenia
Japan	Brazil
Libya	Chile
Mexico	Colombia
New Zealand	Cyprus
Pakistan	Estonia
Philippines	Iraq
Russia	Kazakhstan
Zimbabwe	Jordan
Thailand	Kyrgyzstan
Ukraine	Lebanon
Azerbaijan	Morocco
Australia	Netherlands
Bahrain	Peru
Belarus	Poland
Ghana	Romania
India	Rwanda
Kuwait	Slovenia
Malaysia	South Africa
Nigeria	Spain
Singapore	Sweden
Trinidad and Tobago	Tunisia
Egypt	Turkey
United States	Uruguay
Uzbekistan	

Note: Data from 55 countries where relevant questions were asked in the World Values Survey, 6th Wave (2010–2014).

Restoring voting rights: evidence that reversing felony disenfranchisement increases political efficacy

Victoria Shineman

ABSTRACT

Millions of American citizens are denied the right to vote due to their criminal record. This study finds evidence that restoring the right to vote causes formerly disenfranchised individuals to develop higher levels of internal and external efficacy, generating citizens who are more confident in their own abilities and have stronger tendencies toward democratic engagement. A field experiment is embedded within a panel survey conducted before and after a statewide election in Virginia. All subjects are American citizens with a felony conviction who were once disenfranchised, but are now either eligible to vote, or are eligible to have their voting rights restored. Experimental treatments provide information about recent changes in restored voting rights, along with varying information and assistance with voter registration and turnout. The treatment that included a mobilization element generated the highest levels of efficacy. Additionally, the treatment that only included information about restoring voting rights also generated significant increases in political efficacy on its own. Thus the study finds novel evidence that the right to vote directly increases political efficacy.

Introduction

More than four million American Citizens are currently denied the right to vote due to state laws that disenfranchise citizens who have been convicted of a felony. The vast majority of these citizens continue to be disenfranchised even after they are released from prison. The United States is unique in the civil consequences it applies to its criminal population. As Ewald and Rottinghaus write "the United States is almost certainly the only country in the world that disenfranchises a significant number of people who are either no longer incarcerated or were never in prison at all" (2009, 9–10).

Although the number of these disenfranchised citizens who would vote if they had the right is highly disputed (Miles 2004; Haselswerdt 2009; Hjalmarsson and Lopez 2010; Meredith and Morse 2014; Gerber et al. 2015; Meredith and Morse 2015), at least some of them would likely register and vote. The potential votes blocked by these policies might very well be affecting electoral outcomes at the local and national level (Uggen and Manza 2002; Manza and Uggen 2008; Burch 2011). Previous research has explored possible racialized motivations behind these laws (Behrens, Uggen, and Manza 2003; Ewald and Rottinghaus 2009), and determined that – regardless of intent – disenfranchisement policies disproportionately block voting rights among non-white citizens more often (Manza and Uggen 2008; Uggen, Larson, and Shannon 2016). Studies on public opinion have found that attitudes toward disenfranchisement policies are driven by a number of factors – with racial prejudice driving much of the support for disenfranchisement policies (Pinaire, Heumann, and Bilotta 2002; Manza, Brooks, and Uggen 2004; Manza and Uggen 2008; Wilson, Owens, and Davis 2015; Shineman 2018d) – as is found in many areas of criminal justice policy (Hurwitz and Peffley 1997; Peffley and Hurwitz 2002).

However, another question is often overlooked: how does the experience of being disenfranchised affect citizens at the individual level? Early models of participation argued that voting and participation elicit transformative effects, generating more socially-minded, informed, and active citizens (see Pateman 1970, for example). Empirical studies have demonstrated that increasing voter turnout also increases political information (Shineman 2018a), and political efficacy and trust (Shineman 2018b). Beyond the positive effects generated by the act of voting itself, there are also reasons to expect that the restoration of voting rights would also directly increase pro-social and pro-democratic attitudes. Just being given the right to vote might generate higher levels of political efficacy, even if citizens were never encouraged or mobilized to actually register and vote. Anecdotal evidence suggests that disenfranchised citizens feel resentful and ashamed of their status (Cardinale 2004; Uggen, Manza, and Behrens 2004; Manza and Uggen 2008; Miller and Spillane 2012; Pinkard 2013; Miller and Agnich 2016). Being denied the right to vote creates a lasting stigma, and this can negatively affect the way people view themselves. Although the negative effects of disenfranchisement on individual attitudes have been proposed, no previous empirical study has properly identified and estimated the effects of changes in voting rights. Voting rights and information about voting rights are not random – those whose rights are restored (and those who know when their rights are restored) are not random; they are systematically different from those who are (or who believe they are) disenfranchised. Up until now, no study has estimated the effects of randomly assigning people to receive new information about voting rights. This study seeks to provide the first causal evidence regarding the effects of disenfranchisement policies, and thus fill that gap in the literature.

This paper presents the results from a field experiment embedded within a panel survey conducted before and after a statewide election in Virginia. The experiment recruits a population of citizens with felony convictions who were once disenfranchised, but are now either eligible to vote, or are eligible to have their voting rights restored. Treatments provide information about recent changes in policies regarding the restoration of voting rights, along with varying encouragement and assistance with registration and voting in the upcoming election. The design leverages the high degree of misinformation regarding the restoration of voting rights. By randomly increasing awareness among some subjects that their right to vote has been restored, the experiment is able to isolate and estimate the effects of having one's votes restored. The results suggest that being mobilized to vote and the restoration of voting rights (without mobilization) both cause subjects to develop stronger levels of political efficacy.

Section 1 details the theoretical expectations regarding the effects of restoring voting rights and mobilization on political efficacy. Section 2 presents the design of an original field experiment. Section 3 describes the effects of the treatments on voting rights, information about voting rights, voter registration, and voter turnout. Section 4 presents the results from each model, documenting the effects of each treatment on different estimates of internal and external efficacy. Finally, Section 5 discusses the results as a whole.

Section 1: theory and hypotheses

Early theorists described political efficacy as the "feeling that individual political action does have, or can have, an impact upon the political process, namely, that it is worthwhile to perform one's civic duties" (Campbell, Gurin, and Miller 1954). There has been much debate regarding the conceptual divisions between different types of efficacy, and the appropriate question wordings to capture each of them in surveys (e.g. Balch 1974; Craig and Maggiotto 1982; Abramson 1983; Acock, Clarke, and Stewart 1985; Madsen 1987; Craig, Niemi, and Silver 1990; Niemi, Craig, and Mattei 1991; Morrell 2003). The modern concept of political efficacy is typically divided into two categories: internal efficacy and external efficacy. Internal efficacy refers to an individual's perception of his or her own ability to engage in politics, become informed, and meaningfully participate in the political process. External efficacy refers to an individual's perception of how responsive and accessible the government is to citizen demands.

There are two different pathways through which restoring voting rights should increase political efficacy: (1) through the effect of disenfranchisement on voter turnout (and the effect of voting on efficacy); and (2) through the restoration of rights alone.

First pathway – restoring voting rights increases turnout, and turnout increases efficacy

Disenfranchisement reduces voter turnout, and the restoration of voting rights would increase turnout. Although the exact rate of expected participation among currently disenfranchised citizens (if their rights were restored) is unknown, the restoration of voting rights has been found to increase turnout among at least some members of this population (Manza and Uggen 2008; Gerber et al. 2015; Meredith and Morse 2015; Shineman 2018c).

From a theoretical perspective, there are several reasons why engaging in political participation should cause an increase in political efficacy. Engaging in political participation makes the political world seem less foreign, and causes the individual to feel more included in the democratic process. This inclusion can increase approval of democratic institutions, and increase the perceived legitimacy of the electoral process.

Classical democratic theory contends that political participation plays an "educative role" that promotes civic engagement and democratic values, creating a self-reinforcing cycle of continuing participation (see Pateman 1970). Deliberative theorists (e.g. Fishkin 1991) argue that involvement in deliberation and decision-making can transform individuals, increasing civic-mindedness, and creating more politically aware and engaged citizens.

Engaging in political participation might also motivate an individual to develop a belief that participation is worthwhile, in order to justify one's behaviour to oneself: "those who vote or engage in campaign activities will justify their behaviour by strengthening their belief that the political system responds to citizen involvement" (Clarke and Acock 1989, 553). Engaging in participation might lead citizens "to believe they are ultimately controlling the government" (Olsen 1982, 6). Some argue that the act of engaging with a system causes people to become more likely to consider that system as legitimate and appropriate (Ginsberg 1982).

There is substantial empirical evidence that the act of engaging in political participation causes a person to develop stronger levels of both internal and external efficacy (Finkel 1985; Finkel 1987; Semetko and Valkenburg 1998; Bowler and Donovan 2002; Smith and Tolbert 2009, Chapter 4; Shineman 2018b). Thus, restoring voting rights should not only increase voter turnout – restoring voting rights should also increase political efficacy through its effect on turnout.

Second pathway – the effect of voting rights on political efficacy

The experience of being denied the right to vote also likely causes a direct decrease in political efficacy – regardless as to whether the citizen would choose to vote. A disenfranchised citizen is intentionally disconnected from the democratic process, creating a psychological stigma of "otherness." In a number of focus groups and interviews, citizens with felony convictions report feeling frustrated and isolated, and describe feelings of both sadness and anger about being politically excluded due to disenfranchisement policies (Cardinale 2004; Uggen, Manza, and Behrens 2004; Manza and Uggen 2008; Miller and Spillane 2012; Pinkard 2013; Miller and Agnich 2016). This feeling can make the system feel inaccessible. People build their beliefs regarding their own capabilities partially in reflection of the expectations others place upon them.

The re-entry literature describes how experience in the criminal justice system (such as conviction, sentencing, and time in prison) can cause individuals to transition the way they self-identify – away from an identity as a citizen and toward the identity as a "criminal" or "offender" (Garfinkel 1956). A key element of successful re-entry is developing a new identity as a free citizen (Maruna 2001; Uggen, Manza, and Behrens 2004; Uggen, Manza, and Thompson 2006; Maruna 2011). However, when a person is released from prison but continues to be disenfranchised, it can create a lasting stigma, affecting their confidence in themselves and their own abilities.

Just as the act of voting can cause people to increase their belief in their own political power, being denied the right to vote can have the inverse effect – causing an individual to feel like they are not qualified or capable of engaging the democratic process, or perhaps not even deserving of the right to vote. As Frederick Douglass stated in his famous essay "What the Black Man Wants" (1865):

> [Men] derive their conviction of their own possibilities largely from the estimate formed of them by others. If nothing is expected of a people, that people will find it difficult to contradict that expectation. By depriving us of suffrage, you affirm our incapacity to form intelligent judgments respecting public men and public measures; you declare before the world that we are unfit to exercise the elective franchise, and by this means lead us to undervalue ourselves, to put a low estimate upon ourselves, and to feel that we have no possibilities like other men.

Thus, restoring voting rights should also have a direct positive effect on a person's internal and external efficacy – regardless as to whether or not the person also chooses or is mobilized to vote.

Hypotheses

Informing citizens that their voting rights have been restored (or assisting citizens whose rights have not yet been restored to request restoration of their voting rights) in advance of a statewide election will cause those individuals to:

(H1) … Develop stronger external efficacy – increased confidence in their ability to affect the political system, and that the system will be responsive to citizens. Knowing that they are included in the electoral process will make that person more likely to believe that their vote can make a difference, and will also make that person feel more politically empowered.

(H2) … Develop stronger internal efficacy – an increased confidence in their own ability to participate and engage with the political system. Being granted the right to vote by the government is an affirming experience. That affirmation will make a person more likely to believe that they are qualified and capable to engage the political system.

(H3) … Become more likely to vote in the future. Knowing that one's voting rights have been restored will make them more likely to participate in politics in the future, even beyond the particular election during which the intervention occurred.

(H4) … Become more likely to participate in politics in other ways, beyond the act of voting. Other types of political participation might be non-electoral political acts (like contacting a representative or working with a campaign, for example).

(H5) … Become more likely to participate in non-political activities, like being involved in one's community. Participation is often theorized to be a self-reinforcing and expanding habit. Being included and welcomed into electoral participation should also make a person more likely to seek out participation in other areas of their life – such as involvement in their local community.

(H1 – H5) Similarly, the combination of restoring voting rights along with assistance with voter registration and an encouragement to vote in the upcoming statewide election should also cause individuals to increase their efficacy and participation in all the dimensions specified above. The combined treatment should generate effects through both the direct effect of restoration, and because restoration increases the probability of being registered and voting – and voting increases efficacy. A comparison of effects between the two treatments can isolate whether information about the restoration of voting rights alone is sufficient to increase political efficacy, or if restoration is only effective when it is also combined with mobilization.

Section 2: experimental design

The following section presents the design of a field experiment embedded within a panel survey conducted before and after the November 2017 Virginia Statewide Gubernatorial Election.

In order to isolate the effect of restoring voting rights on political efficacy, one must identify an exogenous increase in the restoration of voting rights. Observational studies are limited because the restoration of voting rights is not randomly assigned. Felony disenfranchisement laws vary widely by state. Given the variation (and frequent changes) in laws across states, there is a high degree of misinformation about the eligibility of citizens with felony convictions – both among the ex-offenders themselves (Drucker and Barreras 2005; Manza and Uggen 2008), and among elites (Ewald 2005; Allen 2011).

In order to isolate random increases in perceived voting rights, this study leverages the high degree of misinformation about eligibility, and randomly assigns some subjects to receive information about a new restoration policy that has already occurred. By generating exogenous increases in awareness of the new restorations of voting rights, this study is uniquely able to estimate how the restoration of voting rights affects the attitudes and behaviours of those who were formerly disenfranchised.

Electoral setting

The experiment was conducted during the November 2017 Virginia (VA) Statewide General Election, during which the state of Virginia elected its Governor, Attorney General, and all 100 members of the State Legislative Assembly. Virginia was an ideal setting to conduct the experiment because of recent changes in voter eligibility. In the state of Virginia, a citizen loses the right to vote when they are convicted of a felony. There is no automatic process for the restoration of rights. In order to restore one's voting rights in Virginia, a citizen with a felony conviction must complete their full term of supervision (e.g. probation), and also receive a personalized exemption from the Governor of Virginia via Executive Order. Historically, VA Governors have waited for eligible applicants to request the restoration of their voting rights, and evaluated each application as it was submitted.

However, in 2016, VA Governor Terry McAuliffe decided to proactively restore the voting rights to anyone who was eligible to have their rights restored by the Governor (e.g. all US Citizens with a felony conviction who had completed their probation). McAuliffe originally tried to restore voting rights to all 206,000 eligible citizens in a single executive order, signed April 22nd 2016. Newly eligible citizens began registering to vote immediately. However, the executive order was challenged by the Republican Party, and overturned by the VA Supreme Court in July 2016. The Court ruled (in a 4–3 split decision) that McAuliffe had the right to restore voting rights to all 206,000 citizens – but he was not allowed to do so in a single executive order. Instead, the Court ruled that McAuliffe would have to process 206,000 separate executive orders – one for each individual. The executive order was overturned, and all 13,000 new voter registrations that had been processed for citizens whose rights had been restored were cancelled.

McAuliffe announced he would process the individual orders one-at-a-time, as quickly as possible – starting with those who had already tried to register. He restored voting rights to 70,000 citizens before the deadline to register and vote in the November 2016 National Presidential Election, and to more than 150,000 citizens before the deadline to register and vote in the November 2017 VA Statewide General Election. The Governor's office sent a certificate of restoration to each citizen after their rights were restored, based on the last known address for each individual. However, ex-offenders are a particularly transient population. Because many of these last known addresses were no longer current, many citizens did not receive their notification letter, and were unaware that their rights had been restored.

Given these circumstances, the Virginia 2017 election presents an ideal setting for estimating the effects of the restoration of voting rights. Given the strict state laws which disenfranchised all citizens with felony convictions after their release, and the former policy from the Governor's Office which limited the restoration of voting rights to a small number of cases, citizens with felonies in Virginia are highly likely to know that they were once disenfranchised. At the time of the 2017 election, more than 150,000 citizens had had their voting rights restored within the last year, with more than half of these restorations occurring after the deadline to register and vote in the high-profile 2016 Presidential Election. Many of these newly-eligible voters did not know that their rights had been restored. Given the initial restoration order being reversed by the VA Supreme Court, the 13,000 new registrations that were processed and then cancelled, the gradual process through which individual restorations were processed over time, and the inconsistency with which citizens received notification of the restoration of their rights – there was a high degree of confusion, misinformation, and suspicion regarding the restoration process. The experiment intentionally leverages this misinformation, in order to capture the experience of having one's rights restored by randomly assigning some subjects to receive information about changes in voting rights that have already happened.

Experimental design

The experiment embedded two mobilization treatments into a panel survey conducted before and after the November 2017 Virginia Statewide Gubernatorial Election. Recruited subjects ($n = 98$) were American Citizens with at least one felony conviction, currently living in Virginia, who had completed their term of supervision – individuals who are eligible to have their voting rights restored by the Governor. The first survey took place about a month before the November 2017 election. A convenience sample was recruited by advertising the study in places potential subjects would be likely to see the invitation to participate.[1] All subjects completed the first survey in person in a private office suite located in downtown Richmond, VA. After completing the first survey, subjects were randomly assigned to receive one of three treatments. All treatments were delivered one-on-one in a private face-to-face setting, after subjects completed the first survey.[2]

(Treatment #1) restoration only

Subjects were provided with information about the Governor's current policy and initiative regarding the restoration of voting rights. The researcher offered to look up the subject's restoration status (which only takes about 15 s through a government website), and did so only if the subject agreed. If the subject agreed to let the researcher look up their voting rights, the researcher would then either confirm the date on which the subject's voting rights had been restored, or – if the subject's rights had not yet been restored – the researcher would offer to assist the subject in submitting a request to restore their voting rights. Such requests would put that citizen's name at the top of the Governor's list, and were typically processed within about 3 weeks.

(Treatment #2) restoration + mobilization

Subjects were provided with all elements of the *Restoration Only* Treatment. Additionally, subjects were informed that a statewide general election was coming up on November 7th, and were provided with information about how to register, locate their polling place, and look up other information about the election. The researcher also offered to look up the subject's registration status (which only takes about 15 s through a government website), and did so only if the subject agreed. If the subject was not registered, the researcher offered to assist the subject in registering to vote.

The two experimental treatments were deliberately designed to differentiate between the effects of knowing one's rights were restored and the effects of being mobilized.

Placebo treatment

The "Placebo" treatment provided subjects with an intensive personalized appeal to volunteer in their communities, along with a list of 14 upcoming volunteer opportunities in the area.[3] The goal of the placebo treatment was to mirror the level of personal contact and connection provided in the two voting rights treatments, and to include a similar pro-participatory message encouraging community involvement, without any reference to voting rights or the upcoming election.

The post-election survey began two days after the election, and could be completed by phone, online, or through the postal mail. Subjects were informed that they would only receive payment after completing both surveys, and were contacted multiple times to maximize the completion rate. Attrition was extremely low: of the 98 subjects who completed the first survey, 93 also completed the 2nd survey. All subjects who completed both surveys were provided with a $25 gift card to a location of their choice.

Section 3: treatment effects on voting rights, information about voting rights, voter registration, and voter turnout

During the delivery of the treatments, the researcher recorded whether the subject thought their voting rights had been restored, whether they allowed the researcher to look up their restoration status, whether their rights had been restored, and if not – whether they completed a request to have their rights restored.

About 65% of subjects said they thought their rights had already been restored, and about 43% of treated subjects allowed the researcher to look up the status of their voting rights. Those that refused typically either insisted they knew their rights were already restored, or expressed disinterest in voting or distrust about the restoration process. Among all treated subjects, 21.4% learned that their right to vote had been restored during the treatment delivery (22.2% in the *Restoration Only* treatment, and 20.7% in the *Restoration with Mobilization* treatment). Just over 16% of subjects verified that their right to vote had *not* yet been restored, and then also filled out a request to have their rights restored during the treatment (18.5% and 13.8% across each treatment). Lastly, 20.7% of subjects who received the *Restoration with Mobilization* treatment filled out a voter registration form – 17.2% to register for the first time, and 3.5% to update their address. By default, all these values were zero in the placebo treatment, as those subjects were not offered these options.

In addition to these on the spot estimates, official data regarding whether each subject had their rights restored, was registered to vote, and voted was attained through official government sources. Overall, both treatments clearly caused increases in knowledge about restored voting rights, new restorations, and new registrations – but neither significantly affected voter turnout in the November 2017 Election.

In comparison to the *Placebo* – where only one new subject had their rights restored during the duration of the experiment (+2.7 pp), the *Restoration Only* treatment increased new restorations by 14.8 percentage points ($p = 0.04$). The *Restoration with Mobilization* treatment increased new restorations by 6.9 pp ($p = 0.212$). Compared to the *Placebo*, the pooled effects of both treatments increased new restorations by 10.7 pp ($p = 0.08$). No new subjects registered to vote in the *Placebo* group. Though subjects in the *Restoration Only* treatment were not offered assistance with voter registration, 14.8 percent of the sample registered on their own ($p = 0.01$) – though notably only one of these subjects registered before the deadline to vote in the November 2017 election. The *Restoration with Mobilization* treatment increased new voter registrations by 13.8 pp ($p = 0.01$) – with one subject registering after the deadline had passed. Overall, the treatments increased *new* registrations by 14.3 pp ($p = 0.01$). The rate of voter turnout was fairly comparable across treatment groups in previous elections, and there were no significant differences in turnout across treatment groups during the November 2017 election.

Section 4: results

Methods for analysis

The post-election survey asked sixteen questions designed to estimate multiple dimensions of political efficacy. Twelve of those questions were also asked in the pre-treatment survey. The estimates are clustered into 5 categories: (1) External efficacy[4]; (2) Internal efficacy[5]; (3) Propensity to vote in the future[6]; (4) Propensity to participate politically in other ways beyond voting[7]; and (5) Propensity to participate in non-electoral activities within the community.[8]

The analyses below estimates the average effects of receiving each treatment, as well as the pooled effects of receiving either treatment. All models are run through ordinary least squares (OLS) regression. In order to further decrease noise and increase the accuracy and precision of the estimates (Pocock et al. 2002), all models include a set of covariates that are likely to affect efficacy,[9] as well as the pre-treatment value of each dependent variable (when available).

The figures below display the predicted post-treatment value for each estimate of political efficacy for a typical subject in each treatment group, as well as the overall effects of both restoration treatments pooled together. Given the directional nature of all hypotheses, all models are evaluated with a 1-tailed (directional) significance test within a 95% confidence interval.[10] Effects within a 90% confidence interval are noted as marginally significant. The effect size and significance thresholds are noted in each figure. To easily facilitate comparisons of magnitude, all estimates of trust are re-scaled to range from 0 to 100, with higher numbers indicating higher levels of trust.

Of the sixteen estimates of political efficacy, twelve were also estimated in the pre-treatment survey. As specified in the pre-analysis plan, additional models estimate the increase in pre v. post survey responses within subjects (for the twelve dependent variables asked in both surveys) – both with and without the same list of pre-registered covariates. The raw effects of receiving each treatment (without covariates) are also estimated. The results are consistent across all four sets of specifications. In the interest of space (and as specified in the pre-analysis plan), the body of the manuscript only presents the estimated predicted values from the OLS models including covariates. The results from all four sets of models are displayed in the appendix.

Results

The first hypothesis predicts that both treatments will cause subjects to increase their external efficacy – their belief that the democratic system is accessible and responsive. Figure 1 displays the results.

The hypothesis is largely confirmed. Subjects were asked whether they agree with the statement: (1A) "My vote can make a difference." Overall, the restoration treatments increased agreement with this statement by 17.2 percentage points (pp) on a 100-point scale ($p \leq 0.01$). The restoration treatment on its own increased agreement with this statement by 13.1 percentage points (pp) on average ($p = 0.06$). When combined with mobilization, the effects of the restoration treatment were substantially stronger – increasing agreement by 21.5 pp ($p \leq 0.01$). Although adding mobilization did indeed generate a larger effect, the restoration treatment also increased efficacy on its own – without the mobilization element. Subjects also indicated their agreement with the statement: (1B) "I feel politically empowered." With regard to feeling empowered, the restoration treatment actually generated the larger effect ($+12.0$, $p = 0.09$). Subjects who received the combined treatment reported higher agreement on average, but it was not a significant increase. The pooled effect of both treatments increased agreement by 10.9 points on average ($p = 0.07$)

The second hypothesis predicts that both treatments will cause subjects to increase their internal efficacy – their confidence in their own ability to engage the political system. Subjects were asked whether they agreed with the statements: (2A) "I consider myself well-qualified to participate in politics" and (2B) "I feel that I could do as good a job in public office as most other people." Figure 2 presents the results.

The restoration treatment on its own dramatically increased subjects' confidence in their own ability to participate in politics ($+26.4$, $p \leq 0.01$). When combined with mobilization, the effects were similarly strong ($+23.7$, $p \leq 0.01$), with a pooled effect of $+24.3$

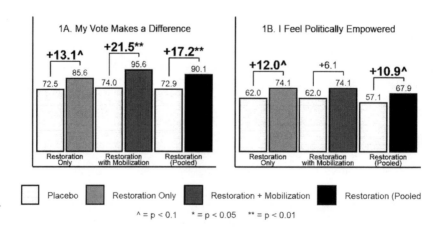

Figure 1. Predicted Post-Treatment Values of Two Estimates of External Efficacy, by Treatment Group. **$p \leq 0.01$; *$p \leq 0.05$; $+p \leq 0.10$.

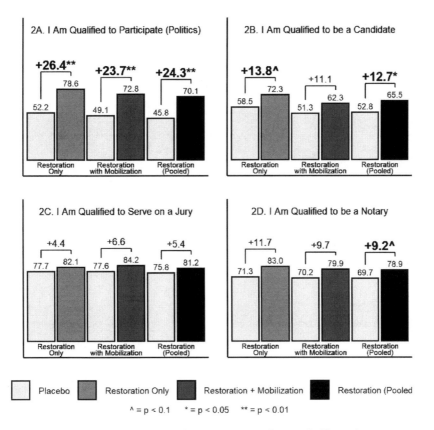

Figure 2. Predicted Post-Treatment Values of Four Estimates of Internal Efficacy, by Treatment Group. **$p \leq 0.01$; *$p \leq 0.05$; +$p \leq 0.10$.

($p \leq 0.01$). Both treatments also increased subjects' agreement that they were just as qualified as most other people to serve in public office – increasing by 13.8 pp in the restoration only treatment ($p \leq 0.05$), by 11.1 pp in the combined treatment ($p \leq 0.11$), and by 12.7 pp overall ($p \leq 0.05$). As such, the second hypothesis is also confirmed.

The restoration of civil rights granted by the Governor also restored subjects' right to serve on a jury, and their right to become a notary. The second survey asked subjects if they believed they were qualified to serve on (2C) a jury or (2D) as a notary, in order to estimate whether the effects of the civil rights extension also affected subjects' confidence in their abilities beyond the realm of electoral participation. Although subjects in both treatment groups reported higher confidence in their own ability to serve as a juror and as a notary on average, these effects did not fall within standard significance thresholds. The only exception is that the pooled effect of both treatments generated an average increase in one's confidence in their ability to serve as a notary by 9.2 points. This effect is considered marginally significant, with a p-value equal to 0.10.

The third hypothesis predicts that both treatments will cause subjects to become more likely to engage in electoral participation in the future, beyond the scope of the current elections. Subjects were asked to indicate how likely they were to vote in the upcoming national elections in November 2018 (3A) and 2020 (3B), and the next Virginia Statewide Gubernatorial Election in November 2021 (3C). Figure 3 displays the results.

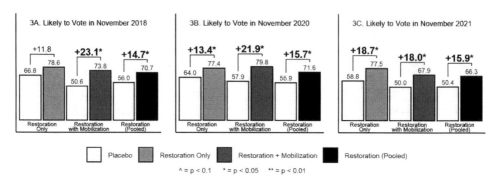

Figure 3. Predicted Post-Treatment Values of Self-Identified Propensity to Vote in Three Upcoming Elections, by Treatment Group. $**p \leq 0.01$; $*p \leq 0.05$; $+p \leq 0.10$.

Again, the hypothesis is largely confirmed. Receiving the restoration treatment alone generated significantly higher predicted probabilities of voting in the November 2020 Election (+13.4, $p \leq 0.05$) and the November 2021 Election (+18.7, $p \leq 0.05$). The reported probability of voting in the 2018 Midterm Election was also higher on average (+11.8, $p = 0.10$). The effects of restoration combined with mobilization on predicted turnout in the future were substantially stronger for both national elections (2018 = +23.1, $p \leq 0.05$; 2020 = +21.9, $p \leq 0.05$), and similarly strong for the next Virginia Gubernatorial Election in 2021 (+18.0, $p \leq 0.05$). The pooled effects were also significant in all three cases. Overall, both treatments caused subjects to predict higher levels of participation in the future, and the treatment that also included a mobilization element generated stronger effects.

The fourth hypothesis predicts that both treatments will cause subjects to become more likely to engage in other types of political participation beyond voting. Subjects were asked how likely they were to (4A) "contribute time or money to a political campaign" or (4B) "contact an elected representative" over the next year. Figure 4 displays the results.

The restoration treatment on its own increased the amount of time or money subjects predicted they would give to a political campaign (+16.3, $p \leq 0.10$). The average effect was similar in the combined treatment (+15.5, $p \leq 0.10$). The restoration treatment on its own

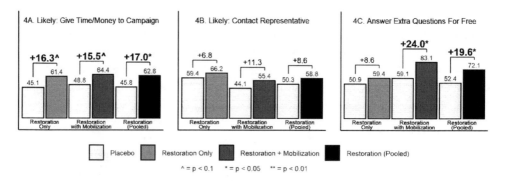

Figure 4. Predicted Post-Treatment Values of Three Estimates of Political Participation other than Turnout, by Treatment Group. $**p \leq 0.01$; $*p \leq 0.05$; $+p \leq 0.10$.

did not significantly increase subjects' expectations regarding contacting their elected representatives, though this value was higher on average among treated subjects (+6.8). When restoration and mobilization were combined, treated subjects did report a higher likelihood of reaching out to their representative on average (+11.3), but this effect was not within standard significance thresholds ($p = 0.11$). The pooled effect was similar (+8.6 on average, with $p = 0.13$).

An additional behavioural test about the effects of the treatments on participation was embedded into the post-election survey. At the end of the survey, subjects were told that the survey was finished and they had satisfied all the requirements to complete the study (and receive the $25 they were promised in compensation for their time). The researcher then asked subjects if they would be willing to answer a few more questions for free. The answers to the extra questions were not studied. Instead, a behavioural estimate of efficacy is generated (4C), based on whether or not the subject was willing to answer extra questions for free. In a sense, agreeing to answer extra questions signals a stronger pro-participatory attitude, and a willingness to give of oneself in order to help the greater good. Subjects who received only the restoration treatment answered these questions more often on average (+8.6 percentage points), but this was not a significant increase over participation among subjects in the placebo group. However, among subjects who received both the restoration and mobilization treatments, willingness to answer extra questions for free increased by 24.0 percentage points on average ($p \leq 0.05$).

While all previous estimates of efficacy are self-reports, this estimate captures an active behavioural response. One caveat is that because subjects knew the post-treatment survey was part of the study, it is possible that their increased willingness to answer extra questions for free was an expression of gratitude toward the researcher (for providing information and assistance regarding voting rights and/or registration), rather than an expression of pro-participatory attitudes toward society as a whole. Although the evidence for the last hypothesis is slightly more mixed, both treatments did appear to increase political participation in matters beyond the realm of voting – and the combination of the restoration treatment along with a mobilization element generated stronger effects overall than restoration alone.

Finally, the fifth hypothesis predicts that both treatments will cause subjects to become more likely to participate in non-political activities, like being involved in one's community. Subjects were asked how likely they are to volunteer in their communities in the future (5A), whether they are aware of opportunities to be involved (5B), whether they were currently involved in their communities (5C), and whether they hoped to be more involved in the future (5D). Figure 5 displays the results.

Overall, neither treatment affected subjects' current levels of community volunteer work. The restoration treatment on its own did not affect subjects' perceived likelihood of engaging in volunteer work in the future, but subjects who received both restoration information and a mobilization appeal did report significantly higher future likelihood of volunteering (+13.3, $p \leq 0.05$). Awareness of volunteer opportunities was actually slightly lower in both treatment groups on average (this makes sense, as the placebo treatment provided subjects with information about upcoming volunteer opportunities). Although the treatments generate little movement with regard to current volunteer activities, the restoration treatment did generate a marginally significant increase in subjects' expressing that they hoped to volunteer in the future (+7.1, $p \leq 0.10$). A similar non-

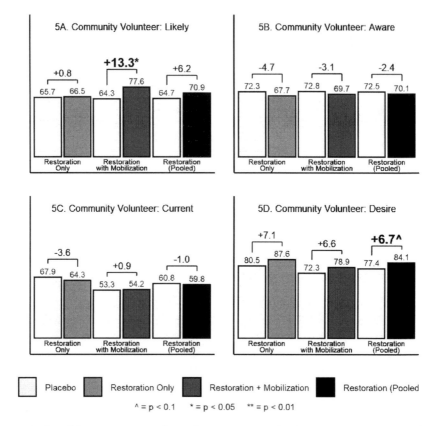

Figure 5. Predicted Post-Treatment Values of Four Estimate of Volunteer Activities Within the Local Community, by Treatment Group. $**p \leq 0.01$; $* p \leq 0.05$; $+ p \leq 0.10$.

significant increase was observed among subjects who received both restoration and mobilization. The pooled effects of both treatments was also marginally significant ($+6.7$, $p \leq 0.10$). Overall, the results suggest that voting rights and voting might generate spillover effects that increase a desire to participate in other non-political ways. However, these last set of effects are fairly weak and inconsistent.

Discussion of results

Overall, this experiment provides strong evidence that restoring voting rights to citizens with felony convictions will cause those citizens to develop stronger levels of political efficacy. Treated subjects reported higher levels of both internal and external efficacy, predicted that they were more likely to vote in the future, and also demonstrated a stronger propensity to engage in other participatory behaviours beyond the act of voting alone.

The treatment generated varying effects on subjects' actual restoration status, knowledge of their restoration status, voter registration, and voter turnout. The effects experienced by each subject depended on whether the subject already had their voting rights restored, whether they knew if their rights had been restored, and whether they allowed the researcher to look up their restoration status. Some subjects were already registered and voting. Others arrived at the survey believing they were disenfranchised, learned their voting rights had already been restored, and registered to vote the same day. There were also many experiences between these two extremes. Both treatments increased overall awareness of newly restored voting rights, and also increased the number of subjects whose rights were restored. As such, the effects of the treatments capture the combined effects of overall increases in voting rights and voting power among this population.[11]

It is worth noting that the mobilization treatment did not generate a significant increase in turnout during the 2017 election. However, registrations and awareness of voting rights both increased. Even though the mobilization treatment did not increase turnout in the short-term, it assisted subjects with voter registration, informed them about the election calendar, and encouraged them to participate. As such, the current study adds support to the existing body of evidence that suggests that encouraging and increasing participation also increases political efficacy. It is also likely that turnout among treated subjects might increase in the future, perhaps during more high-profile national elections.

Previous research has demonstrated that mobilizing individuals to participate in politics can cause an increase in political efficacy (Shineman 2018b). The current study adds further confidence to this result, by replicating this previous finding among a different subject population in a different political setting. Although the restoration treatment generated significant increases in efficacy on its own, treatment effects were consistently stronger when a mobilization element was added.

The final novel contribution of this study is providing evidence that the restoration of voting rights alone (without mobilization) also increases political efficacy. Subjects who received only information about the restoration of their voting rights – with no mention of the upcoming election or assistance with registration or voting – reported significantly higher levels of external efficacy and internal efficacy, and higher expectations of participating in the future both as a voter, and in a wider participatory context.

These results suggest that felony disenfranchisement laws are directly decreasing political efficacy through the act of disenfranchisement – and not only through the decrease in turnout they generate. Some argue that the effects of disenfranchisement are less severe because of the low voter turnout among eligible ex-offenders (e.g. Miles 2004). While other estimates of the electoral power of the ex-offender population refute this critique (e.g. Manza and Uggen 2008), the current study offers an additional response. Regardless as to whether citizens choose to exercise their voting rights, the act of restoring rights alone causes citizens to feel more empowered, more capable, and to be more likely to seek out opportunities for participatory engagement in the future.

The limited sample size does place some restrictions regarding the level of confidence we can place in the magnitude of these estimates. Small samples provide a more difficult barrier to revealing existing effects, increasing the risk of false negatives (Vadillo, Konstantinidis, and Shanks 2016). Thus we should not consider observed null effects as conclusive evidence of no real effect taking place. Additionally, small samples are also more susceptible to over-estimating effect sizes, so we should also approach the magnitude of the significant findings with caution. The appendix provides power statistics for each model. Although two models were sufficiently powered above 90%, three significant effects were estimated in models with limited power (between 0.70–0.79), and three significant effects were estimated in models with power between 0.60 and 0.69.[12]

A natural question one might ask is whether the effects demonstrated in this study can be generalized to all citizens with felony convictions who were once disenfranchised and might have their voting rights restored. Because the rules restricting the voting rights of citizens with felony convictions vary between states, the population of possible subjects in Virginia is different from the population of subjects with comparable status in other states. This study was also conducted within the city of Richmond – a single city within the state of Virginia. Lastly, because of the hard-to-reach nature of the subject population and the desire to recruit subjects who were not registered to vote or in other consumer databases, the study recruited a convenience sample, not a representative sample of the full Richmond population. Thus we cannot infer from this single study that all citizens who are eligible to have their voting rights restored in Richmond would experience effects of similar magnitude in response to these treatments. However, the results do show that the citizens in this study did increase their political efficacy in response to the treatments – which means at least some members of this population would experience these effects. The average effect across all possible subjects nationwide might be larger, or might be smaller, compared to the effects documented among this particular sample.

Future studies can expand and apply the template provided in this study to other populations in other states and other elections. Future studies could also vary the content and intensity of the treatments. Such analyses could provide additional information regarding how robust these effects are across different types of citizens in different types of settings. Furthermore, it would be worthwhile to explore whether the size of the treatment effects varies across different types of citizens (e.g. by age, by gender, or by race). The sample size in this experiment was not large enough to facilitate estimating heterogeneous treatment effects. Future studies could increase the sample size in order to estimate which types of citizens experience the highest increases in efficacy when their rights are restored.

Conclusion

Felony disenfranchisement laws restrict the voting rights of over four million American Citizens, likely altering some electoral outcomes, and generating unknown effects at the individual level. Scholars and policymakers have long suspected that disenfranchisement causes a sense of otherness, ripples into disengagement beyond the electoral arena, and can affect overall political efficacy, as well as recidivism. This study presents the first empirical evidence of a causal relationship between the restoration of voting rights and political efficacy. This paper finds that both voting and voting rights increase efficacy.

Many scholars have endorsed civic engagement and reintegration as key elements of successful post-prison re-entry (Orr 1998; Bazemore and Stinchcomb 2004; Uggen, Manza, and Thompson 2006). Because pro-social attitudes like internal and external efficacy are thought to increase a citizen's chances of successfully reintegrating into society after being released from prison, the results from this study also suggest that disenfranchisement policies might be inadvertently preventing citizens with felony convictions from successfully integrating into society after being released from prison – thus potentially making a return to crime more likely.

Shineman (2018d) finds that attitudes toward felony disenfranchisement are largely racially motivated. However, that study also finds that public opposition to full voting rights would be reduced if evidence suggests that allowing citizens with felony convictions to participate would help them reintegrate into society, and decrease recidivism. Although felony disenfranchisement has historically been a fairly partisan issue, bipartisan alliances have recently found common ground in their shared goal to create successful re-entry programmes. This study suggests that the right to vote doesn't only affect whether a person registers and votes – it also affects their participatory attitudes and their confidence in their own abilities – attitudes which help people transition into society after being released from prison. Thus this research also has the potential to bridge the historical partisan divide in public opinion on felony disenfranchisement policies, by introducing new evidence that suggests a further unintended consequence of these laws.

Notes

1. Recruitment materials were placed online and in print in a variety of newspapers (Urban Views Weekly; Richmond News; Richmond Free Press), job search websites (indeed.com; craigslist.org; classifiedads.com), through Facebook ads, and were also distributed through flyers posted at outdoor street festivals, public transportation hubs, bodegas, and in offices and organizations that provided public services. Recruitment materials did not mention voting rights or any other political content. A sample recruitment ad is provided in the Appendix.
2. The complete materials for all experimental treatments can be viewed in the Appendix.
3. All volunteer opportunities were for events taking place between October 14th (the voter registration deadline) and November 7th (Election Day).
4. How strongly do you agree or disagree with the following statements: "My vote can make a difference"; "I feel politically empowered"
5. How strongly do you agree or disagree with the following statements: "I consider myself well-qualified to participate in politics"; "I feel that I could do as good a job in public office as most other people"; "I am just as qualified to serve on a jury as most other people"; "I am just as qualified to serve as a notary public as other people"
6. "How likely are you to vote in the upcoming [November 2018 General Midterm Election] / [November 2020 Presidential Election] / [November 2021 Virginia Statewide Election]?"
7. "Over the next year, how likely are you to [contribute time or money to a political campaign] / [contact an elected representative]"; "Are you willing to answer some extra survey questions for free?"
8. How strongly do you agree or disagree with the following statements: "I am currently active in my community"; " I am aware of opportunities to be involved in my community"; "Over the next year, how likely are you to engage in the following types of participation ... Volunteer Within Your Community"; "In the future, I would like to be active in my community".
9. As specified in the pre-analysis plan, covariates include age, age^2, gender, race, education, employment, and number of years at current address.
10. All directional hypothesis tests were pre-registered and specified in the pre-analysis plan.
11. One might be tempted to estimate effects among subgroups within the sample, such as generating a complier average causal effect (CACE) estimating the effects of learning one's right to vote was restored. However, such analyses rely on the exclusion restriction to be unbiased, and this assumption is not met with the current design. There are several reasons to suspect that the treatments generated increases in efficacy beyond the effects they had through the increases in awareness of voting rights they generated. For example, subjects were informed that the Governor proactively restored voting rights to 150,000 citizens with felony convictions in Virginia. Learning about this policy (among those who had not heard of it before) might increase efficacy and confidence in oneself and one's peer group – as the Governor made a statement that this community should be eligible to vote. Because the treatments likely caused direct increases in efficacy, models estimating complier effects would provide

over-estimates. Estimating the average effect of receiving each treatment is the more conservative approach, and the estimated effects of receiving either treatment are also unbiased.
12. Overall, of the eight estimates where the pooled analysis estimated statistically significant treatment effects (1A, 2A, 2B, 3A, 3B, 3C, 4A, and 4C), the average level of power was 0.75.

Acknowledgements

Thank you to Ray Dutch, Lisa Hill, Marc Meredith, Melissa Michelson, Paul Legunas, Amy Lerman, Dave Nickerson, and Jill Sheppard for vital input and feedback during various stages of designing and analyzing this project. The experimental designs also benefitted from feedback received at the ISPS Experimental Research Methods seminar at Yale University, Bobst-CSDP Workshop on Experimental Research Design at Princeton University, Center for the Study of American Politics Workshop at Yale University, American Politics Seminar at New York University, Workshop on Experimental Research Design at the University of Pittsburgh, and the Evidence in Governance and Policy Workshop in Bogota, Colombia. The field experiment was funded through the Stephen D. Manners Faculty Development Award at the University of Pittsburgh. The field experiment was preregistered with a pre-analysis plan through EGAP: ID #20171109AA.

Disclosure statement

No potential conflict of interest was reported by the author.

Funding

This work was supported by The field experiment was funded through the Stephen D. Manners Faculty Development Award.

References

Abramson, Paul R. 1983. *Political Attitudes in America*. San Francisco: Freeman.
Acock, Alan, Harold D. Clarke, and Marianne C. Stewart. 1985. "A New Model for Old Measures: A Covariance Structure Analysis of Political Efficacy." *The Journal of Politics* 47 (4): 1062–1084.
Allen, Jessie. 2011. "Documentary Disenfranchisement." *Tulane Law Review* 86: 389.
Balch, George I. 1974. "Multiple Indicators in Survey Research: The Concept 'Sense of Political Efficacy'." *Political Methodology* 1 (Spring): 1–43.
Bazemore, Gordon, and Jeanne Stinchcomb. 2004. "A Civic Engagement Model of Reentry: Involving Community Through Service and Restorative Justice." *Federal Probation* 68 (2): 14–24.
Behrens, Angela, Christopher Uggen, and Jeff Manza. 2003. "Ballot Manipulation and the 'Menace of Negro Domination': Racial Threat and Felon Disenfranchisement in the United States, 1850-2002." *American Journal of Sociology* 109 (3): 559–605.
Bowler, Shaun, and Todd Donovan. 2002. "Democracy, Institutions and Attitudes About Citizen Influence on Government." *British Journal of Political Science* 32 (2): 371–390.
Burch, Traci. 2011. "Turnout and Party Registration among Criminal Offenders in the 2008 General Election." *Law & Society Review* 45 (3): 699–730.
Campbell, Angus, Gerald Gurin, and Warren E. Miller. 1954. "The Voter Decides."
Cardinale, Matthew. 2004. *Triple-Decker Disenfranchisement: First-Person Accounts of Losing the Right to Vote among Poor, Homeless Americans with a Felony Conviction*. Washington, DC: The Sentencing Project.

Clarke, Harold D., and Alan C. Acock. 1989. "National Elections and Political Attitudes: The Case of Political Efficacy." *British Journal of Political Science* 19 (4): 551–562.

Craig, Stephen, and Michael Maggiotto. 1982. "Measuring Political Efficacy." *Political Methodology* 8 (3): 85–110.

Craig, Stephen C., Richard G. Niemi, and Glenn E. Silver. 1990. "Political Efficacy and Trust: A Report on the NES Pilot Study Items." *Political Behavior* 12 (3): 289–314.

Douglass, Frederick. 1865. "What the Black Man Wants." Speech Delivered at the Annual Meeting of the Massachusetts Anti-Slavery Society in Boston, MA. Retrieved November. Vol. 10.

Drucker, Ernest, and Ricardo Barreras. 2005. "Studies of Voting Behavior and Felony Disenfranchisement among Individuals in the Criminal Justice System in New York, Connecticut, and Ohio." The Sentencing Project.

Ewald, Alec. 2005. "A Crazy-Quilt of Tiny Pieces: State and Local Administration of American Criminal Disenfranchisement Law." Vol. 16. Sentencing Project.

Ewald, Alec C., and Brandon Rottinghaus, eds. 2009. *Criminal Disenfranchisement in an International Perspective*. Cambridge: Cambridge University Press.

Finkel, Steven E. 1985. "Reciprocal Effects of Participation and Political Efficacy: A Panel Analysis." *American Journal of Political Science* 29: 891–913.

Finkel, Steven E. 1987. "The Effects of Participation on Political Efficacy and Political Support: Evidence from a West German Panel." *The Journal of Politics* 49 (2): 441–464.

Fishkin, James S. 1991. *Democracy and Deliberation. New Directions for Democratic Reform*. New Haven: Yale University Press.

Garfinkel, Harold. 1956. "Conditions of Successful Degradation Ceremonies." *American Journal of Sociology* 61 (5): 420–424.

Gerber, Alan S., Gregory A. Huber, Marc Meredith, Daniel R. Biggers, and David J. Henry. 2015. "Can Incarcerated Felons Be (Re)Integrated Into the Political System? Results from a Field Experiment." *American Journal of Political Science* 59 (4): 912–926.

Ginsberg, Benjamin. 1982. *The Consequences of Consent*. Reading, MA: Addison Wesley.

Haselswerdt, Michael V. 2009. "Con Job: An Estimate of Ex-Felon Voter Turnout Using Document-Based Data." *Social Science Quarterly* 90 (2): 262–273.

Hjalmarsson, Randi, and Mark Lopez. 2010. "The Voting Behavior of Young Disenfranchised Felons: Would They Vote if they Could?" *American Law and Economics Review* 12 (2): 356–393.

Hurwitz, Jon, and Mark Peffley. 1997. "Public Perceptions of Race and Crime: The Role of Racial Stereotypes." *American Journal of Political Science* 41: 375–401.

Madsen, Douglas. 1987. "Political Self-Efficacy Tested." *American Political Science Review* 81 (2): 571–581.

Manza, Jeff, Clem Brooks, and Christopher Uggen. 2004. "Public Attitudes Toward Felon Disenfranchisement in the United States." *Public Opinion Quarterly* 68: 275–286.

Manza, Jeff, and Christopher Uggen. 2008. *Locked out: Felon Disenfranchisement and American Democracy*. Oxford: Oxford University Press.

Maruna, S. 2001. *Making Good: How Ex-Convicts Reform and Rebuild Their Lives*. Washington, DC: American Psychological Association.

Maruna, Shadd. 2011. "Reentry as a Rite of Passage." *Punishment & Society* 13 (1): 3–28.

Meredith, Marc, and Michael Morse. 2014. "Do Voting Rights Notification Laws Increase Ex-Felon Turnout?" *The ANNALS of the American Academy of Political and Social Science* 651 (1): 220–249.

Meredith, Marc, and Michael Morse. 2015. "The Politics of the Restoration of Ex-Felon Voting Rights: The Case of Iowa." *Quarterly Journal of Political Science* 10 (1): 41–100.

Miles, Thomas J. 2004. "Felon Disenfranchisement and Voter Turnout." *Journal Legal Studies* 33 (1): 85–129.

Miller, Bryan Lee, and Laura E. Agnich. 2016. "Unpaid Debt to Society: Exploring how Ex-Felons View Restrictions on Voting Rights After the Completion of their Sentence." *Contemporary Justice Review* 19 (1): 69–85.

Miller, B. L., and J. Spillane. 2012. "Civil Death: An Examination of Ex-Felon Disenfranchisement and Reintegration." *Punishment & Society* 14: 402–428.

Morrell, Michael E. 2003. "Survey and Experimental Evidence for a Reliable and Valid Measure of Internal Political Efficacy." *The Public Opinion Quarterly* 67 (4): 589–602.

Niemi, Richard G., Stephen C. Craig, and Franco Mattei. 1991. "Measuring Internal Political Efficacy in the 1988 National Election Study." *American Political Science Review* 85 (4): 1407–1413.

Olsen, Marvin E. 1982. *Participatory Pluralism*. Chicago: Nelson-Hall.

Orr, G. 1998. "Ballotless and Behind Bars: The Denial of the Franchise to Prisoners." *Federal Law Review* 26 (1): 56–82.

Pateman, Carole. 1970. *Participation and Democratic Theory*. Cambridge: Cambridge University Press.

Peffley, Mark, and Jon Hurwitz. 2002. "The Racial Components of "Race-Neutral" Crime Policy Attitudes." *Political Psychology* 23 (1): 59–75.

Pinaire, Brian, Milton Heumann, and Laura Bilotta. 2002. "Barred from the Vote: Public Attitudes Toward the Disenfranchisement of Felons." *Fordham Urban Law Journal* 30: 1519–1550.

Pinkard, John E. 2013. *African American Felon Disenfranchisement: Case Studies in Modern Racism and Political Exclusion*. El Paso: LFB Scholarly Publishing LLC.

Pocock, Stuart J., Susan E. Assmann, Laura E. Enos, and Linda E. Kasten. 2002. "Subgroup Analysis, Covariate Adjustment and Baseline Comparisons in Clinical Trial Reporting: Current Practice and Problems." *Statistics in Medicine* 21 (19): 2917–2930.

Semetko, Holli, and Patti Valkenburg. 1998. "The Impact of Attentiveness on Political Efficacy: Evidence from a Three-Year German Panel Study." *International Journal of Public Opinion Research* 10 (3): 195–210.

Shineman, Victoria Anne. 2018a. "If you Mobilize Them, they will Become Informed: Experimental Evidence that Information Acquisition is Endogenous to Costs and Incentives to Participate." *British Journal of Political Science* 48 (1): 189–211.

Shineman, Victoria. 2018b. "Evidence that Casting a Ballot Increases Political Trust and Efficacy: Isolating the Downstream Effects of Voting by Generating Exogenous Shocks in Turnout." October 25, 2018. doi:10.2139/ssrn.3272681.

Shineman, Victoria. 2018c. "Restoring Rights, Restoring Trust: Evidence that Reversing Felony Disenfranchisement Penalties Increases Both Trust and Cooperation with Government." October 25, 2018. doi:10.2139/ssrn.3272694.

Shineman, Victoria. 2018d. "Racial Animus Is Decreasing Support for the Voting Rights of Citizens with Felony Convictions." October 25, 2018. doi:10.2139/ssrn.3272685.

Smith, Daniel A., and Caroline Tolbert. 2009. *Educated by Initiative: The Effects of Direct Democracy on Citizens and Political Organizations in the American States*. Ann Arbor, MI: University of Michigan Press.

Uggen, Christopher, Ryan Larson, and Sarah Shannon. 2016. "Million lost Voters: State-Level Estimates of Felony Disenfranchisement." Research and Advocacy for Reform (6).

Uggen, Christopher, and Jeff Manza. 2002. "Democratic Contraction? Political Consequences of Felon Disenfranchisement in the United States." *American Sociological Review* 67: 777–803.

Uggen, Christopher, Jeff Manza, and Angela Behrens. 2004. "'Less than the Average Citizens': Stigma, Role Transition, and the Civic Reintegration of Convicted Felons." In *After Crime and Punishment: Pathways to Offender Reintegration*, edited by Shadd Maruna, and Russell Immarigeon, 261–293. Portland, OR: Willan Publishing.

Uggen, Christopher, Jeff Manza, and Melissa Thompson. 2006. "Citizenship, Democracy, and the Civic Reintegration of Criminal Offenders." *The Annals of the American Academy of Political and Social Science* 605 (1): 281–310.

Vadillo, Miguel A., Emmanouil Konstantinidis, and David R. Shanks. 2016. "Underpowered Samples, False Negatives, and Unconscious Learning." *Psychonomic Bulletin & Review* 23 (1): 87–102.

Wilson, David C., Michael L. Owens, and Darren W. Davis. 2015. "How Racial Attitudes and Ideology Affect Political Rights for Felons." *DuBois Review* 12: 73–94.

Are inequalities in representation lower under compulsory voting?

Eric Guntermann ⓘ, Ruth Dassonneville ⓘ and Peter Miller ⓘ

ABSTRACT
In recent years, there has been considerable scholarly interest in inequalities in representation between rich and poor citizens. Just over 20 years ago, Lijphart argued that compulsory voting could reduce such inequalities by boosting the turnout of the poor. We measure the efficacy of Lijphart's proposal with regard to three measures of representation; (1) ideological congruence, (2) an indicator of whether a citizen's preferred party enters government and (3) an indicator of how much citizens like governing parties compared to opposition parties. We find that the extent to which the rich are better represented than the poor varies strongly across countries. We also find that the income gap in representation is smaller in the compulsory voting countries in our sample. However, turnout is not a significant predictor of inequalities in representation.

In recent years, a number of authors have expressed concern that economic inequalities produce political inequalities. Their research has shown that the policy preferences of better-off citizens have more influence on representatives' votes (Ellis 2012; Bartels 2016) and on government policy (Gilens 2012) than those of the poor in the United States and in comparative contexts (Giger, Rosset, and Bernauer 2012; Rosset, Giger, and Bernauer 2013; Lupu and Warner 2017).

A plausible explanation for unequal influence is that the rich vote more often and in greater numbers than the poor, giving them more governmental influence. There is considerable evidence of a temporally durable socioeconomic bias in turnout (Verba and Nie 1972; Leighley and Nagler 2013). While the size of the income gap in turnout varies between countries (Kasara and Suryanarayan 2015), a meta-analysis shows that a large majority of studies that consider the impact of income on electoral participation find that the rich vote more than the poor (Smets and van Ham 2013).[1] The consequences of an economic bias in electoral participation are not a recent concern. The most cited example is Lijphart's (1997) Presidential Address to the American Political Science Association, in which he argued that inequalities in turnout translate into unequal political influence. As a solution, Lijphart advocated the introduction of compulsory voting. He argued that it would boost turnout and, in turn, improve the representation of the poor.

Dozens of scholars have empirically tested Lijphart's (1997) arguments. Strong evidence substantiates the claim that inequalities in income (or correlates of income, such as education) are reduced when turnout is high (Gallego 2010; Persson, Solevid, and Öhrvall 2013) and when turnout is compulsory (Dassonneville, Hooghe, and Miller 2017). Whether compelling citizens to vote has an effect on inequalities in political representation, however, is unclear.[2]

We contribute a comprehensive analysis of income differences in representation to this debate and we assess the extent to which government composition reflects the preferences of rich and poor in the presence of compulsory voting rules. We expect that better-off citizens are more successful than the poor at getting governments that reflect their preferences (Giger, Rosset, and Bernauer 2012). We also expect income inequalities to be smaller when turnout is high and that countries that compel citizens to vote to have lower inequalities in representation between rich and poor citizens (Lijphart 1997).

We analyse the influence on government composition using different types of indicators. We first use the dominant measure of representation in comparative studies: ideological (left-right) congruence (Huber and Bingham Powell 1994; Golder and Stramski 2010; Ferland 2016). To address the limitations of a focus on a single ideological dimension, we complement the congruence-measure with an analysis of measures of correspondence based on party preferences (Blais, Guntermann, and Bodet 2017).

To test our expectations, we use survey data from modules 2–4 of the Comparative Study of Electoral Systems (CSES) project. Our results show that the rich are better represented than the poor in about a third of elections. We also find that the gap between rich and poor on both of the party preference measures of representation is significantly smaller in the compulsory voting countries in our sample. It is not clear, however, that the mechanism is increased turnout of the poor, as Lijphart (1997) proposed.

Preferences of the rich and the poor and government composition

It is likely that income inequalities in turnout are consequential for government representation because conventional wisdom has it that "who votes and who doesn't, has important consequences for who gets elected" (Lijphart 1997, 4). Given that the rich are more likely to turn out than the poor (Verba and Nie 1972; Leighley and Nagler 1992; Smets and van Ham 2013), we suspect that they will end up being better represented than the poor. In particular, a difference in representation will emerge if rich and poor have different political preferences. Given that research on voting behaviour beginning with Lazarsfeld, Berelson, and Gaudet (1968) has long shown that demographic characteristics – such as class or income – influence vote choice, it is possible that the rich's higher likelihood to vote translates into a stronger impact on electoral results and on who ends up in government. The preferences of the rich – who vote more – should be more strongly expressed on election day, giving them a representation advantage.

This assumption, however, should be tested. A number of scholarly findings cast doubt on the thesis that income differences in turnout lead to unequal representation. Several authors indicate that citizens with different income levels have similar policy preferences (Soroka and Wlezien 2008; Bashir 2015; Enns 2015; Branham, Soroka, and Wlezien 2017). If the preferences of the poor are similar to those of the rich, they might be well represented even if they do not turn out to vote.

Work that has focused on who gets elected when turnout is higher has also produced mixed results. While it is commonly expected that left-of-centre parties – representing the poor – will do better when turnout is high, only a handful of studies find evidence that fits such a pattern (Pacek and Radcliff 1995; Brunell and DiNardo 2004; Fowler 2013). Others find no (Citrin, Schickler, and Sides 2003; van der Eijk and van Egmond 2007) or even reverse effects (Ferland 2016; Miller and Dassonneville 2016).

Given these doubts, we verify empirically whether the poor are represented in Pitkin's (1967, 8–9) sense of making apparent "something which is nevertheless not present literally or in fact." In the political realm, this consists of giving citizens a presence in government.

A dominant way for studying representation assesses the proximity of government to citizens' policy preferences (Achen 1978; Powell 2000). We focus on ideological congruence, like most work in the comparative representation literature (Ferland 2016; Golder and Stramski 2010; Huber and Bingham Powell 1994). It involves assessing the proximity between the party (or parties) in government and citizens' ideological positions. Congruence is usually operationalized as proximity to the median citizen or as the average proximity to individual citizens (Golder and Stramski 2010). This approach has previously been used to study income inequalities in representation (Giger, Rosset, and Bernauer 2012; Rosset, Giger, and Bernauer 2013). We determine whether governments are less ideologically congruent with the poor than to the rich.

A focus on a single ideological dimension has important limitations. As Converse (1964) showed, it is far from clear that most citizens think about politics in an ideological way. Moreover, in many countries politics is known to be multi-dimensional (Medeiros, Gauvin, and Chhim 2015). Furthermore, Stecker and Tausendpfund (2016) have argued that to fully understand citizens' political attitudes in European democracies, it is essential to take into account citizens' and parties' positions on different dimensions. Finally, ideology is only one of many factors that influence vote choice (Campbell et al. 1960; Clarke et al. 2004; Lewis-Beck and Stegmaier 2007).

To address the limitations of ideological congruence, Blais, Guntermann, and Bodet (2017) have argued that scholars should consider alternative indicators of representation. They suggest relying on indicators of citizens' party preferences; they show that citizens have diverse evaluations of different parties and that a representative government should include parties that are more liked and exclude parties that are less liked. To evaluate the representativeness of the government in terms of party preferences, Blais, Guntermann, and Bodet (2017) propose three criteria: the proportion of citizens whose highest-rated party enters government, whether the party that is highest rated in the aggregate enters government, and a summary measure of how much more citizens like government parties than opposition parties.[3] They argue that the third measure is the most complete measure, because it includes evaluations of all parties and it assesses the intensity of preferences for each of them (Blais, Guntermann, and Bodet 2017, 318).

We integrate this work into our analyses and investigate income inequalities in representation in terms of ideological congruence and party preferences. We focus on the two party preference criteria proposed by Blais, Guntermann, and Bodet (2017) that can be measured at the individual level: whether citizens' most preferred party is in government and the extent to which they like government parties more than opposition parties.

Testing the conventional wisdom that the rich are better represented than the poor, and focusing on indicators of ideological congruence and party preference measures of representation, our expectations are the following: Parties to which the rich are ideologically closer or that they like more should end up with more seats in the legislature and, in turn, in government. Our first hypothesis is that the rich do better than the poor on the three criteria of representation.

Hypothesis 1 Rich citizens are better represented on each criterion than poor citizens.

More equal representation under compulsory voting, and under high turnout

We expect the poor to be less well represented than the rich. This disadvantage likely varies by context. There are good theoretical reasons for assuming that representation will be more equal in high-turnout settings and, consequently, in countries that mandate voting (Lijphart 1997).

The argument is based on what scholars refer to as "Tingsten's law of dispersion" (Lijphart 1997; Persson, Solevid, and Öhrvall 2013; Dassonneville and Hooghe 2017). That is, differences between who votes and who does not – such as income-based biases – will be smaller when turnout is higher (Tingsten 1937). Turnout-inequalities in education or income are indeed found to be smaller in high turnout elections compared to elections with low turnout (Persson, Solevid, and Öhrvall 2013; Dassonneville and Hooghe 2017). Building on this work, and assuming that participation improves representation, we expect income-based differences in representation to be reduced under high turnout. Given that compulsory voting "is a particularly effective method to achieve high turnout" (Lijphart 1997, 2) we also expect that compulsory voting will equalize inequalities in representation.

Previous work offers some insights into the validity of these expectations. First, the mobilizing effect of compulsory voting has not been challenged. Comparative work (Blais and Dobrzynska 1998), research that studies the effects of the abolition or introduction of compulsory voting in single countries (Hirczy 1994; Ferland 2016; Miller and Dassonneville 2016) as well as meta-analyses (Cancela and Geys 2016) all show evidence of the strong and positive effect of compulsory voting on electoral participation.

There is substantial variation in the rules and implementation of compulsory voting between countries, however. In some countries voting is mandatory by law, but the sanction is not enforced (Jackman 2001; Panagopoulos 2008). There is, furthermore, substantial heterogeneity in terms of the sanctions for abstainers. In some compulsory voting countries, non-voters have to pay a fine, in other settings non-voters are simply excluded from the electoral register, or are excluded from certain government services or government jobs (Jackman 2001; Panagopoulos 2008; Dassonneville et al. 2019). The impact of compulsory voting on turnout varies accordingly, with the strongest positive effects of mandatory voting in countries that enforce it (Birch 2009; Singh 2011).

There is also evidence that compelling citizens to vote reduces inequalities between citizens who are more or less likely to vote. Under compulsory voting, gaps in turnout between citizens who are young and old, who have high and low knowledge, who are rich and poor, who have high and low efficacy as well as partisans and non-partisans are lower (Singh 2015; Dassonneville, Hooghe, and Miller 2017).

However, a number of authors have expressed concern that the "quality" of the vote choice by variously disadvantaged citizens is lower when they are compelled to vote (Selb and Lachat 2009).[4] Focusing on proximity voting as an indicator of the quality of the vote, studies show that the quality of the vote choice is lower in compulsory voting countries (Singh 2016; Dassonneville, Hooghe, and Miller 2017). Studies that explore variation within compulsory voting settings find that those who would not turn out to vote if it was not mandatory have a lower likelihood of voting for the most proximate party (Dassonneville et al. 2019). This concern is particularly important when focusing on ideological congruence, but should matter less when focusing on representation in terms of party preferences.

It is important to consider both ideological and party preference measures of representation. Ideological preference measures are limited because voters' ideologies are partly endogenous to their vote choice (Brody and Page 1972; Lenz 2012). Citizens, in particular those with high levels of political knowledge, adopt their preferred party's policy positions (Zaller 1992). Since we know that compulsory voting compels many less sophisticated voters to vote, it is possible that the lower quality of votes under compulsory voting is a result of less sophisticated voters' lower motivation to adapt their ideology to their vote choice. Ideological proximity to the party one votes for may reflect as much about one's ideological positioning as about the "quality" of vote choice. Ideology should, therefore, not be considered an absolute benchmark against which to judge representation. Party preferences are just as important.

Building on the insights of Tingsten (1937), we expect that income-inequalities in representation will be reduced under high turnout. Given the mobilizing impact of compulsory voting, we also expect that representation is more equal in countries that mandate voting. These expectations lead to the following hypotheses about the representation advantage of rich citizens over poor citizens (i.e. how much better represented the former are than the latter):

Hypothesis 2 The representation advantage of rich citizens over poor citizens is smaller under compulsory voting than under voluntary voting.

Hypothesis 3 The representation advantage of rich citizens over poor citizens is smaller when turnout is higher.

Data and methods

We rely on data from modules 2, 3 and 4 of the Comparative Study of Electoral Systems (CSES) project.[5] The CSES project coordinates a common module of questions that are fielded in representative post-electoral surveys worldwide. The data are ideally suited for a comparative analysis of voters' electoral behaviour and their political preferences.

To compare the extent to which low- and high-income groups are represented, we first code – at the individual level – the ideological distance between a citizen and the government, whether or not a citizen's preferred party is in government, and a citizen's relative evaluation of government and opposition parties. These indicators constitute our three dependent variables.

To operationalize the indicators, we use two sets of survey variables: respondents' left-right placements as well as their placements of each party on the same scale, from 0 (left) to 10 (right), and respondents' evaluations of each of the parties, measured on a scale from 0 (strongly dislike) to 10 (strongly like).

We then consider how well the ideological or party preferences of each income group were reflected in the governments that formed following each election. To distinguish between groups, we use the income variable included in the CSES dataset, which placed respondents in income quintiles. Data on government composition come from a variety of sources.[6]

We follow previous studies and focus on non-presidential democracies (Blais, Guntermann, and Bodet 2017; Ferland 2016; Golder and Stramski 2010). We include parliamentary systems and the premier-presidential variant of semi-presidentialism. In the latter, the legislature has more influence over government composition relative to the president (Shugart 2005). We are primarily interested in the party (or parties) which enter government after an election, and therefore do not include cases where the chief executive is elected and then selects the members of the cabinet independently from the legislature.[7]

We operationalized congruence by first calculating the ideological position of each party. We did so by taking the perception of each party's position by the median survey respondent. The position of governments was obtained by weighting each cabinet party by the proportion of seats it has in the legislature. We then calculated the absolute distance between each survey respondent and the government. This way of proceeding corresponds to "absolute citizens congruence", which unlike the more common "absolute median congruence"[8] can be calculated at the individual level, allowing us to compare congruence between the rich and the poor. Finally, we subtracted these distance measures from 10 to make them measures of proximity to government (min = 0, mean = 7.3, max = 10, stdev = 2.1).

For the second criterion, we determined the party (or parties) each citizen rated highest. We considered up to two parties when there was a tie.[9] Respondents who gave more than two parties the highest rating were coded as not having their preferred party in government, because they did not have a clear preference. We then determined whether the party or one of the two parties a respondent rated the highest ended up in the cabinet following the election. Overall, 54.4% of respondents found their preferred party in government.

For the third criterion, we calculated like/dislike scores for government and opposition parties. To calculate the former, we weighted each respondent's evaluations of each government party by the proportion of seats among cabinet parties they had in the legislature. For the latter, we weighted evaluations of each opposition party by their proportion of legislative seats among all parties that are excluded from government. We then took the difference between evaluations of government parties and of opposition parties (min= −10, mean = 1.1, max = 10, stdev = 4.0). To construct the measures of criteria 2 and 3, we follow the procedures of Blais, Guntermann, and Bodet (2017). Details about the dataset, the variables used, and how we recoded variables are in the supporting materials.

Our analyses follow a two-step strategy to compare the representation of respondents in the top and bottom income quintiles. First, we assess the existence of inequalities in representation in the government formed after the election. To do so, we ran a series of bivariate individual-level regressions of each criterion of representation on a dummy variable for the fifth income quintile in reference to the lowest quintile. For the first and the third criteria, which take continuous values, we use Ordinary Least Squares (OLS) regression. The coefficient on the top income quintile dummy variable shows us how much better represented the richest respondents were on each criterion than those in the lowest income quintile. For the second criterion, we use logistic regression and focus on the difference between the predicted probabilities of a rich respondent and a poor respondent having their preferred party in government. For each election sample in the dataset, we estimate regression models for each of the three dependent variables.

In a second step, we run multi-level regressions to determine whether compulsory voting reduces gaps in representation between the rich and the poor. We regress each dependent variable on a dummy variable distinguishing high-income respondents (i.e. top quintile in a given country) from low-income (i.e. bottom quintile in the same country) as well as interactions between that dummy and macro-level variables.[10]

Our sample includes four countries that mandate voting: Australia, Greece, Thailand and Turkey, which we indicate using a simple dummy variable. In the supplementary materials, we validate the robustness of the results to alternative ways of operationalizing compulsory voting rules.[11]

We add relevant control variables to the multilevel models. First, we account for the proportionality of the electoral system in a country using the mean district magnitude. Proportionality of the electoral system significantly determines party preference representation (Blais, Guntermann, and Bodet 2017). Iversen and Soskice (2006) have shown that left-wing governments are more common under proportional electoral rules, which might be more favourable to the poor.

We also control for variables assessing how close the preferences of middle-income respondents are to those of high-income respondents than to those with low incomes.[12] An extreme income category (either low or high) will be better represented if it happens to share preferences with other categories more than with the other extreme income group. We calculated such measures for both the left-right dimension and for party evaluations. For the left-right scale, we subtracted the average ideology scores of respondents in the middle-income quintile from those of respondents in the top quintile. We then subtracted the average ideology score of respondents in the middle-income quintile from respondents in the bottom income quintile. Subsequently, we subtracted the absolute value of the former from the latter. In this way, we generated a measure that captures how much closer middle income citizens' preferences are to those of the rich than to those of the poor.

We created an analogous measure for party evaluations. We calculated the differences between average evaluations of each party by middle income respondents on the one hand, and high- and low-income respondents on the other. We then took the difference between the absolute values of the latter and the former difference for each party. We calculated this measure for each party and combined information on all parties by taking a weighted mean, where weights are each party's vote share. Like the ideology measure, it is important to include this variable because it determines the extent to which each income group shares its preferences with other respondents, which likely determines how well they are represented.

Results

Income, voting, and preferences

Unequal participation of rich and poor citizens implies unequal representation of the two groups if, and only if, their opinions and party preferences are at least partly structured by income categories. We first investigate whether rich and poor citizens have significantly different ideological positions and party preferences.

First, we regress left-right self-placement on a dummy variable contrasting respondents in the top- and bottom-income quintiles. We were able to reject the null that ideology does not differ between rich and poor citizens at the .05 level for 52.4% of elections (the coefficients from these models are listed in the supplementary materials).

Second, we regress evaluations of each party on the high-income dummy. We were able to reject the null hypothesis that coefficients for that dummy are 0 for 51.4% of the 774 parties for which we have information. The mean absolute coefficient was 0.66 (recall that the scale is from 0 to 10). There was at least one party that was significantly more or less liked by respondents with incomes in the top quintile than by those in the bottom quintile in all elections except one (see supplementary materials).

Most of the time ideology and party preferences differ between income groups, in particular when focusing on party preferences.

Are high-income groups better represented?

Having confirmed that there are income differences in ideology and party preferences, we now turn to investigating whether these differences translate into gaps in government representation.

We estimate – for each election in the dataset – models regressing each representation criterion on a dummy variable indicating the highest income quintile in reference to respondents in the low-income quintile. We run OLS models for criteria 1 and 3, and present coefficients on the dummy identifying the top income category. These coefficients show how much better or worse the richest respondents are represented compared to the poorest. We estimate logistic regression models for criterion 2 and calculate the difference between the predicted probabilities that the preferred party of a top- and bottom-quintile respondent, respectively, is in government. We present all coefficients graphically, and include 95% confidence intervals. If confidence intervals do not overlap 0, we assert that the rich are significantly better (or worse) represented on a given measure than the poor.

We first consider how ideologically proximate each income group is to the government. Figure 1 shows the coefficients and confidence intervals of the high-income dummy. Positive (negative) coefficients indicate that the rich are better (worse) represented than the poor. The richest are significantly better represented than the poorest in 43.1% of elections. In 7.8% of all elections respondents in the lowest income quintile were significantly better represented. The rich are better represented than the poor more than four times as often as the poor are better represented than the rich.

We next consider whether rich citizens are more likely to find their preferred parties in government than the poor, a fear expressed by authors like Bartels (2016). The results in Figure 2 indicate that the rich were significantly better represented on this criterion than the poor in 39.0% of elections. The poor were significantly better off than the rich in 16.2% of cases. There are twice as many elections where the rich are better represented than the poor than there are elections where the reverse holds.

Finally, we consider whether high-income respondents have a greater preference for parties that enter government than those that are excluded. The coefficients for this

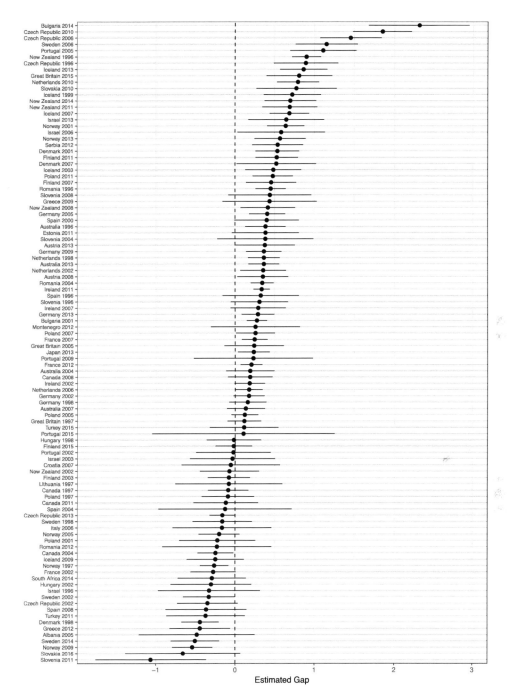

Figure 1. Income differences in ideological congruence, coefficient on high-income dummy.

dependent variable are reported in Figure 3. For this criterion, the advantage of the rich over the poor is least pronounced. While we find that the rich are better represented than the poor in 39.0% of elections, the poor were better represented than the rich in 24.8% of elections.

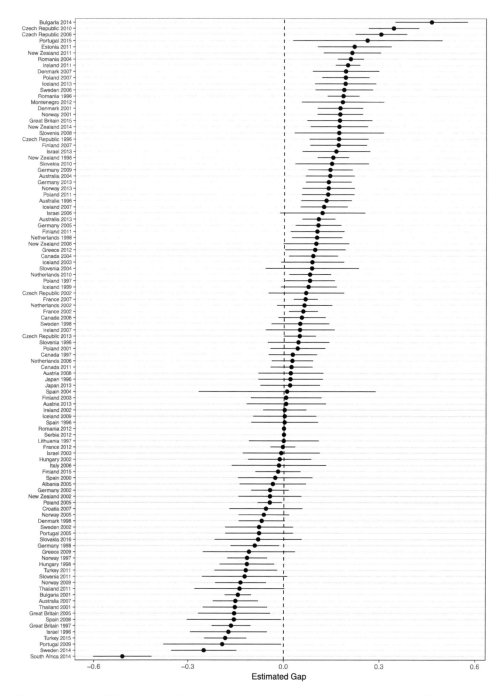

Figure 2. Income differences in seeing one's most preferred party in government, coefficient on high-income dummy.

The results in these three figures show that high-income citizens are somewhat better represented than those with low incomes – as we hypothesized. The rich are better represented than the poor in over a third of elections, but – depending on the criterion –

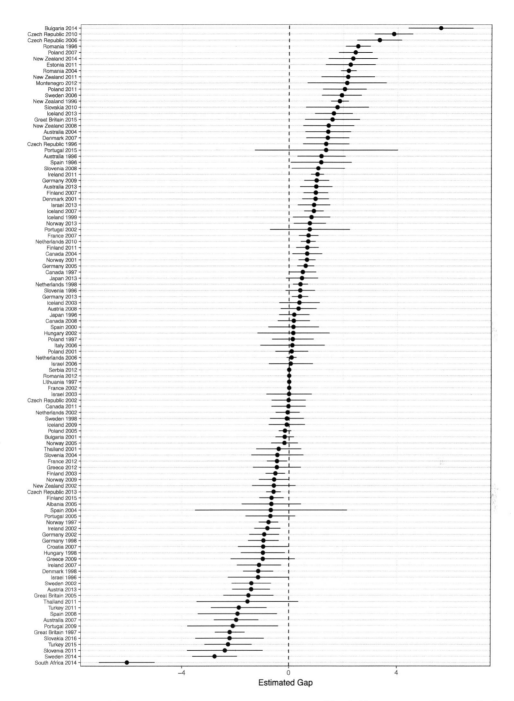

Figure 3. Income differences in relative government/opposition like/dislike scores, coefficient on high income dummy.

we find that in up to a quarter of elections the poor are significantly better represented than the rich.[13] Income gaps in representation vary strongly between countries, and elections, and this variance remains to be explained. Do turnout levels and compulsory voting rules help explain the over-representation of the rich?

Is the gap between rich and poor citizens smaller in compulsory voting countries?

Out of concern for inequalities in representation, Lijphart (1997) favoured the introduction of mandatory voting. Is there any evidence that compulsory voting rules are indeed an effective means to limit inequalities in representation? We answer this question by comparing income gaps in representation in the compulsory and non-compulsory voting elections in our dataset.

We first assess this question descriptively and consider the distributions of the gaps between high- and low-income respondents that are presented in Figures 1–3 for elections in voluntary and compulsory countries. The three graphs in Figure 4 show the distributions of gaps in each measure for the two sets of countries. The density plots in graph (a) suggest that compulsory voting is associated with essentially no difference in how congruent governments are to rich and poor citizens. The mean gap in representation between rich and poor citizens is 0.10 when voting is compulsory, while it is 0.24 when it is voluntary. Recall that positive gaps indicate that the rich are better represented.

Graph (b) in Figure 4 shows a larger difference when focusing on income gaps in a respondent's highest rated party entering government. The density plot for elections with voluntary voting is clearly located to the right of that for elections in compulsory voting countries, suggesting the advantage of the high-income group is larger under voluntary voting. The mean gap between the highest and lowest income quintile is 0.05 when voting is voluntary and −0.04 under mandatory voting rules.

Graph (c) in Figure 4 shows important differences between elections in voluntary and compulsory voting countries on the third criterion. The density plot for non-compulsory voting countries is situated to the right of the plot for compulsory voting countries, indicating the income gap is larger in the former set of countries. More precisely, the rich do significantly better than the poor 40.0% of the time when voting is voluntary. In compulsory voting countries, the proportion of elections in which the rich are significantly advantaged is reduced to 30.0%.

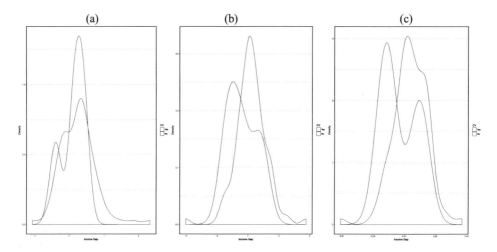

Figure 4. Density plots of distribution of high-income dummy coefficients.

In summary, the density plots included in Figure 4 offer suggestive evidence that inequalities in representation are smaller when voting is compulsory. We do not find indications of a difference when studying ideological congruence. But on the two measures of party preference representation, the representation-advantage of the rich appears to be smaller in mandatory voting settings.

To test the significance of these differences, we estimate multilevel models with individuals nested in elections. We regress each measure of representation on the dummy distinguishing high- from low-income citizens and allow the coefficient on that variable and the intercept to vary across elections. All models include the controls described above. To account for the fact that observations in elections within the same country are not independent, we cluster standard errors at the country level.[14]

The results of these analyses are summarized in Table 1. For each criterion of representation, we first estimate a model that includes the compulsory voting dummy but no interactions (models 1, 3 and 5). For each criterion of representation the rich tend to do better than the poor. The coefficients for the high-income dummy are consistently positive – though it is not significant at conventional levels for the third criterion. These tests on the pooled dataset are in line with what we observed in Figures 1–3. That is, there is clearly a trend towards the rich being better represented than the poor, but that gap is least pronounced for the third indicator of representation. Importantly, there is substantial variation between countries and elections. Thus, the logical next step is to look for macro variables like compulsory voting that account for such variations.

Table 1. Income inequalities in representation and compulsory voting.

	(1)	(2)	(3)	(4)	(5)	(6)
	Criterion 1		Criterion 2		Criterion 3	
High income	0.250***	0.182*	0.135*	0.141*	0.206	0.406*
	(0.049)	(0.071)	(0.056)	(0.063)	(0.174)	(0.205)
Compulsory voting (CV)	−0.109	−0.103	0.410	0.475*	0.597	0.622
	(0.205)	(0.202)	(0.232)	(0.224)	(0.636)	(0.648)
Log MDM	−0.089	−0.091	0.077	0.077	0.013	0.015
	(0.093)	(0.092)	(0.048)	(0.048)	(0.081)	(0.082)
Relative LR proximity	−0.117	−0.099				
	(0.201)	(0.209)				
Relative LD proximity			0.263	0.354*	0.558	0.583
			(0.172)	(0.175)	(0.668)	(0.695)
High income × CV		−0.141		−0.461*		−1.140*
		(0.130)		(0.211)		(0.481)
High income × MDM		0.031		0.001		−0.071
		(0.027)		(0.043)		(0.095)
High income × LR proximity		−0.189				
		(0.229)				
High income × LD proximity				−0.225		−0.661
				(0.332)		(0.911)
Intercept	7.538***	7.542***	−0.090	−0.097	0.897***	0.891***
	(0.216)	(0.215)	(0.098)	(0.096)	(0.163)	(0.164)
σ^2 high income	0.214	0.202	0.336	0.325	2.203	2.072
σ^2 election	0.620	0.620	0.228	0.220	1.249	1.247
(N) individuals	47,241	47,241	47,599	47,599	54,307	54,307
(N) elections	83	83	82	82	84	84

Note: Relative LR proximity is relative left-right proximity and Relative LD proximity stands for relative proximity in terms of party like/dislike ratings. Cluster-robust standard errors (by country) are reported in parentheses. Significance levels: *$p < 0.05$, **$p < 0.01$, ***$p < 0.001$.

We can evaluate whether the differences between voluntary and compulsory voting countries that we observed in Figure 4 are significant in Models 2, 4, and 6 in Table 1. The coefficients on the interaction between the high-income dummy and compulsory voting, show that these are negative for each of the three criteria. As such, the results confirm that compulsory voting is associated with less overrepresentation of the rich relative to the poor. In line with what the graphs in Figure 4 suggested, this difference between compulsory and non-compulsory settings fails to reach significance on ideological congruence. However, for the two party preference criteria, the difference between voluntary and mandatory voting context is significant.

The results in Table 1 might be challenged in a number of ways. In particular, the fact that we only have information from four countries that mandate voting might lead some to question the stability of our estimates. To address such challenges, we first ran jackknife tests in which we estimated the models excluding one country at a time. We also estimated models in which we excluded one election at a time. While removing compulsory voting countries and elections did weaken the results, we were able to reject the null that the coefficient of the "high-income × compulsory voting" interaction is 0 in the model explaining representation (at the 0.06 level or below) on the third criterion, which, by considering ratings of both government and opposition parties, is the most complete measure. The p-values of these additional models are reported in the supporting materials.

We also verified whether the results were robust to controlling for GDP per capita, and Freedom House scores, and found similar results (see the supporting materials).

Our results offer mild support for the second hypothesis. Income inequalities in representation are significantly smaller in compulsory voting countries compared to voluntary voting countries, at least when considering indicators of party preference. However, before concluding that Lijphart had it right when arguing in favour of the introduction of compulsory voting, we also need to verify that turnout, the mechanism Lijphart suggested, receives support.

Is the gap between rich and poor citizens smaller under high turnout?

Concerned about inequalities in representation, Lijphart argued for the introduction of compulsory voting because it "is the only institutional mechanism, (...), that can assure high turnout virtually by itself" (Lijphart 1997, 10). That is, he thought of compulsory voting as a means to increase turnout – and improve the political representation of the poor.

A full assessment of Lijphart's argument should take into account differences in turnout. In Table 2, we add turnout – as a proportion of registered voters[15] – and its interaction with the high-income dummy to the models. According to the conventional causal mediation approach (Baron and Kenny 1986), if turnout mediates the relationship between compulsory voting inequalities and inequalities in representation, the coefficient on the "income × compulsory voting" interaction should weaken and become non-significant when accounting for turnout. The results in Table 2 show, however, that the coefficient on the compulsory-voting interaction only weakens modestly, and it remains significant, casting doubt on the notion that turnout is the mediator. While we find that income inequalities in representation are smaller in compulsory voting countries, we cannot confirm our third hypothesis. In the next section, we elaborate on this counter-intuitive finding.

Table 2. Compulsory voting, turnout and inequalities in representation

	(1) Criterion 1	(2) Criterion 2	(3) Criterion 3
High income	0.209	0.286	0.560
	(0.142)	(0.151)	(0.306)
Compulsory voting (CV)	−0.119	0.472*	0.607
	(0.211)	(0.222)	(0.643)
Turnout	0.093	−0.005	0.098
	(0.103)	(0.089)	(0.163)
Log MDM	−0.091	0.078	0.015
	(0.091)	(0.048)	(0.082)
Relative LR Proximity	−0.093		
	(0.211)		
Relative LD Proximity		0.362*	0.582
		(0.176)	(0.693)
High income × CV	−0.134	−0.437*	−1.107*
	(0.132)	(0.209)	(0.476)
High income × Turnout	−0.039	−0.198	−0.224
	(0.157)	(0.189)	(0.303)
High income × Log MDM	0.031	0.002	−0.072
	(0.027)	(0.043)	(0.095)
High income × Relative LR proximity	−0.192		
	(0.235)		
High income × Relative LD proximity		−0.211	−0.659
		(0.328)	(0.907)
Intercept	7.479***	−0.086	0.824***
	(0.195)	(0.124)	(0.192)
σ^2 high income	0.200	0.324	2.067
σ^2 election	0.615	0.218	1.246
(N) individuals	47241	47599	54307
(N) elections	83	82	84

Note: Relative LR proximity is relative left-right proximity and Relative LD proximity stands for relative proximity in terms of party like/dislike ratings. Cluster-robust standard errors (by country) are reported in parentheses. Significance levels: *$p <$ 0.05, **$p < 0.01$, ***$p < 0.001$.

Discussion

Over 20 years ago, Lijphart (1997) made a compelling case for the introduction of compulsory voting. Worried about the consequences of unequal participation, he favoured mandatory voting to ensure high, and more equal, turnout and – in this way – more equal representation. Since the publication of Lijphart's Presidential Address, we have gained important insights into the effects of compulsory voting rules. We are now even more certain of the mobilizing effects of compulsory voting (Cancela and Geys 2016). In addition, there is work that empirically shows that compelling citizens to vote reduces inequalities between citizens who are more or less likely to vote. It has been found that, under mandatory voting, turnout gaps between young and old citizens, between rich and poor citizens, between those with high and low political knowledge or efficacy, as well as between partisans and non-partisans are all substantially smaller (Dassonneville, Hooghe, and Miller 2017). Scholars have also pointed out the possible disadvantages of compulsory rules, however, such as a cost in terms of the "quality" of the vote choices (Selb and Lachat 2009; Dassonneville et al. 2019) or a strengthening of anti-democratic attitudes (Singh 2018).

The extent to which compulsory voting rules effectively reduce inequalities in representation, however, has not yet received scholars' attention. We set out to test whether there are indications that compulsory voting rules indeed contribute to more equal representation. Having focused on income inequalities, and having studied three different measures of representation in government, our conclusions are mixed. On the one hand, we find consistent and robust evidence that the poor are significantly better represented (in terms of party preference measures) when voting is mandatory. On the other hand, the fact that we fail to find support for increased turnout as the mechanism linking compulsory voting rules to more equal representation might cast doubt on our conclusions.

How can we explain the fact that we find support for our second hypothesis, but not for the third hypothesis? One explanation might be that Tingsten's law only holds when comparing very low and very high turnout. Gradual increases in turnout are not necessarily related with increased participation of the poor and an improvement in their representation. The strongest empirical support in favour of Tingsten's law comes from studies that have compared high and low turnout settings (Bhatti et al. 2019; Persson, Solevid, and Öhrvall 2013). Such an interpretation is also consistent with Gallego's (2015) analyses of the relationship between turnout and inequalities in education. Most contextual variables that influence turnout, such as changes in voter registration, electoral competitiveness, or the complexity of voting, have a modest (Lijphart 1997) but also heterogeneous (Gallego 2015) effect on turnout. We have explored the possibility that the effect of turnout is not linear, but have failed to find evidence that the poor are significantly better represented in the high turnout elections in our sample (see supporting materials).

What alternative theories might explain the equalizing role of compulsory voting rules? We can think of three in particular. First, some scholars have argued that compulsory voting rules have the potential to improve citizens' knowledge of politics (Sheppard 2015; Shineman 2018). Perhaps the poor are better prepared to choose parties that will represent them well when voting is compulsory. Second, it is likely that parties in a compulsory voting context will have additional incentives to appeal to broad segments of the electorate, some of which may have been previously neglected due to a lower propensity to vote (Bugarin and Portugal 2015; Somer-Topcu 2015;). Third, perhaps societies that value more equality choose to make voting compulsory in an effort to reduce political inequalities. Whether there is indeed a link between valuing equality and opting for compulsory voting, however, is uncertain. On the one hand, it can be pointed out that compulsory voting emerged in Catholic Europe (i.e. Austria, Belgium, and Italy) based on an ethic of civic ideals of participation in politics. However, discussions in countries that abolished compulsory revolved around a logic of personal emancipation to engage in politics - without much reference to the issue of political inequality (Ferland 2016; Miller and Dassonneville 2016). More research is needed to evaluate whether one of these mechanisms indeed serves as the connection between compulsory voting rules and more equal representation.

Conclusion

Previous studies have shown that compulsory voting boosts turnout and reduces inequalities in electoral participation. We contribute to the literature on the effects of compulsory voting by investigating whether compulsory voting is associated with smaller income inequalities in representation.

We considered three measures of representation that allow evaluating whether a citizen's views are represented in government. We found evidence of income inequalities in representation; in about a third of elections, high-income citizens are significantly better represented than those with low incomes, the reverse holds true only about a quarter of the time.

Evaluating differences between countries in income inequalities in representation, our results suggest that the poor are better represented when voting is compulsory. We found that the income gap in party preferences was significantly smaller in elections in the four compulsory voting countries. This result is robust to alternative operationalizations, additional controls or estimations on subsamples. We are confident that this difference is "real".

However, our results do not allow us to validate the mechanism that Lijphart (1997) argued connects compulsory voting to an improved representation of the poor. We do not find evidence that the poor are better represented when turnout is high. This set of results leaves us with a puzzle: inequalities in representation are smaller in compulsory voting countries, but how these countries achieve this level of equality in representation remains an open question.

Our analyses are limited to the four parliamentary cases with compulsory voting rules within the CSES data. We, unfortunately, do not have in our analyses cases from Latin and South America, where compulsory voting rules are common (Power 2009). Evidence from Brazil, where abstainers are fined, suggests this sanction actually *increases* inequality in the electorate by incentivizing the better educated to vote to a higher degree than less educated voters (Cepaluni and Hidalgo 2016). That being said, our four cases demonstrate variability across two pertinent dimensions that give us confidence the results we report are generalizable to the set of compulsory voting countries. First, two of the four (Australia and Turkey) have a strict sanction for abstaining, while Greece and Thailand have no such sanction. Second, three of our four cases are relatively small economies compared to Australia, while only Thailand is not a member of the Organization for Economic Cooperation and Development.

Notes

1. Inequalities in participation are not limited to electoral participation. The resource model generally applies to different forms of participation, implying that the poor will participate less. Empirical work that compares inequalities in forms of institutionalized participation (e.g. voting or membership of a party) and non-institutionalized participation (e.g. donating money, demonstrating, or boycotting products) suggests that gender and age inequalities are smaller or reversed for some types of non-institutionalized participation, other sources of inequality – such as inequalities based on education or income – remain present in both forms of participation (Gallego, 2007; Marien, Hooghe and Quintelier, 2010).
2. While Lijphart (1997) was particularly concerned with influence on government policy, our focus is on political representation in terms of the parties that form government. Equality in representation can be thought of as an important cause of equality in influence on policy, though we acknowledge that there are other ways to influence policy, such as donating money to politicians (Bartels 2016; Gilens 2012).
3. In this criterion, evaluations of government and opposition parties are weighted by the proportion of seats each party has among parties in government and opposition.
4. Following Lau and Redlawsk (1997), we use the term "quality" to refer to the "correctness" of a citizen's vote, or voting according to one's values and beliefs.
5. We excluded Module 1 because most (97%) of the election studies in that module asked respondents to rate six or fewer parties. About half of the later studies asked respondents to evaluate

more than six parties. Comparisons among modules would thus be problematic if preferences for the parties that were excluded from the first module are associated with income.

6. When available, we used data from the *European Journal of Political Research*'s Political Data Yearbook. Data for other elections came from the Economist Intelligence Unit.
7. Austria is a special case within these categories; we treat the country as premier-presidential in our analyses. Austrian parties effectively control the recruitment of presidents, and power is shared between two parties, all of which limit the power of the president (Müller 1999; cited in Shugart 2005). See the Supplementary information for a list of all elections included.
8. For background on these measures, see Golder and Stramski (2010, 92–93).
9. Blais, Guntermann, and Bodet (2017) broke ties at random. However, doing so is problematic for evaluating inequalities in representation if some income groups have more decisive preferences than others.
10. We excluded respondents in the middle-income categories in this step. We can safely do so, because the middle group does not influence results for the gap between the low- and high-income quintiles.
11. We show the results when only focusing on strict compulsory voting systems in Australia and Turkey. We also validate the robustness of our results to including a continuous compulsory voting variable that takes the value of 0 if voting is voluntary, 1 if CV is weak and 2 if CV is strict.
12. Excluding these variables from our models, however, the results are substantively the same (see supplementary materials).
13. The poor tend to be better represented when governments are left-of-centre.
14. We also ran models entering income as a continuous variable and found similar results (see supporting materials).
15. Using an indicator of turnout expressed as a percent of the voting age population leads to substantively the same results. See the supporting materials.

Disclosure statement

All interpretations and conclusions are the responsibility of the authors and do not necessarily reflect the institutional positions of the Brennan Center for Justice at New York University School of Law.

Funding

This work was supported by the Canada Research Chairs [grant number 950-231173].

ORCID

Eric Guntermann ⓘ http://orcid.org/0000-0003-4877-0963
Ruth Dassonneville ⓘ http://orcid.org/0000-0003-2511-0129
Peter Miller ⓘ http://orcid.org/0000-0003-3929-8417

References

Achen, C. H. 1978. "Measuring Representation." *American Journal of Political Science* 22: 475–510.

Baron, Reuben M., and David A. Kenny. 1986. "The Moderator-Mediator Variable Distinction in Social Psychological Research: Conceptual, Strategic and Statistical Considerations." *Journal of Personality and Social Psychology* 51: 1173–1182.

Bartels, Larry. 2016. *Unequal Democracy: The Political Economy of the New Guilded Age.* Princeton: Princeton University Press.

Bashir, Omar S. 2015. "Testing Inferences about American Politics: A Review of the "Oligarchy" Result." *Research & Politics* 2, doi:10.1177/205316801560889.

Bhatti, Yosef, Jens Olav Dahlgaard, Jonas Hedegaard Hansen, and Kasper M. Hansen. 2019. "Core and Peripheral Voters: Predictors of Turnout Across Three Types of Elections." *Political Studies* 67 (2): 348–366.

Birch, Sarah. 2009. *Full Participation. A Comparative Study of Compulsory Voting.* Manchester: Manchester University Press.

Blais, André, and Agnieszka Dobrzynska. 1998. "Turnout in Electoral Democracies." *European Journal of Political Research* 33: 239–261.

Blais, André, Eric Guntermann, and Marc André Bodet. 2017. "Linking Party Preferences and the Composition of Government: A New Standard for Evaluating the Performance of Electoral Democracy." *Political Science Research and Methods* 5: 315–331.

Branham, J. Alexander, Stuart N. Soroka, and Christopher Wlezien. 2017. "When Do the Rich Win?" *American Political Science Review* 66: 450–458.

Brody, Richard A., and Benjamin I. Page. 1972. "Comment: The Assessment of Policy Voting." *American Political Science Review* 66: 450–458.

Brunell, Thomas, and John DiNardo. 2004. "A Propensity Score Reweighting Approach to Estimate the Partisan Effects of Full Turnout in American Presidential Elections." *Political Analysis* 12: 28–45.

Bugarin, Mauricio, and Adriana Portugal. 2015. "Should Voting be Mandatory? The Effect of Compulsory Voting Rules on Candidates' Political Platforms." *Journal of Applied Economics* 18: 1–29.

Campbell, Angus, Philip Converse, Warren Miller, and Donald Stokes. 1960. *The American Voter.* New York: John Wiley & Sons.

Cancela, Joao, and Benny Geys. 2016. "Explaining Voter Turnout: A Meta-Analysis of National and Subnational Elections." *Electoral Studies* 42: 264–275.

Cepaluni, Gabriel, and F. Daniel Hidalgo. 2016. "Compulsory Voting can Increase Political Inequality: Evidence from Brazil." *Political Analysis* 24: 273–280.

Citrin, Jack, Eric Schickler, and John Sides. 2003. "What if Everyone Voted? Simulating the Impact of Increased Turnout in Senate Elections." *American Journal of Political Science* 47: 75–90.

Clarke, Harold D., David Sanders, Marianne C. Stewart, and Paul Whiteley. 2004. *Political Choice in Britain.* Oxford: Oxford University Press.

Converse, Philip E. 1964. "The Nature of Belief Systems in Mass Publics." In *Ideology and Discontent*, edited by David E. Apter, 206–261. New York: Free Press.

Dassonneville, Ruth, Fernando Feitosa, Marc Hooghe, Richard Lau, and Dieter Stiers. 2019. "Compulsory Voting Rules, Reluctant Voters and Ideological Proximity Voting." *Political Behavior* 41: 1–22.

Dassonneville, Ruth, and Marc Hooghe. 2017. "Voter Turnout Decline and Stratification: Quasi-Experimental and Comparative Evidence of a Growing Educational Gap." *Politics* 37: 184–200.

Dassonneville, Ruth, Marc Hooghe, and Peter Miller. 2017. "The Impact of Compulsory Voting on Inequality and the Quality of the Vote." *West European Politics* 40: 621–644.

Ellis, Christopher. 2012. "Understanding Economic Biases in Representation: Income, Resources, and Policy Representation in the 110th House." *Political Research Quarterly* 65: 938–951.

Enns, Peter K. 2015. "Reconsidering the Middle: A Reply to Martin Gilens." *Perspectives on Politics* 13: 1072–1074.

Ferland, Benjamin. 2016. "Revisiting the Ideological Congruence Controversy." *European Journal of Political Research* 55 (2): 358–373.

Fowler, Anthony. 2013. "Electoral and Policy Consequences of Voter Turnout: Evidence from Compulsory Voting in Australia." *Quarterly Journal of Political Science* 8: 159–182.

Gallego, Aina. 2007. "Unequal Political Participation in Europe." *International Journal of Sociology* 37: 10–25.

Gallego, Aina. 2010. "Understanding Unequal Turnout: Education and Voting in Comparative Perspective." *Electoral Studies* 29: 239–248.

Gallego, Aina. 2015. *Unequal Participation Worldwide*. Cambridge: Cambridge University Press.

Giger, Nathalie, Jan Rosset, and Julian Bernauer. 2012. "The Poor Political Representation of the Poor in a Comparative Perspective." *Representation* 48: 47–61.

Gilens, Martin. 2012. *Affluence and Influence: Economic Inequality and Political Power in America*. Princeton: Princeton University Press.

Golder, Matt, and Jacek Stramski. 2010. "Ideological Congruence and Electoral Institutions." *American Journal of Political Science* 54: 90–106.

Hirczy, Wolfang. 1994. "The Impact of Mandatory Voting Laws on Turnout: A Quasi-Experimental Approach." *Electoral Studies* 13: 64–76.

Huber, John D., and G. Bingham Powell. 1994. "Congruence Between Citizens and Policy-Makers in Two Visions of Liberal Democracy." *World Politics* 46: 291–326.

Iversen, Torben, and David Soskice. 2006. "Electoral Institutions and the Politics of Coalitions: Why Some Democracies Redistribute More than Others." *American Political Science Review* 100: 165–181.

Jackman, Simon. 2001. "Compulsory Voting." In *International Encyclopedia of the Social and Behavioral Sciences*, edited by Neil J. Smelser and Paul B. Bates, 16314–16318. Amsterdam: Elsevier.

Kasara, Kimuli, and Pavithra Suryanarayan. 2015. "When Do the Rich Vote Less than the Poor and Why? Explaining Turnout Inequality across the World." *American Journal of Political Science* 59: 613–627.

Lau, Richard R., and David P Redlawsk. 1997. "Voting Correctly." *American Political Science Review* 91: 585–598.

Lazarsfeld, Paul F., Bernard Berelson, and Hazel Gaudet. 1968. *The People's Choice: How the Voter Makes Up His Mind in a Presidential Campaign*. New York: Columbia University Press.

Leighley, Jan E., and Jonathan Nagler. 1992. "Socioeconomic Class Bias in Turnout, 1964–1988: The Voters Remain the Same." *American Political Science Review* 86: 725–736.

Leighley, Jan E., and Jonathan Nagler. 2013. *Who Votes Now? Demographics, Issues, Inequality and Turnout in the United States*. Princeton: Princeton University Press.

Lenz, Gabriel S. 2012. *Follow the Leader? How Voters Respond to Politicians' Policies and Performance*. Chicago: University of Chicago Press.

Lewis-Beck, Michael S., and Mary Stegmaier. 2007. "Economic Models of the Vote." In *The Oxford Handbook of Political Behavior*, edited by Russell J. Dalton and Hans-Dieter Klingemann, 518–537. Oxford: Oxford University Press.

Lijphart, Arend. 1997. "Unequal Participation: Democracy's Unresolved Dilemma. Presidential Address, American Political Science Association, 1996." *American Political Science Review* 91: 1–14.

Lupu, Noam, and Zach Warner. 2017. *Affluence and Congruence: Unequal Representation around the World*. Working Paper.

Marien, Sofie, Marc Hooghe, and Ellen Quintelier. 2010. "Inequalities in Non-Institutionalised Forms of Political Participation: A Multi-Level Analysis of 25 Countries." *Political Studies* 58: 187–213.

Medeiros, Mike, Jean-Philippe Gauvin, and Chris Chhim. 2015. "Refining Vote Choice in an Ethno-Regionalist Context: Three-Dimensional Ideological Voting in Catalonia and Quebec." *Electoral Studies* 40: 14–22.

Miller, Peter, and Ruth Dassonneville. 2016. "High Turnout in the Low Countries: Partisan Effects of the Abolition of Compulsory Voting in the Netherlands." *Electoral Studies* 44: 132–143.

Müller, W. C. 1999. "Austria." In *Semi-Presidentialism in Europe*, edited by Robert Elgie. Oxford: Oxford University Press.

Pacek, Alexander, and Benjamin Radcliff. 1995. "Turnout and the Vote for Left-of-Centre Parties: A Cross-National Analysis." *British Journal of Political Science* 25: 137–143.

Panagopoulos, Costas. 2008. "The Calculus of Voting in Compulsory Voting Systems." *Political Behavior* 30: 455–467.

Persson, Mikael, Maria Solevid, and Richard Öhrvall. 2013. "Voter Turnout and Political Equality: Testing the 'Law of Dispersion' in a Swedish Natural Experiment." *Politics* 33: 172–184.

Pitkin, Hanna F. 1967. *The Concept of Representation.* Berkeley: University of California Press.

Powell, G. Bingham. 2000. *Elections as Instruments of Democracy: Majoritarian and Proportional Visions.* New Haven: Yale University Press.

Power, Timothy. 2009. "Compulsory for Whom? Mandatory Voting and Electoral Participation in Brazil, 1986–2006." *Journal of Politics in Latin America* 1: 97–122.

Rosset, Jan, Nathalie Giger, and Julian Bernauer. 2013. "More Money, Few Problems? Cross-Level Effects of Economic Deprivation on Political Representation." *West European Politics* 36: 817–835.

Selb, Peter, and Romain Lachat. 2009. "The More, the Better? Counterfactual Evidence on the Effects of Compulsory Voting on the Consistency of Party Choice." *European Journal of Political Research* 48: 573–597.

Sheppard, Jill. 2015. "Compulsory Voting and Political Knowledge: Testing a 'Compelled Engagement' Hypothesis." *Electoral Studies* 40: 300–307.

Shineman, Victoria Anne. 2018. "If You Mobilize Them, The Will Become Informed: Experimental Evidence that Information Acquisition is Endogenous to Costs and Incentives to Participate." *British Journal of Political Science* 48: 189–211.

Shugart, Mattew Søberg. 2005. "Semi-Presidential Systems: Dual Executive and Mixed Authority Patterns." *French Politics* 3: 323–351.

Singh, Shane. 2011. "How Compelling is Compulsory Voting? A Multilevel Analysis of Turnout." *Political Behavior* 33: 95–111.

Singh, Shane. 2015. "Compulsory Voting and the Turnout Decision Calculus." *Political Studies* 63: 548–568.

Singh, Shane. 2016. "Elections as Poorer Reflections of Preferences Under Compulsory Voting." *Electoral Studies* 44: 56–65.

Singh, Shane P. 2018. "Compulsory Voting and Dissatisfaction with Democracy." *British Journal of Political Science* 48 (3): 843–854.

Smets, Kaat, and Carolien van Ham. 2013. "The Embarrassment of Riches? A Meta-Analysis of Individual-Level Research on Voter Turnout." *Electoral Studies* 32: 344–359.

Somer-Topcu, Zeynep. 2015. "Everything to Everyone: The Electoral Consequences of the Broad-Appeal Strategy in Europe." *American Journal of Political Science* 59: 841–854.

Soroka, Stuart N., and Christopher Wlezien. 2008. "On the Limits to Inequality in Representation." *PS: Political Science & Politics* 41: 319–327.

Stecker, Christian, and Markus Tausendpfund. 2016. "Multidimensional Government-Citizen Congruence and Satisfaction with Democracy." *European Journal of Political Research* 55: 492–511.

Tingsten, Herbert. 1937. *Political Behavior: Studies in Election Statistics.* London: P.S. King & Son.

van der Eijk, Cees, and Marcel van Egmond. 2007. "Political Effects of Low Turnout in National and European Elections." *Electoral Studies* 26: 561–573.

Verba, Sidney, and Norman H. Nie. 1972. *Participation in America: Political Democracy and Social Equality.* New York: Harper and Row.

Zaller, John. 1992. *The Nature and Origins of Mass Opinion.* Cambridge: Cambridge University Press.

Conceptualizing more inclusive elections: violence against women in elections and gendered electoral violence

Paige Schneider ⓘ and David Carroll

ABSTRACT

Violence against women in politics and throughout the election cycle has been documented as an impediment to the free and equal political participation of women, and to the conduct of inclusive elections. Academic research and practitioner assessments have raised the profile of this global problem, and draw attention to key challenges in theory development, the operationalization of concepts, and the creation of shared measures for data collection. This article seeks to contribute to the scholarship by positing a theoretical framework that situates violence against women in elections (VAWE) at the intersection of gender-based violence and political violence. We examine the role of gender in relationship to targets, perpetrators, motives, and forms of electoral violence to demonstrate the importance of studying violence motivated by gender discrimination alongside more conventional motives of electoral violence. The analysis is informed by examples drawn from field research in Uganda.

Introduction

The study of the relationship between gender and political violence has flourished in the last decade with more scholars interested in women's experiences with violence, but also in their roles as political actors on the international stage (Enloe 1990; Cockburn 1998; Moser and Clark 2001; Mazurana, Raven-Roberts, and Parpart 2005; Sjoberg 2014, 2016; Davis 2017). Gender is relevant to our understanding of political violence in a multitude of contexts such as war, peacekeeping operations, and acts of terrorism. It is increasingly clear that gender also matters to our understanding of electoral violence (SAP 2008; Valverde 2011; Bardall 2013, 2015; 2016; Cerna 2014; Zabiliute 2014; Drummond 2015; Piscopo 2015, 2016; Bjarnegard 2016; Krook and Sanin 2016a; Krook 2017). Scholars and practitioners working at the intersection of gender and electoral violence have provided evidence from the field that documents violence against women in the context of campaigning and elections, and suggests that it is a global problem (Bardall 2011, 2015; Ballington 2016; Bjarnegard 2016). Violence against women in elections undermines the integrity of elections by inhibiting women's equal participation as voters, election officials, candidates, and party leaders, among other roles. Reflecting the growing awareness of the problem, the United Nations Special Rapporteur on Violence against Women recently convened a working group and announced a new initiative to develop global indicators and gather data on the phenomena.[1]

Traditional gender roles, along with conceptions of masculinity and femininity that place men and women in roles associated with different social spheres, means that public political activity is often perceived as a *male preserve* in many countries around the world (Sheard and Dunning 1973; Matthews 2016).[2] Politics as a male preserve becomes a domain where men may feel entitled to lay claim to positions of power, and women who transgress these expectations may face ridicule, harassment, or worse. This sense of entitlement can lead to male resistance to women's incursions into these spaces. This *backlash effect* (Mansbridge and Shames 2008; Krook and Sanin 2016a, 126) results in threats and actual acts of violence against women in politics. The movement of women into male preserves can be perceived as a challenge to the social order and to gendered power relations. This suggests that violence against women in politics and during elections is more than just a case of individual men attempting to deter individual women from participating. When motivated by systemic gender discrimination and misogyny, violence against women in politics and during elections becomes an instance where men *as a group* consolidate and monopolize political power, and limit or prohibit the participation of women *as a group*.

The backlash against women in politics is a serious threat, nonetheless women continue to enter politics and exercise political agency in a variety of roles. Studies of political violence during civil wars, in revolutionary movements and in other types of conflict scenarios find that females are not only the victims of violence, but may perpetrate violence (Moser and Clark 2001; Sjoberg 2016). The increasing numbers of women participating in electoral politics may subsequently increase the potential for conflict and violence *between* women, who often compete for power under constraints such as limited resources and limited numbers of elected or appointed positions (Expert Group Meeting 2018, 15). Studying election related violence requires a gendered lens if we are to uncover and better understand patterns of targeting and perpetration, and clarify when and how gender matters. Existing frameworks in the conventional study of electoral violence fail to consider its gendered dimensions. This results in an incomplete understanding of who is affected by election related violence and the range of harms involved in the different forms and types of violence.

This article offers a new theoretical and conceptual framework for considering the relationship between gender and electoral violence. The framework posits that violence against women in elections (VAWE) is a subset of gendered electoral violence and as well as a subset of both political violence and electoral violence.[3] We draw examples from field work conducted in Uganda in 2018 and 2019 to elucidate the extent to which electoral violence may be gendered, including instances in which women perpetrate violence against their opponents.

In the first section of the article, we review the literature on the relationship between electoral violence and the integrity of elections, and consider the place of gender as a variable in conventional studies of electoral violence. In this review we also summarize the emerging scholarship on women's experiences with violence, intimidation, and harassment in their roles as voters, candidates, and other political stakeholders. Then, we turn to a discussion of our methods for the Uganda case material included in the analysis. Finally, we offer an alternative gender sensitive conceptual framework which draws on insights from both academic scholarship and practitioner assessments to suggest a more inclusive and intersectional approach to the study of election violence.

Electoral integrity and electoral violence

Electoral integrity can be undercut by a wide variety of irregularities or "electoral malfunctions" that can undermine democratic processes and inclusive participation, including vote buying, suppressing voter turnout, unequal access to media across parties and candidates, or tampering with vote counts at the ballot box (Birch 2011; Norris 2014). In addition to these and other such efforts to manipulate or subvert the electoral process, electoral violence constitutes an especially serious threat to electoral integrity due to the potential for threats and acts of violence to deter voters, candidates, and other stakeholders from participating in the process.

The last decade has witnessed a surge in scholarly interest in electoral violence, drawing on a range of literatures related to democratization and elections, ethnic and political conflict, civil war, and post-conflict elections, among others. This research has examined a wide range of issues, including causal factors for electoral violence operating not only at the micro individual and political levels but also at the macro institutional and structural levels (Goldsmith 2015; Fjelde and Höglund 2016; Taylor, Pevehouse, and Straus 2017). Research has assessed electoral violence as a strategic choice from a menu of election manipulation options (Norris, Frank, and Martinez i Coma 2015; Van Ham and Lindberg 2015), examined the interaction effects from the presence of election observers (Daxecker 2012, 2014; Smidt 2016), and the increased risks of electoral violence associated with holding post-conflict elections (Brancati and Snyder 2013).

Although there is no single widely agreed upon definition of electoral violence, Fischer's (2001) definition has been widely employed and is summarized as any act or threat of action, that involves physical harm or psychological intimidation, with the intention of delaying or influencing the electoral process or outcomes. Incidents that involve actual physical harm (including sexual violence) are of particular concern because of the potential for large scale mortality and morbidity among the civilian population (Smith 2009; Dercon and Gutiérrez-Romero 2012; Goldsmith 2015), but threats of violence, or other acts such as psychological intimidation, are much more common. Consequently, the concept of electoral violence is understood by most scholars as encompassing a range of other non-physical types of harm including *threats* of physical assault, as well as psychological intimidation and harassment, and economic damage or loss (Höglund 2009, 417; Bardall 2011, 6–8, 22). These non-physical forms of violence are nonetheless quite serious. They can take the form of thinly veiled threats to destroy property, harm children or other family members, or humiliate or shame someone in front of the community, and can be as effective as actual physical violence in deterring someone from participating in the political process[4] (Höglund 2009, 417; Bardall 2011, 18).

Birch and Muchlinski (2017) offer another definition of electoral violence in their work, worth quoting at length, as it explicitly subsumes electoral violence under the rubric of political violence, and connects the temporal aspect of the election process to the causal link that assumes acts of electoral violence are motivated by political goals to manipulate or control the outcomes of the electoral process:

... our definition of electoral violence is: coercive force, directed towards electoral actors and/ or objects, that occurs in the context of electoral competition. This definition can be justified on the grounds that virtually all political violence that occurs during the electoral period can be expected to be conditioned by the electoral process either directly or indirectly, and conversely, the electoral process can be expected to be conditioned by virtually all political violence that occurs during this period (3).

The reference to coercive force is an important one, because it implies intentionality which is one of the necessary attributes that distinguishes violence from more general acts that result in *harm* which may occur without a motive or intention.

The importance of intentionality in definitions of violence is also found in the World Health Organization's (WHO) approach that defines violence as

the intentional use of physical force or power, threatened or actual, against oneself, another person, or against a group or community, that either results in or has a high likelihood of resulting in injury, death, psychological harm, maldevelopment or deprivation. (Rutherford et al. 2007, 676)

The WHO definition adds the notion of *deprivation* which is less commonly included in analyses of forms of electoral violence. We believe that the notion of deprivation aptly describes the effects or consequences of a well-established category of electoral violence – economic violence – and is a useful addition in specifying a particular form of economic violence. For example, typical examples of economic violence such as destruction of property require the active use of physical force to destroy something. In contrast, depriving an individual of shelter, or family or entire village of access to a market to purchase food in retaliation for refusal to support a particular candidate, for example, constitutes loss and harm in a way that does not directly require the use of any physical force. Scholars of intimate partner violence have long understood that deprivation is a crucial tactic in the repertoire of harms that may occur more frequently in the context of interpersonal violence and family relationships – contexts in which women are disproportionately represented as targets (but may also serve as perpetrators).

In sum, we offer the following gender sensitive definition of electoral violence that covers a range of types of targets, perpetrators, and forms of violence, as well as timing and motive:

Electoral violence constitutes any purposeful or calculated act of physical, sexual, psychological or economic harm against a person or property, including threats, harassment, intimidation, or deprivation that occurs at any point throughout the election cycle with the intent to discourage or prevent an individual or group from participating, or to alter an election process or outcome.

Gender and electoral violence

Electoral violence is perpetrated by individuals or groups who seek to manipulate or control the electoral process or election outcomes, and this often results in actions intended to dissuade or prevent citizens from participating in the political process. Conventional political science scholarship on electoral violence typically ignores its gendered dimensions such that acts of violence, intimidation, or harassment motivated by gender discrimination are often not included as instances of electoral violence (Dercon and Gutiérrez-Romero 2012; Daxecker 2014; Goldsmith 2015; Van Ham and Lindberg

2015; Birch and Muchlinski 2017; Taylor, Pevehouse, and Straus 2017). This is problematic, as over the last decade scholars and practitioners have documented that women experience a wide range of harms during elections both in private and public spaces *because they are women*, with the intent to discourage their participation as voters, candidates, elected officials, party leaders, activists, and supporters or agents of candidates (National Democratic Institute 2018; Report of the Special Rapporteur 2018, 9–10). Furthermore, scholars have documented cases in which women are perpetrators of political violence, complicating our notions of the relationship between gender and violence, women's positionality, and culpability (Lorentzen and Turpin 1998; Moser and Clark 2001; Bardall 2011; Mackenzie 2012; Sjoberg 2016).

Scholars and practitioners have documented serious incidents of violence against women during elections (VAWE) at least as far back as 2010 (SAP 2008; Kellow 2010; Valverde 2011; RUA 2010; Bardall 2011, 2013, 2016; Valverde 2011; Cerna 2014; Drummond 2015; Piscopo 2015, 2016; Ballington 2016; Bjarnegard 2016; Krook and Sanin 2016a, 2016b; Krook 2017). Bardall's (2011) report, *Breaking the Mold: Understanding Gender and Electoral Violence* was the first comprehensive examination of the relationship between gender and election violence, and from this work the acronym VAWE gained traction. Utilizing International Foundation for Electoral Assistance (IFES) data from six country contexts, Bardall examined in detail the forms and frequencies of electoral violence by gender of the target[5] and the perpetrator. Data from Bardall (2011) and others clearly demonstrate gendered patterns of perpetration and victimization (Figures 4–7, 10–14; UN Women Programming Guide 2017, 31–35; Report of the Special Rapporteur 2018, 9–10). While women are frequently the targets of gendered electoral violence, and males frequently the perpetrators, there are exceptions to this pattern. Bardall (2011) finds (albeit limited) evidence that under some conditions, women can perpetrate violence often against other females, and especially when they are part of group violence (1–2).

As many scholars have already noted, intentions are hard to measure, and the targets of violence may perceive the motivation behind the attack in a way quite different from the perpetrator(s) (Krook and Sanin 2016a, 147; Piscopo 2016, 446). To untangle the complex interplay between intent and action, and determine whether an attack was motivated by political power struggles on the one hand, or embedded in gendered power relations, on the other, requires a considerable amount of detail about the incident. Motivations are obviously more difficult to validate empirically than say, reporting the location of an incident. Some degree of error in the data is likely unavoidable. Minimizing error in assigning motives to acts of violence requires a methodological approach that includes careful questioning and follow up with the respondent, and gathering data at a level of detail rarely found in existing electoral violence studies.

Birch and Muchlinski (2017) point out the weaknesses of existing methodologies by stating,

> many broad measures of electoral violence currently in use obscure the identity of the actors involved, gloss over the tactics employed, do not report on the nature of the violence itself, or otherwise provide indicators of electoral violence at quite high levels of aggregation and generality. Because of this lack of detailed data, important puzzles still remain about the perpetrators, timing, causes, consequences, and nature of electoral violence. (2)

Fjelde and Höglund (2016, 9) and Norris, Frank, and Martinez i Coma (2015, 146–147) make similar arguments in their analyses of methodological challenges in the measurement of electoral violence, and in their recommendations for future research.

The alternative and gender sensitive conceptual framework that we propose below promotes the collection of data on individual and group perpetrated violence at levels of specificity necessary to expose the complex relationship between gender and electoral violence. At the same time, it retains the flexibility and logical properties necessary to cover cases in which a weak relationship between gender and election violence exists. To demonstrate how a gender sensitive framework improves our understanding of the nature and extent of violence during elections, in the analysis below we provide examples of cases of various types of gendered and non-gendered violence.

Methods

To elucidate how a gender sensitive conceptual framework contributes to our understanding of the motives, types, and forms of election violence, we draw examples from two main sources. The first source comprises reports and assessments by professional practitioners in the fields of democratic participation, and international election observation. Practitioner-scholars like Bardall (2011) observed and studied VAWE at the community level, and were the first individuals to call attention through their work to the various forms of violence and harassment experienced by women political stakeholders during the election process.

The second source of data is from one of the authors' (Schneider) ethnographic field research in Uganda conducted during July and August of 2018, and March of 2019. As mentioned above, the literature on election violence is dominated by studies that draw upon large N databases that have broad geographic coverage, but which lack the level of detail necessary to document first hand, important manifestations of violence. These include the gender of perpetrator or target, certain temporal qualities such as if violence is perpetrated over a sustained period of time, or the perceived motivations behind the violence. Ethnographic methods can overcome some of the limitations of large N studies by facilitating collection of detailed qualitative data.

Schneider, with the assistance of Ugandan human rights defender Lina Zedriga Waru, conducted sixteen focus group discussions with one hundred and sixteen participants, and fourteen key informant interviews. Focus group participants comprised men and women who were politically active at some level in local councilor (LC1-V) elections serving in one or more of the following roles: candidates, campaign managers, party officials, candidate mobilizers or "agents," current and former elected officials, or voters. Key informants included staff at women's rights organizations, a media representative (radio talk show host), and current and former elected officials and party leaders. Participants were identified through convenience and snowball sampling techniques and sampled from five electoral districts representing a diverse group of counties, sub-counties, and villages in northeastern (Moroto), northern (Gulu), central (Soroti), and southcentral (Wakiso; Mityana) regions of the country. Ugandan graduate assistants provided language translation for speakers of Karamojong (Moroto), Acholi/Lango (Gulu), Teso (Soroti), and Luganda (Wakiso; Mityana).

In addition to these qualitative sources, 134 respondents completed detailed election incident reports indicating whether or not they had experienced any election related violence, threats, intimidation, or harassment during the 2016 or 2018 election cycles (including during voter education, candidate certification or nomination, voter registration efforts, the primary election, election day, or during the immediate post-election period). For those who reported election related incidents, detailed information was gathered about the type, timing, location, target, perpetrator and other characteristics relevant to understanding the incident.

A gender sensitive conceptual framework for the study of electoral violence

The varied and complex ways in which sex and gender condition social interactions within any given society, presents significant methodological challenges for scholars who seek to empirically document sex- differentiated and gendered political behaviour. The framework that we propose addresses some of these challenges by defining key concepts and clarifying logical relationships between concepts and assumptions in the study of gender and electoral violence.

Violence against women in politics (VAWP) or elections (VAWE) is generally understood to be a category or sub-type of *gender-based violence* because the motivation for the behaviour is assumed to be embedded in unequal gendered power relations and gender discrimination. It is also a sub-type of *violence against women* (VAW) as women are assumed to be the primary targets. Gender-based violence is violence that is perpetrated against an individual for transgressing dominant gender roles, norms, or expectations of behaviour in a given society (Bloom 2008, 14) which means that heterosexual/cis-gendered, homosexual, transgender men, and non-binary individuals may be targets. Under this definition of gender-based violence, even male supporters of women's rights may be targeted if their views transgress dominant gender norms in their communities.

For our purposes, the concept *gendered violence* is defined as violence in which the gender of the perpetrator(s) or target(s) emerge in the data as a predictor of types or patterns of violence. The motivation behind the violence can involve a range of different instrumental concerns, including gender discrimination or sexism. Or, the motivation could be the result of political or partisan attempts to control the outcome of an election or resources, or something else altogether such as animus directed at religious or ethnic minorities.

Theories of gendered political behaviour, such as the previously discussed notion of a *male preserve,* predict that males will be overrepresented in public and political spaces because these spaces remain male dominated and controlled, especially in many lower income countries. Other theories of gendered behaviour predict that males will be at higher risk of committing violence in groups, than when acting alone (Reeves Sanday 1990; Lombard 2017). Group or gang violence in which males are disproportionately represented are considered cases of gendered violence for purposes of this research, because if gender did not matter we would expect to find a relatively random distribution of males and females participating in group violence.

Both of these theories predict a form of electoral violence documented in our field research in Uganda. Respondents reported a large number of instances of male (or

predominantly male) youth gangs paid as party agents to threaten supporters of an opposition candidate.[6] When asked who was perpetrating violence during elections, one female
councilor responded that in her community, "the agents of candidates are perpetrating the
violence. Mostly males. Mostly youth and drunk" (focus group discussion, women councilors, LCIII, Gulu, August 2 2018). A male agent of a candidate in Soroti remarked, "I was
surrounded at my candidate's rally by the opposition and they started throwing rocks at
us. These are men – youth – who were the perpetrators" (focus group discussion, Soroti,
July 26 2018). A community radio host who interviews candidates on the air during elections remarked, "Agents are mostly the perpetrators. An agent wants to show that they are
working for their candidate so they actually go out and start trouble with the other side.
Mostly men are agents and perpetrators of this kind of sabotage" (key informant interview,
community radio host, Gulu, July 31 2018). There were some instances in which women
(often very low-income women) were paid agents involved in gang violence. However,
men and boys were more often perceived to be the main perpetrators of this form of
violence.

   Another example that reflects gendered patterns of violence is the case in which male
party members propositioned female candidates or elected officials within the same party.
This type of harassment was reported as pervasive among key informants and focus group
participants in Uganda, and is also documented by the Ugandan women's human rights
group Forum for Women in Democracy (FOWODE) in a recent publication (FOWEDE
2018, 39). Here, the gender of both the target and the perpetrator emerge as important in
the pattern of violence. The motivation for sexually harassing female candidates is clearly
grounded in gendered power relations and is a form of sex discrimination. We argue that it
is also a form of gendered election violence that can result in psychological and emotional
harm, and deter women from participating in elections, and in the political process more
broadly.

   Female candidates and elected officials in Uganda reported widespread sexual harassment, unwanted sexual contact, and expectations of sexual favours in exchange for votes
(from community members) or party support (male fellow party members). One informant who had served two terms in an LCIII women's seat stated that transactional sex
was a fact of life for female candidates who lacked money to run a campaign. She said,
"To run, to get party support, you must end up giving in and agreeing" (focus group discussion, women councilors, Soroti, July 27 2018). Another female candidate in the same
group stated, "It is pervasive that women candidates are expected to sleep with party
leaders. That is why some husbands do not want their wives to be candidates because
they assume that they will have to sleep with the men" (focus group discussion, women
councilors, Soroti, July 27 2018).

Gender and electoral violence, the conventional approach

As mentioned above, violence against women in elections motivated by gender discrimination or misogyny is generally understood to be a subset of both violence against women
in politics, and violence against women more generally. However, it has not been included
as a category of electoral violence in the political violence scholarship. Figure 1 is a visual
representation of what we argue is the conventional approach in the political violence literature to the study of the relationship between gender and electoral violence. Why is this?

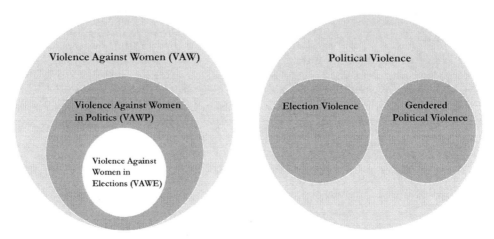

Figure 1. Conventional approach to the relationship between violence against women in elections (VAWE) and political/electoral violence.

There are feminist scholars writing on political violence, who study its gendered forms and types, however their work tends to be *outside of the field of electoral studies* (Moser and Clark 2001; Mazurana, Raven-Roberts, and Parpart 2005; Cheldelin and Eliatamby 2011; Cohn 2012; Guichaoua 2012; Sjoberg 2016; Davis 2017). When gender is included in electoral studies the research tends to focus on questions of women's political behaviour as voters and candidates, such as studies that examine the impact of electoral quotas on women's political representation (Dahlerup and Frei-denvall 2005; Krook 2009; Paxton, Hughes, and Painter 2010). The work of scholars such as Bardall (2011) and Krook (2017) who have documented violence and harass-ment against women politicians in national legislatures, rightly situate their scholarship at the intersection of feminist studies of women and politics, and political violence. However, the conventional political/electoral violence scholarship has generally failed to include violence and harms motivated by gender discrimination against women can-didates and elected officials *as acts of political violence.*

To better understand how the conventional approach to the study of political violence may overlook important gendered aspects of electoral violence, we can consider the case of female Afghan politician Sitara Achakzai, a women's rights activist and local councilor who was assassinated in 2009 by an extremist group. (Boone 2009). Violence studies scholars might record her death as an instance of political violence, but fail to con-sider it an instance of gender-based violence motivated by misogyny or sex discrimination, neglecting a crucial aspect of the case. The assassination of Achakzai resulted in a tremen-dous loss, and not only to her family. It likely had a chilling effect on the political ambi-tions of untold other women in the region. Indeed, both our findings from Uganda, and evidence from a large Interparliamentary Union (IPU) (2016) study suggests that for every instance of actual harm, there are many more cases in which women candidates or elected officials are *threatened* with physical harm because they are women. As mentioned pre-viously, threats of harm are serious forms of intimidation and harassment that, depending upon the severity of the threat, can be experienced as psychological terror by those who are targeted. Acts of violence against politically active women constitute not only harm to a single individual, but also by extension, to an entire class of citizens whose participation is essential to upholding fundamental democratic principles (Krook 2017).

An alternative approach to conceptualizing gender and electoral violence

In an effort to strengthen the explanatory power of the conventional approach we offer an alternate framework (Figure 2) that conceptualizes violence against women in elections and politics as a logical subset of the political violence set. This alternative approach strengthens the existing framework in at least two important ways. From a methodological perspective, it encourages the inclusion of a wider range of independent variables, such as gender, that facilitates a more detailed and comprehensive understanding of the causes and consequences of the violence. Secondly, it eliminates the artificial segregation of studies of violence against women in politics/elections *as women,* from the political and electoral violence sets. By including additional motivations for electoral violence, such as gender discrimination and misogyny, we expand the range of violent acts included in the study of political violence, including those for which women may be at greater risk of victimization. This speaks to longstanding feminist critiques of the marginalization of violence against women in political violence literature, and challenges assumptions that violence against women *as women* is outside of the scope of legitimate political violence.

Of course, not all incidents or patterns of violence correlate with gender, and when gender fails to predict or explain any significant level of variation in the data we categorize this as *non-gendered* electoral violence. In such instances, the motive of the violence would be purely political in nature, rather than a function of gendered power relations. An example of non-gendered electoral violence from our field work is a case where a man stood as an independent candidate in a local council race in a district that is a stronghold of the ruling National Resistance Movement (NRM) party. He received threats of physical harm from family and community members, who feared losing payments from the party if the village failed to show unified support for the NRM. While all of the participants in this

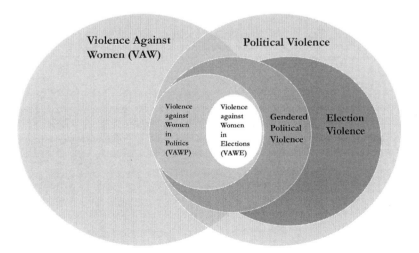

Figure 2. Alternative approach to the relationship between violence against women in elections (VAWE) and political/electoral violence.

incident have a sex/gender, there is nothing in the details of the incident to suggest that sex/gender was a particularly important factor in understanding or explaining the nature of the violence.

Lastly, Figure 3 supplements the conceptual framework in Figure 2, by illustrating in more detail the gendered dimensions of the electoral environment. The flow chart posits that the motivation for electoral violence can predict or explain some of the variation in patterns of targeting, perpetration, type of violence, and even the location of violence. For instance, reading from left to right, the **first motivation** listed for electoral violence is that of gender discrimination or misogyny. The violence is motivated by an

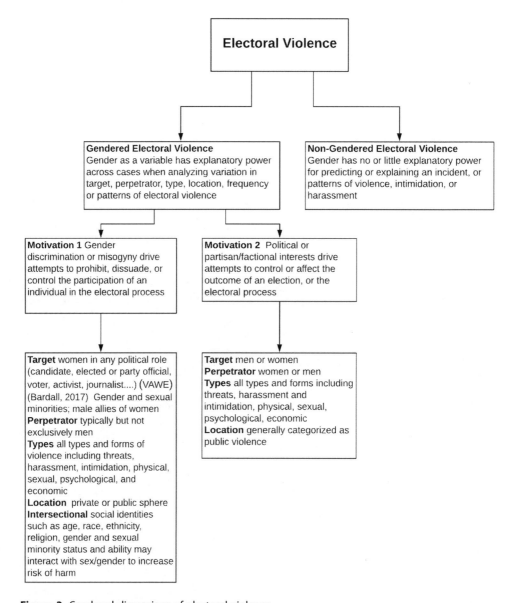

Figure 3. Gendered dimensions of electoral violence.

attempt to prohibit or dissuade individuals from participating in the election process based upon sex/gender. This motive predicts that women are more frequently the primary targets of violence, and men, the primary perpetrators. An example of this target-perpetrator combination was discussed above in the stories of women candidates who were targets of sexual harassment, coercion, and unwanted sexual contact from male candidates and party leaders.

Another category of incidents in which women are the primary targets and men the primary perpetrators are those involving intimate partners who seek to control the political choices, or behaviour of spouses. This type of electoral violence is unique in that it occurs primarily in the home, or private sphere, and thus it is unlikely to be documented in conventional studies of electoral violence. A number of respondents in Uganda shared stories of women who experienced serious physical injury from male partners over election related disputes. For instance, two market women who were agents for a female candidate in their subcounty in Soroti stated, "The husbands control the time that a woman can go to the polls," and, "If your candidate wins, and your husband's loses, then you cannot rejoice or you will get beaten" (focus group discussion, market women's association, Soroti, July 26 2018). In Gulu, the female director of a field office for a national women's rights organization stated,

> Women also face challenges to choose their own candidate—especially if they are illiterate. Two women from a village came to my office just recently wanting advice about how to deal with their husbands! The lining up behind [method of voting as an alternative to the use of secret ballot] meant that some women got beat up when they lined up behind the candidate they wanted, rather than their husbands. We know that this happened for a fact! (key informant interview, director of women's rights organization, Gulu, July 31 2018).

While less common, it is certainly possible for women to perpetrate election related violence against other women, motivated by gender discrimination. Although we have no examples of this type from our field work in Uganda, there are a number of violent cultural practices globally in which female relatives perpetrate violence against other females to defend traditional gender roles, privilege, and gender hierarchies (Engle Merry 2009, 127). Violence motivated by gender discrimination and unequal gendered power relations could also *target males* who are perceived as male allies of women's rights, as gender non-conforming, or sexual minorities. In this case, males or females could be perpetrators of violence (Weiss and Bosia 2013).

Gender and sexual minorities are at greater risk than others of being targets of violence, and this is an understudied form of gendered violence. Weiss and Bosia (2013) demonstrate in their groundbreaking work on global homophobia that lesbians, gay men, bisexuals, and transgender (LGBT) individuals are most often targeted *as gender and sexual minorities* rather than for explicitly political or partisan reasons. Recent events in a range of countries (e.g. Iran, Russia, Poland, Uganda, Cameroon) complicate the interpretation of the motivation behind the targeting of LGBT individuals, suggesting that sexual minorities may be used as scapegoats during political campaigns to deflect attention away from creeping authoritarianism. Our proposed framework attempts to account for some of the more common forms of political violence against LGBTQ individuals, as gendered electoral violence. This framework can also account for possible interaction effects between gender and other marginalized social identities such as age, ability, ethnic minority status, or others which may operate to place some individuals at higher risk of violence.

The **second motivation** for gendered electoral violence comprises political or partisan interests to control or affect the electoral process, or election outcome. We argue that violence motivated by political factors is gendered if gender has some explanatory power in predicting or explaining patterns of targeting, perpetration, or forms of violence. A number of examples from the Uganda case support this assertion. The first is the case of a female candidate targeting another female candidate in a race for a women's reserved seat in the local council election. In our field research in northern Uganda, we found extensive evidence of female perpetrated violence against other female candidates, or their agents/supporters. Female perpetrated violence was much more common in local municipal council (LC) contests for a "woman's (quota/reserved) seat" than in contests where women competed against men for a direct or open seat.

One female respondent who was an agent for a female candidate admitted that she would intentionally start physical altercations to prove to her candidate that she was a good agent, so she could get money to feed her children (focus group discussion, mixed, Soroti, July 26 2018). A female candidate for the woman's disabled seat recounted how two women agents of her female opponent followed her home after a campaign event, beat her, and cut her face, pointing to a prominent scar (incident report, case 13, female respondent, Gulu). Another respondent who was an agent for an LC1 female candidate reported that she and other supporters were chased by a group of ten male and female youth supporters of a different female candidate. One woman in their group fell behind and was physically attacked and had her arm broken (incident report, case 25, female respondent, Soroti). Unlike instances of violence against women in elections that is motivated by sexism or gender discrimination, the motivation behind violence perpetrated by female candidates or their agents, against other female candidates or agents was clearly political or partisan in nature.

Gender is important factor in cases of female perpetrated violence against other females for at least two reasons. First, female perpetrated violence is still considered an anomaly in some contexts, and electoral violence is one of them. Uncovering and explaining patterns of female perpetration are important from both an empirical and a theoretical perspective. Secondly, the violence occurred within the context of an election for a woman's reserved (quota) seat. This has implications for our understanding of how institutional reforms affect women's political participation and representation, and whether certain institutional reforms might predict higher levels of (gendered) election violence.

As mentioned previously, we also found many instances in which all male youth gangs carried out sustained threats, harassment and intimidation against opposition candidates or their supporters. This pattern of perpetration (youth gangs) has been documented in accounts of election violence, but the gender of the perpetrators is rarely if ever   mentioned, nor examined or interrogated as an important characteristic for understanding the nature of the violence (Bekoe 2012, 222; Burchard 2015, 28).[7] We found a number of incidents in Uganda in which targets reported that perpetrators were mixed male and female groups or gangs, or even all female groups of supporters of female candidates. Using a gendered lens can complicate both our expectations about perpetrators of electoral violence, and our assumptions of why the violence occurs.

In sum, our alternative conceptual framework offers a gender sensitive approach to the study of violence that clarifies why gender matters in the study of electoral violence. It demonstrates how analysing elections with a gendered lens exposes types and patterns of violence that might otherwise be missed, and thus increases the explanatory power of models that seek to document and understand electoral violence. A conceptual framework that more accurately captures and documents the range of harms experienced by individuals in contentious elections brings us closer to the goals of understanding how to ensure safer and more inclusive elections for all.

Conclusion

In this article we have proposed and defended a gender sensitive conceptual framework that clarifies and refines the complex relationship between gender and election violence. The framework illuminates how gendered election violence may be motivated by political or factional concerns, or by sex discrimination. When motivated by sex discrimination, violence may circumscribe or limit women's political participation and threaten the integrity of democratic elections. Violence against women in elections is a global problem deserving of greater attention from scholars and practitioners. The types of violence motivated by gender discrimination and which target female voters, candidates, and other actors can be serious, and even fatal, making its exclusion from the electoral violence literature especially problematic. Furthermore, gendered election violence can have real and serious consequences not only for individual women, but also for *women as a group* who can be dissuaded from participating in politics out of fear of retribution or retaliation. These incidents of violence usually entail violations to one or more of a wide range of human rights and state obligations for democratic elections, including the right to participate in political affairs, to vote and be elected, equality between men and women, freedom from discrimination, the right to the security of the person, among others.

The failure to consider sex/gender as a variable in research on electoral violence can lead to important gaps in our understanding of patterns of perpetration, victimization and harm. Such patterns include widely observed instances of all male groups perpetrating violence, but also cases in which females perpetrate violence against other females during campaigning or elections. These gaps must be addressed in order to develop more effective policies aimed at mitigating electoral violence, and securing safer, and more inclusive elections. Such policies could include legislation or electoral regulations to address violence against women in elections, and other types of gendered election violence such as attacks on sexual minorities; creation of appropriate enforcement entities; sanctions for non-compliance as well as avenues for administrative or judicial remedies; the adoption of codes of conduct by political parties and other election stakeholders; public awareness campaigns about VAWE ; and over the long-term, efforts to further strengthen the international normative framework related to VAWE and other forms of gendered election violence.

Notes

1. https://www.ohchr.org/Documents/Issues/Women/ViolenceAgainstWomeninPoliticsReport.pdf
2. As far as we can determine, the use of the concept of a *male preserve* was first introduced in the academic scholarship devoted to the study of sport and gendered power relations and is attributed to Sheard and Dunning. Christopher R. Matthews resurrects the term in his insightful 2016 article in the journal *Gender & Society*.

3. In the interest of coalescing around a single set of acronyms, we use the acronyms for violence against women in politics (VAWP) and violence against women in elections (VAWE), or in some cases VAWP/E, that is utilized by UN Women in the recent comprehensive programming guide, *Preventing Violence against Women in Elections,* that can be found here, http://www.unwomen.org/-/media/headquarters/attachments/sections/library/publications/2017/preventingvaw-in-elections.pdf?la=en&vs=2640

4. In recent field work in northern Uganda, one of the authors (Schneider) heard compelling stories from informants about the effectiveness of the use of threats. Acts of violence, while they did occur, were not necessary to undermine the sense of safety of voters and candidates and dissuade individuals from participating in the electoral process.

5. Following Höglund (2009 , 417) and others in the field of election and conflict studies, we employ the term *target* to denote victims of violence. While the term *survivor* has been widely adopted in the public health literature--particularly for victims of intimate partner violence and especially sexual assault, we argue that *target* is a generic and more appropriate concept to describe victims of the wide range electoral violence documented in the present study.

6. In Uganda we found that out of 90 acts of election violence reported by informants in Soroti, Moroto and Gulu, 44 were instances of group perpetrated violence. Of these, four groups are all female, nineteen are all male, and twenty- one are mixed, with "mostly male" but some female members.

7. In fact, there is no mention of *gender* or *women* in the index of either of these volumes.

Acknowledgements

We would like to thank Gabrielle Bardall, Toby James, Holly Ann Garnett, and the anonymous reviewers at *Policy Studies* for their many helpful comments on earlier versions of this work. We also benefitted greatly from the insights shared by participants at the 2018 Uppsala University workshop on *Gender, Politics and Violence,* and the 2018 workshop, *Measuring Violence against Women in Elections,* hosted by the Institute for Developing Nations (IDN) at Emory University, and The Carter Center. We also owe a debt of gratitude to colleagues who participated in the European Consortium for Political Research (ECPR) workshop, Violence Against Political Actors: New Research Directions, especially organizers Elin Bjarnegård and Mona Lena Krook, and discussant Pär Zetterberg. Research assistant Sophie Clark cheerfully and efficiently addressed our every request. Finally, ethnographic data that informs this study was made possible because of the assistance of Ugandan human rights defender and magistrate Lina Zedriga Waru whose expansive professional network greatly facilitated the data collection effort during Schneider's field work in Uganda.

Disclosure statement

No potential conflict of interest was reported by the authors.

Fieldwork data

Focus group discussion, women councilors LCIII, Gulu, Uganda, 2 August 2018.
Focus group discussion, mixed candidates, agents, and voters, Soroti, Uganda, 26 July 2018.
Focus group discussion, market women's association, Soroti, Uganda, 26 July 2018.
Focus group discussion, women councilors LC mixed, Soroti, Uganda, 27 July 2018.
Key informant interview, community radio host, Gulu, Uganda, 31 July 2018.
Key informant interview, director of women's rights organization, Gulu, Uganda, 31 July 2018.

Incident report, case 13, female respondent, Gulu Uganda.

Incident report, case 25, female respondent, Soroti, Uganda.

ORCID

Paige Schneider ⓘD http://orcid.org/0000-0001-7540-5027

References

Ballington, Julie. 2016. "Turning the Tide on Violence Against Women in Politics: How are we Measuring Up?" Paper presented at the 24th annual meeting for the international political science association world congress, Poznan, July 23–28.

Bardall, Gabrielle. 2011. *Breaking the Mold: Understanding Gender and Electoral Violence*. Washington, DC: International Foundation for Electoral Systems. http://ifes.org/sites/default/files/gender_and_electoral_violence_2011.pdf.

Bardall, Gabrielle. 2013. "Gender-specific Election Violence: The Role of Information and Communication Technologies." *Stability: International Journal of Security and Development* 2 (3): 1–11. doi:10.5334/sta.cs.

Bardall, Gabrielle. 2015. "Towards a More Complete Understanding of Election Violence: Introducing a Gender Lens to Electoral Conflict Research." Paper presented to the 4th European conference on politics and gender (ECPG), Uppsala, June 11–13.

Bardall, Gabrielle. 2016. "Gender Based Distinctions and Motivations in Political Violence." In Voices, Votes and Violence: Essays on Selected Dynamics of Electoral Authoritarianism. PhD diss., University of Montreal.

Bekoe, Dorina. 2012. *Voting In Fear*. Washington, DC: United States Institute of Peace.

Birch, Sarah. 2011. *Electoral Malpractice*. Oxford: Oxford University Press.

Birch, Sarah, and David Muchlinski. 2017. "The Dataset of Countries at Risk of Electoral Violence." *Terrorism and Political Violence*. doi:10.1080/09546553.2017.1364636.

Bjarnegard, Elin. 2016. "Gender and Election Violence: The Case of the Maldives." Paper presented at the annual meeting of the world congress of the international political science association, Poznan, July 23–28.

Bloom, Shelah S. 2008. "Violence Against Women and Girls: A Compendium of Monitoring and Evaluation Indicators." USAID. East Africa Regional Office. Accessed January 2018. https://www.measureevaluation.org/resources/publications/ms-08-30.

Boone, Jon. 2009. "Taliban Shoot Dead Afghan Politician Who Championed Women's Rights." *The Guardian* April 12.

Brancati, D., and J. L. Snyder. 2013. "Time to Kill: The Impact of Election Timing on Post-conflict Stability." *Journal of Conflict Resolution* 57 (5): 822–853. doi:10.1177/0022002712449328.

Burchard, Stephanie M. 2015. *Electoral Violence in Sub-Saharan Africa*. London: First Forum Press.

Cerna, Daniela Cerva. 2014. "Political Participation and Gender Violence in Mexico." *Revista Mexicana de Ciencias Politicas y Sociales*. Universidad Nacional Autonoma de Mexico Nueva Epoca. LIX, num. 222. Septiembre-diciembre. LIX (222): 117–140.

Cheldelin, Sandra I., and Maneshka Eliatamby. 2011. *Women Waging War and Peace*. New York: Continuum International Publishing.

Cockburn, Cynthia. 1998. *The Space Between Us: Negotiating Gender and National Identities in Conflict*. London: Zed Books.

Cohn, Carol. 2012. *Women & Wars*. Cambridge: Polity.

Dahlerup, Drude, and Lenita Freidenvall. 2005. "Quotas as a 'Fast Track' to Equal Representation for Women." *International Feminist Journal of Politics* 7 (1): 26–48. doi:10.1080/1461674042000324673.

Davis, Jessica. 2017. *Women in Modern Terrorism*. New York: Rowman Littlefield.

Daxecker, Ursula E. 2012. "The Cost of Exposing Cheating: International Election Monitoring, Fraud, and Post-Election Violence in Africa." *Journal of Peace Research* 49 (4): 503–516.

Daxecker, Ursula E. 2014. "All Quiet on Election Day? International Election Observation and Incentives for Pre-Election Violence in African Elections." *Electoral Studies* 34: 232–243.

Dercon, Stefan, and Roxana Gutiérrez-Romero. 2012. "Triggers and Characteristics of the 2007 Kenyan Electoral Violence." *World Development* 40 (4): 731–744.

Drummond, Paula. 2015. "Promoting Democracy in Preventing Electoral Violence: The Women's Situation Room." Programme on Gender and Global Change. The Graduate Institute Geneva.

Enloe, Cynthia. 1990. "'Womanandchildren': Making Feminist Sense of the Persian Gulf Crisis." *The Village Voice*. September 25.

Expert Group Meeting. 2018. "Violence Against Women in Politics." Report of the United Nations Human Rights, Office of the High Commissioner. March 8–9. New York.

Fischer, Jeff. 2001. "Electoral Conflict and Violence." White Paper. International Foundation for Electoral Systems (IFES). United States.

Fjelde, Hanne, and Kristine Höglund. 2016. "Electoral Violence: The Emergence of a Research Field." Newsletter of the Comparative Democratization section of the American Political Science Association. National Endowment for Democracy (NED).

Forum for Women in Democracy. 2018. "Deterred Not Barred: Unmasking Violence Against Women in the 2016 General Elections in Uganda." ISBN: 978-9970-14-019-0.

Goldsmith, Arthur A. 2015. "Elections and Civil Violence in New Multiparty Regimes: Evidence from Africa." *Journal of Peace Research* 52 (5): 607–621.

Guichaoua, Yvan. 2012. *Understanding Collective Political Violence*. New York: Palgrave Macmillan.

Höglund, Kristine. 2009. "Election Violence in Conflict-Ridden Societies: Concepts, Causes, and Consequences." *Terrorism and Political Violence* 21 (3): 412–427.

Inter-Parliamentary Union. 2016. "Sexism, Harassment, and Violence Against Women Parliamentarians Brief." Accessed March 18, 2018. http://www.ipu.org/pdf/publications/ issues-brief-e.pdf.

Kellow, Tim. 2010. *Women, Elections and Violence in West Africa: Assessing Women's Political Participation in Liberia and Sierra Leone*. London: International Alert.

Krook, Mona Lena. 2009. *Quotas for Women in Politics: Gender and Candidate Selection Reform Worldwide*. New York: Oxford University Press.

Krook, Mona Lena. 2017. "Violence Against Women in Politics." *Journal of Democracy* 28 (1): 74–88.

Krook, Mona Lena, and Juliana Restrepo Sanin. 2016a. "Gender and Political Violence in Latin America: Concepts, Debates, and Solutions." *Política y Gobierno* 13 (1): 125–157.

Krook, Mona Lena, and Juliana Restrepo Sanin. 2016b. "Violence Against Women in Politics: A Defense of a Concept." *Politica y Gobierno* 23 (2): 459–490.

Lombard, Nancy. 2017. *The Routledge Handbook on Gender and Violence*. London: Routledge University Press.

Lorentzen, Lois Ann, and Jennifer Turpin. 1998. *The Women & War Reader*. New York: New York University Press.

Mackenzie, Megan H. 2012. *Female Soldiers in Sierra Leone*. New York: New York University Press.

Mansbridge, Jane, and Shauna Shames. 2008. "Toward a Theory of Backlash: Dynamic Resistance and the Central Role of Power." *Politics & Gender* 4 (4): 623–634.

Matthews, R. Christopher. 2016. "The Tyranny of the Male Preserve." *Gender & Society* 30 (2): 312–333.

Mazurana, Dyan, Angela Raven-Roberts, and Jane Parpart. 2005. *Gender, Conflict, and Peacekeeping*. Lanham: Rowman and Littlefield.

Merry, Sally Engle. 2009. *Gender Violence: A Cultural Perspective*. West Sussex: Wiley Blackwell.

Moser, Caroline O. N., and Fiona C. Clark. 2001. *Victims, Perpetrators or Actors? Gender, Armed Conflict and Political Violence*. London: Zed Publishers.

National Democratic Institute. 2018. "Votes Without Violence." Accessed May 5, 2018. https://www.voteswithoutviolence.org/cross-country-analysis.

Norris, Pippa. 2014. *Why Electoral Integrity Matters*. Cambridge: Cambridge University Press.

Norris, Pippa, Richard Frank, and Ferran Martinez i Coma. 2015. *Contentious Elections. From Ballots to Barricades*. New York: Routledge.

Paxton, Pamela, Melanie M. Hughes, and Matthew A. Painter. 2010. "Growth in Women's Political Representation: A Longitudinal Exploration of Democracy, Electoral Systems, and Gender Quotas." *European Journal of Political Research* 49 (1): 25–52.

Piscopo, Jennifer M. 2015. "The Challenges with Legislation as Enforcement: Rethinking Responses to Violence Against Women in Politics." Paper presented at the international seminar violence in politics against women in Latin America: diagnostics, dialogues, and strategies, Mexico City, November 11–13.

Piscopo, Jennifer M. 2016. "State Capacity, Criminal Justice, and Political Rights: Rethinking Violence Against Women in Politics." *Politica y gobierno* 23 (2): 437–458.

RAU. 2010. "Preying on the 'Weaker' Sex: Political Violence against Women in Zimbabwe." International Center for Transitional Justice [ICTJ]. Research and Advocacy Unit. Accessed June 4, 2018. http://www.researchandadvocacyunit.org/index.php?option=com_docman&task=doc_download&gid=96&Itemid=90.

Reeves Sanday, Peggy. 1990. *Fraternity Gang Rape*. New York: New York University Press.

Report of the Special Rapporteur on Violence Against Women. 2018. United Nations Office of the High Commissioner. Accessed September 20, 2018. https://www.ohchr.org/EN/Issues/Women/SRWomen/Pages/ViolenceAgainstWomeninPolitics.asp.

Rutherford, A., A. B. Zwi, N. J. Grove, and A. Butchart. 2007. "Violence: A Glossary." *Journal of Epidemiology and Community Health* 61 (8): 676–680. doi:10.1136/jech.2005.043711.

SAP International and International IDEA. 2008. "Women, Representation and Violence: Exploring Constituent Assembly Election in Nepal." August. http://iknowpolitics.org/sites/default/files/vawip-report.pdf.

Sheard, K. G., and Eric G. Dunning, 1973. "The Rugby Football Club as a Type of "Male Preserve": Some Sociological Notes." *The International Review for the Sociology of Sport* 8 (3): 5–24.

Sjoberg, Laura. 2014. *Gender, War and Conflict*. Cambridge: Polity.

Sjoberg, Laura. 2016. *Women as Wartime Rapists*. New York: New York University Press.

Smidt, Hannah. 2016. "From a Perpetrator's Perspective: International Election Observers and Post- Electoral Violence." *Journal of Peace Research* 53 (2): 226–241.

Smith, Lahra. 2009. "Explaining Violence After Recent Elections in Ethiopia and Kenya." *Democratization* 16 (5): 867–897.

Taylor, Charles Fernandes, Jon C. W. Pevehouse, and Scott Straus. 2017. "Perils of Pluralism: Electoral Violence and Incumbency in Sub-Saharan Africa." *Journal of Peace Research* 54 (3): 397–411.

UN Women. 2017. "Preventing Violence Against Women in Elections: A Programming Guide." UNWomen/UNDP. Accessed June 19, 2018. http://www.unwomen.org/en/digital-library/publications/2017/11/preventing-violence-against-women-in-elections#view.

Valverde, María Eugenia Rojas. 2011. "Gender-Based Political Harassment and Violence: Effects on the Political Work and Public Roles of Women." *NEW SOLUTIONS: A Journal of Environmental and Occupational Health Policy* 20 (4): 527–535.

Van Ham, Carolien, and Staffan I. Lindberg. 2015. "From Sticks to Carrots: Electoral Manipulation in Africa, 1986–2012." *Government and Opposition* 50 (03): 521–548.

Weiss, Meredith L., and Michael L. Bosia. 2013. *Global Homophobia*. Urbana Champagne: University of Illinois Press.

Zabiliute, Emilija. 2014. "Notes From the Field: Delhi Assembly Elections Daru and Politisation of Violence Against Women." *Feminist Review* 107: 90–97.

Electoral integrity, voter fraud and voter ID in polling stations: lessons from English local elections

Toby S. James and Alistair Clark

ABSTRACT
Polling stations are at the fulcrum of the democratic process. They are the location where most voters exercise their democratic rights, but also one place where electoral fraud and irregularities may occur, both in consolidating and established democracies. This study provides a detailed analysis of the nature and frequency of electoral irregularities that are found in English local elections using original surveys of poll workers in 2018 and 2019 ($n = 5659$). It also identifies the effects of recent attempts to improve electoral integrity through the introduction of voter identification requirements on a pilot basis. Elections are found to be broadly well run but problems are reported with names missing from the electoral register and polling station accessibility requirements. Some more infrequent problems were reported with inappropriate behaviour from party agents/candidate – and some gender-based intimidation amongst voters. Attempted impersonation was exceptionally rare, however, and measures to introduce voter identification requirements therefore had little effect on the security of the electoral process. In fact, they led to some voters not casting their ballot, either for reasons of convenience and availability of suitable forms of ID, or reasons of principle and protest. There are therefore important implications for the wider literature on electoral integrity and the design of democratic practices.

Introduction

Polling stations are at the fulcrum of the democratic process. They are the location where most voters exercise their democratic right by casting their vote and therefore have an iconic and symbolic place within democratic practices. They are also the location where electoral fraud and irregularities are thought to occur, both in consolidating and established democracies. These irregularities might include outright attempts to rig the electoral process through ballot box stuffing, carousel voting and voter intimidation (Schedler 2002). They might also involve bureaucratic hurdles that makes voting more difficult than it otherwise needs to be. Practice and procedure could also more heavily disadvantage some individuals or groups of voters more than others if polling practices are not inclusive

(James and Garnett 2020b). For example, polling stations might lack accessibility requirements (Schur, Ameri, and Adya 2017) or onerous voter identification requirements might exist (Burden 2018).

The extent and nature of these irregularities are commonly subject to speculation. Evidence about the frequency of them is less common, however. This study provides a detailed analysis of the nature and frequency of electoral irregularities that are reported in English local elections using original surveys of poll workers in 2018 and 2019 ($n =$ 5659). It also identifies the implications of recent attempts to improve electoral integrity through the introduction of voter identification requirements on a pilot basis in a selection of local government areas. This was the first time that voter identification requirements had been used in Britain and allows broader lessons to be learnt about the consequences of the reform.

Elections are found to be broadly well run but problems are reported with names missing from the electoral register, polling station accessibility requirements and ballot secrecy problems. Attempted impersonation was exceptionally rare, however, and provided no evidence to support the introduction of voter identification requirements. In fact, these voter identification requirements led to some voters not casting their ballot when they arrived at the polling place, either for reasons of convenience and availability of suitable forms of ID, or reasons of principle and protest. This article therefore contributes to the international literature about the nature of electoral integrity in established democracies, the literature on inclusive voting practices, and the effects of voter identification requirements – where the number of studies remain limited.

The article proceeds by presenting a five-part typology of problems that are regularly thought to occur in polling stations. It then reviews the literature on the known effects of voter identification requirements. The way in which English local elections are run is then explained with the pilot schemes explained in historical context. The research design is set out before the results of the study are introduced.

Existing literature on polling place problems

Elections are an essential part of the democratic process (Beetham 1994; Dahl 1971; James 2020a; Przeworski 2018). They provide citizens with the opportunity to hold governments to account and choose their elected representatives. Polling stations are the physical location where citizens have the opportunity to cast their ballot. As well as providing the functional purpose of providing citizens with their opportunity to have their say, this also provides an important ritual (Orr 2016). For Coleman (2013) the act of voting is a social performance which can generate different emotions, memories and anxieties. The act of voting following the toppling of an autocratic regime, for example, can provide cathartic moments. Media images, beamed worldwide, can show people who had been "long denied the vote, forming winding queues to assert their entry into the enfranchised world stand as semiotic markers of political progress" (2).

Nonetheless, problems with electoral integrity are often found in polling stations, as well as other stages of the electoral process. These are important because the consequences can be far reaching, including undermining the legitimacy of government, affecting voter behaviour and set in motion a series of events that might undermine peace and security (Norris 2014). We argue that there are five overlapping themes of problems that are often thought to occur in polling stations, all of which could potentially undermine the quality of the electoral and democratic process. In recent years, there have been some concern about each of these in the UK.

Firstly, given the huge volume of ballot papers, staff and complex laws involved – there is considerable potential for administrative problems. There is increasing cross-national evidence of variations in standards of electoral management (James 2020a; James et al. 2019; Norris, Martinez i Coma, and Gromping 2016). These are not necessarily the consequence of deliberate partisan efforts to alter the result of elections. Instead, they might result from human error, under–resourcing or poor performance management systems and/or leadership. These are important because individuals can inadvertently lose their ability to exercise their right to vote as a consequence of such difficulties. The UK made international headlines on the night of the 2010 general election when citizens were locked out of polling stations as they closed at 10pm, and they were inconsistently dealt with by officials. Legal clarity was subsequently provided, but there remains evidence of variation in the quality of delivery (Clark 2015, 2017). James argued that the UK compared unfavourably in many respects against Canada, using a comparative framework to evaluate electoral management (James 2020a).

Secondly, there might be bureaucratic hurdles to citizens casting their vote, which might ultimately determine whether they decide whether to vote – or are even able to do so. As the introduction to the special issue sets out, voters find themselves within a strategic-relational environment which might make voting more or less likely. The administrative time involved in voting can make voting more or less likely. Early voter registration deadlines, limited polling hours and long distances to polling stations are amongst the factors that have been shown to affect whether or not individuals vote (Gimpel and Schuknecht 2003; Hall 2013; James 2012; Orford et al. 2011; Pallister 2017; Wolfinger and Rosenstone 1980). The introduction of individual electoral registration into Britain caused concern that students and younger citizens might be adversely affected (James 2014a). These concerns eventually proved to be well founded with the completeness of the electoral register affected amongst younger groups (James 2020a). Campaigners therefore argued strongly for voter registration reform (Bite the Ballot, James, and ClearView Research 2016) to address this.

Thirdly, there might be accessibility problems with polling stations and polling materials which makes it more difficult for citizens with disabilities to cast their vote. Such an experience might send "the message that people with disabilities are not expected to participate in the political sphere" (Schur, Ameri, and Adya 2017, 1374). Studies have shown that individuals with disabilities are often reported to be less likely to vote and have experienced problems in polling stations (van Hees, Boeije, and de Putter 2019). Convenience voting mechanisms such as absentee voting have therefore been found to increase turnout among those with disabilities (Miller and Powell 2016). The UK Electoral Commission report on the 2015 general election found that 5% of people with disabilities were dissatisfied with the voting process, by contrast with 2% for those without a disability (Electoral Commission 2015, 47–48). Despite this, research on disabled voters' experience in polling stations has been relatively sparse.

Fourthly, polling stations are often highlighted as the physical spaces where parties, state agents and the public might try to exert voter intimidation (Birch 2011; Frye, Reuter, and Szakonyi 2019). Threats of physical violence are often made well in advance of the day of the election, so that the day of the election can itself be relatively free of intimidation. Nonetheless, historical studies from older democracies (Argersinger 1985) and cross-national analyses (Birch et al. 2018) reveal the persistence of intimidation and violence in and around polling stations. UK elections were historically long thought to be free from electoral malpractices of this type. An evaluation of the 2016 EU referendum, however, did find some problems with inappropriate campaigning at polling stations, such as the placement of posters close to polling stations (Clark and James 2016). Physical intimidation inside polling stations was alleged in a court case regarding elections in a London borough (Mawrey 2015).

Fifth, polling stations have been pointed to as a site where electoral fraud might be conducted. This could involve include ballot-box stuffing in favour of one party or candidate, carousel-voting or impersonation (Birch 2011; Lehoucq 2003; Lehoucq and Molina 2002; Schedler 2002). In response to this, some advocate increased security provisions, such as voter identification requirements, removing convenience voting provisions such as mail-in ballots or asking citizens or the use of election monitors (Fund 2008). Critics, however, argue that actual cases of electoral fraud in the older established democracies are fewer and further between than media coverage often implies (Minnite 2010). In the UK, Wilks-Heeg (2008) argued that provisions for postal voting provided opportunities for electoral fraud. Meanwhile, Sobolewska et al. (2015) argued that the structure of Pakistani and Bangladeshi origin communities provided opportunities for undue influence. These findings are not always found in other studies, however (Clark and James 2016).

Existing literature on voter ID requirements

Voter ID requirements have often been proposed to improve electoral integrity in polling stations, but have been one of the most contested aspects of electoral administration in the US and at the heart of fiercely political "voting wars" (Hasen 2012; James 2012) Proponents claimed that they are necessary to reduce voter fraud (Fund 2008), while opponents claim that they amount to voter suppression and can or have had a disproportionate effect on minority voters less likely to have the required form of ID (Hajnal, Lajevardi, and Nielson 2017; Minnite 2010; Piven, Minnite, and Groarke 2009). In a review of the US literature Highton (2017) concluded that "a small number of studies have employed suitable research designs and generally find modest, if any, turnout effects of voter identification laws." (149)

Identifying the effects of voter ID requirements on participation is difficult because of a number of methodological problems (Burden 2018; Erikson and Minnite 2009; Highton 2017). As Highton noted, only a few US states initially introduced strict voter ID laws. These reforms were relatively recent and often in tandem with other simultaneous reforms. There is therefore no strict experimental method as voter ID is introduced in states with specific political contexts (Highton 2017). The relative absence of cross-national data on voting requirements has limited the study of other states. There have been important moves to introduce biometric identification in many countries – but there has been relatively little focussing on the impact on turnout (Gelb and Diofasi 2016).

One approach is to examine who has the required form of identification. Hood and Bullock (2008) estimated which registered voters in Georgia lacked a Department of Motor Vehicles-issued form of ID. In the UK, pressure groups such as the Electoral

Reform Society criticized the voter identification scheme on the basis that 9.5 million people did not hold a passport in 2011 and 9 million did not have a driving licence in 2013/14. The reforms, they argued, would have a disproportionate effect on those without the necessary forms of ID (Electoral Reform Society 2019). This provides a useful "worst-case scenario" but makes crude assumptions about whether those with the required form of ID will vote, and makes no allowances for the systems that electoral officials introduce for those without ID. For example, provisional ballots could be granted. Alternatively, other forms of ID could be made available on request – but it would be unclear whether/how many people would apply.

A second approach is to use surveys of citizens' experiences, but citizens may not always report their experiences accurately. One advance has been to use surveys where responses are checked against voter registration files. Hajnal, Lajevardi, and Nielson (2017) therefore used the Cooperative Congressional Election Study and concluded that strict identification laws did have a differentially negative impact on turnout. Grimmer et al. (2018), however, argued that there were data inaccuracies as there are problems in matching the data records. Atkeson et al. (2010) undertook a survey of citizens in New Mexico to identify whether Hispanic and other minority voters were more likely to have been asked for ID than others. Surveys of citizens have been used in Northern Ireland where photographic requirements were introduced in 2002. An Electoral Commission survey suggested that one percent of voters experienced problems with voter ID in the 2007 Northern Ireland Assembly election (Electoral Commission 2014, 25). This would be approximately 11,000 citizens.[1]

A third approach has been to use surveys of poll workers. Atkeson et al. (2010), for example, surveyed poll workers in New Mexico to ask how frequently they asked for voter ID and why they did so. They concluded that neither the partisan or demographic characteristics of the poll worker affected whether they asked for voter ID (Atkeson et al. 2010, 71). Their survey didn't, however, identify the number of people who were unable to vote because they didn't have the required form of voter identification. Poll worker surveys have not been used to identify the effects of voter ID outside of the US.

In summary, there has been some evidence of the impact of voter identification requirements on turnout, especially minority populations but there remain few studies outside of the US. A variety of available methods have been established, but poll worker studies have not been used to explore the effects of voter identification in different polities.

Inclusive electoral practices in the UK?

This article empirically focuses on electoral integrity in English polling stations. Elections in England are run by Returning Officers who are appointed by local government units. Returning Officers are responsible for the conduct of the poll and have some discretion over the timing of the count. An Electoral Registration Officer is responsible for compiling the electoral register. Both Returning Officers and Electoral Registration Officers are local government employees but are independent of both central and local government with respect to their electoral duties. They are instead accountable to the courts system as an independent statutory officer and can be prosecuted for being in breach of their duties. Electoral Registration Officers and Returning Officers implement elections according to electoral law which is determined by Parliament in Westminster and appropriate additional secondary legislation set out by the Minister of State. Since 2000, a UK Electoral

Commission has provided advice and guidance for election administration, served as the chief counting officer for referendums and has had a statutory duty to evaluate any electoral pilots undertaken by the government. In normal electoral circumstances, with the exception of referendums, the Electoral Commission has no power of direction over electoral administrators on the ground. Electoral justice is primarily dealt with by the court system. Election Courts can be convened by the High Court if a petition is raised challenging the result of an election. There are some important variations across the UK, with different arrangements in Northern Ireland and Scotland, but the focus of this study is solely on local elections in England for reasons that the methods section will explain.

The franchise for local elections is different to general elections, with EU citizens also eligible to vote. Polling stations are open for local elections between 7.00am and 10.00pm on the day of the poll, with the count usually taking place immediately afterwards. Electors need to have applied to be registered no later than 12 days before the poll. These applications are processed by local government units who maintain 381 separate local registers in Britain. Votes can also be cast by post if an application is made no later than 11 days before the poll. Proxy votes can be applied for on the basis of disability or absence on the day of the poll 11 days before the poll. Citizens can, however, also apply to cast an emergency proxy vote as late as 5pm on election day (Electoral Commission 2019). These procedures were the result of efforts by the New Labour governments to make it easier for citizens to cast their ballot (James 2011).

A different policy agenda emerged from the mid-2000s following some high-profile cases of electoral fraud. Six councillors were found guilty of postal vote fraud in Birmingham in 2004, although one successfully appealed. The case caught the headlines after the judge presiding over the election court declared that the levels of fraud would shame a "banana republic" (Stewart 2006). The same judge also oversaw a case where a candidate for mayor of the London Borough of Tower Hamlets was found guilty of a variety of electoral offences (Mawrey 2015). The Labour governments introduced some measures to tackle vulnerabilities for fraud such as tighter provision for postal votes and initiated the move towards individual electoral registration. This momentum was sped up under the Conservative led governments from 2010. Individual electoral registration was legislated for in 2013 and the government asked former Conservative Party chair and Secretary of State for Communities & Local Government, Eric Pickles, to author a report recommending measures to reduce electoral fraud. One of his recommendations was voter identification (Pickles 2016).

A first step was the introduction of pilot voter ID schemes in the 2018 and 2019 local elections in England. Pilots were run in five authorities in 2018,[2] ten in 2019[3] with different models being used in different councils (Cabinet Office 2019, 5–6; Electoral Commission 2018) as set out in Table 1. These pilots were voluntary, with participating councils effectively self-selecting in applying to participate (Cabinet Office 2018a). The vast majority of councils chose not to do so. Two councils – Watford and Woking – participated in both rounds of pilots. Critics of the 2018 pilots noted that most of the participating councils were located in the South of England, traditionally a Conservative-voting region. Indeed, four of the five pilot authorities had Conservative majorities in the 2018 local elections (Dempsey 2018).[4] In 2019 this regional distribution changed with four in the Midlands – Broxtowe, Derby, North Kesteven and North West Leicestershire – and two in the north – Craven and Pendle – and the remaining four in the South. The Conservative Party were the largest in all but one of the councils after the 2019 elections, being the majority

Table 1. Voter-ID pilots.

Model type	Description	Usage
Poll card model	Electors were required to present their poll card, an item which is posted to all electors, before being issued a ballot paper. Replacement poll cards were available on demand. Should they not be able to produce a poll card then alternatives included photographic identification such as a passport.	2018: Swindon, Watford2019: Mid-Sussex, Watford, North West Leicestershire
Photo ID model	Electors were required to show a form of photographic identification. If they could not produce one then they were required to apply for an electoral identify document, up until 5pm, the day prior to the poll	2018: Bromley, Gosport, Woking2019: Pendle and Woking
Mixed model	Electors could provide one form of listed photographic ID or two forms non-photographic ID such as a bank card, council tax demand, mortgage statement or birth certificate.	2019: Braintree, North Kesteven, Craven, Broxtowe and Derby.

Source: authors based on (Cabinet Office 2019, 5–6; Electoral Commission 2018).

in three, and the largest party in a no overall control situation in a further six (Uberoi 2019). With the exception of the London Borough of Bromley, and Swindon and Derby which are unitary councils, the remainder were all district councils. Notable by their absence were both Labour controlled councils, and large metropolitan councils where many groups argued to be potentially disadvantaged by voter ID were most likely to be resident.

The aim of the voter identification pilots was therefore to reduce opportunities for electoral fraud – notably personation. Critical voices, however, argued that the piloting of ID was unlawful (Green 2019) and in breach of human rights commitments (Stanford 2018).

Research methods

This article aims to address the following questions:

(1) What problems are reported in polling stations at English local elections?
(2) To what extent did the introduction of voter identification requirements help or hinder these problems?

Poll worker studies have become an established method for identifying the frequency and nature of problems with electoral integrity in polling stations (Clark and James 2017). The officials who were present in polling stations on the day can be conceived as "street level bureaucrats" (Lipsky 1980) who have intimate frontline knowledge of the mundane everyday practice of elections (Durose 2009). They therefore have a different vantage point from which we can see the electoral process than voter surveys. They are also actors who are much closer "to the ground" than experts, whose opinions are often used to assess the frequency of other forms of electoral integrity (James 2020a, 33–58; Martínez i Coma and van Ham 2015). Poll worker surveys may, however, *underestimate* the effects of voter ID on participation. Electors may decide not to travel to the polls because of the ID requirements and their actions would not feature in the experience of poll workers. Poll worker studies therefore provide a conservative estimate of the effects.

Poll worker surveys were conducted in the 2018 and 2019 English local elections based on a questionnaire design used in the 2015 general election (Clark and James 2017). The Electoral Commission has a statutory duty to undertake evaluations of electoral pilots and therefore they conducted a poll worker survey, partially based on the questionnaire design proposed by the authors, in the pilot areas. The authors approached all returning officers in remaining non-participating local authorities via email, asking them to circulate the survey to their poll workers. The surveys contained many identical questions about the frequency of problems in polling stations.

The surveys provided a greater number of responses than any previous poll worker survey undertaken in the UK. The authors' surveys generated 2,276 responses in 2018 and a further 460 in 2019. The surveys therefore provided extensive information about the frequencies of problems at polling stations. These also included qualitative responses that could be used to expand on the nature of the problems experienced at polling stations. Qualitative comments were read by the authors and then selected to illustrate examples. A formal coding system was not therefore used. The 2019 surveys saw a lower response rate because European Parliament elections followed shortly after the local elections. This meant that fewer local authorities circulated the survey due to the increased pressure. In addition, the Electoral Commission surveys generated 1,436 in 2018 and 1,803 in 2019. This provides a total of 5,973 responses. The sample was broadly representative of the population in terms of the coverage of local authorities included.[5]

Data collected from non-pilot areas can be compared against the pilot areas to examine what effect, if any, the different voter ID requirements had on the running of the elections. The pilots brought considerable investment in publicity about the form of voter identification that was required in each pilot area, which might not be replicated at other events. Written evidence to the House of Commons Public Administration and Constitutional Affairs Committee suggested that around £353,000 had been spent on awareness raising in the five pilot authorities in 2018, while additional administrative costs amounted to £1,385,934.[6] Voter ID also featured prominently in the national media as critics such as the Electoral Reform Society and Labour Party argued that it would disenfranchize voters (Walker 2019). This may have increased awareness of the voting procedures and boosted turnout to be higher than it might otherwise have been. The effects of voter identification in a pilot situation might also be very different to a permanent reform, where voters would become used to the requirements over several elections and might therefore be more likely to bring the required identification. Nonetheless, the pilots provide an important opportunity to establish the likely effects of permanent reforms.

Results: polling station problems in English local elections

The article now reports on the quantitative and qualitative evidence found from the surveys with respect to the five different themes of potential problems.

Administrative problems

Table 2 summarizes responses about whether some possible administrative problems occurred. The general picture was very similar to earlier studies on the 2015 general election in that few problems were reported (Clark and James 2017). The polling process was described as going smoothly with few problems setting up or closing polling stations. In some cases, this was because problems were identified in advance and solutions found. In one case there were major problems with incorrectly printed electoral registers, but this was identified the day before the register was collected, for example.

Table 2. Administrative problems experienced.

	Strongly disagree	Disagree	Neither agree or disagree	Agree	Strongly agree	N
Problems setting up polling station	67.7	23.5	3.5	3.9	1.4	2609
Problems closing polling station	72.6	23.3	2.4	.8	.8	2606
Poll workers worked well together	1.9	1.0	2.2	20.4	74.5	2616
Voting process went smoothly at my polling station	2.1	.5	1.5	24.3	71.6	2613
Problems with queues during the day	75.0	20.5	2.4	.4	1.6	2602
Problems with queues towards end of the day	77.3	19.4	1.8	.3	1.3	2596

Note: Author's data only.

This is not to say that the day was without incident. One polling station, for example, had to be evacuated as the fire alarm had developed a faulty sensor. A temporary polling station therefore had to be set up in the back of a car until the alarm was silenced and the building was confirmed as safe to enter.

Access to the buildings was sometimes problematic. One poll worker noted that:

> School gates were closed and no one was there to open them so voters, disabled or not, were having to walk a long distance to get to us. Some even said they were going to turn around and go home rather than coming in. Some voters could have done this without our knowledge.

In other cases, facilities were poor which meant that working conditions for poll workers were cramped. Buildings would sometimes also be used for several purposes on the day which might have undermined the quality of service. In one instance "a wake was being held in the same building and it got a bit heated."

Poll workers generally described themselves as working well together. "My team worked very well together and it was a fantastic day/experience," said one. The "feeling of camaraderie" was praised while one poll worker pointed out that their presiding officer "was friendly and taught me a lot of extras." But relations were not always harmonious. This potentially led to the quality of service to the voter being undermined:

> One of the workers is quite rude and insensitive and regularly upsets voters … . Although I've mentioned it nobody seems concerned. I often have to diffuse situations and have decided I am going to ask to work at another station next time as I find it embarrassing and hard work.

One issue that has been thought to have made running elections more difficult has been the complexity of electoral law. Earlier research found that this was a problem which could lead to errors in the electoral process and drain resources (James 2014b) and the Law Commission subsequently published recommendations to consolidate electoral law (Law Commissions 2016). The non-pilot surveys asked about whether the law was too complex to understand quickly and easily. Although no problems were directly linked to this, there was a significant proportion of 15.9% of responding poll workers who found electoral law difficult to understand and follow quickly, while a further 31.5% were neutral, neither agreeing nor disagreeing.

Bureaucratic hurdles

One form of bureaucratic hurdle that voters might experience is a queue or long wait time (King 2020). Table 2 illustrates that these were relatively rare. Polling stations may have been put under less pressure than they would be at a general election because of lower turnout (although more staff might have been employed at a general election). Where they did occur, logistical problems were often the cause. One poll worker explained that:

> it took time to get a second ballot box hence holding the queue because we had to ensure the ballot papers are pushed right inside into the box.

There were also some isolated case of citizens "who turned up after the polls were closed, around 10:05, and insisted to vote," but were presumably refused since the law only permits those already in a queue to vote to cast their ballot after the 10pm close of poll. A positive correlation was found between queues and population density. Queues were more likely in higher density urban areas.[7]

Poll workers were asked whether they experienced people asking to vote who were not on the register (see Table 3). In a legal sense, poll workers correctly turn prospective voters away in these circumstances. However, this is a bureaucratic hurdle for citizens because in some polities they could vote without prior voter registration at any polling station (James 2019). This was one of the more frequent problems with roughly half of polling stations reporting a problem with at least one voter. Pearson's correlations also showed that it was more likely to be reported in urban areas ($\beta = .226$, $p < 0.01$).[8] Electoral Commission data for 2018 suggest that around 1400 voters were affected in those local elections.[9] Poll workers cited various examples this. For instance:

> Someone had moved recently from one area of [location given] to another, he assumed because he pays his council tax on new house his election rights automatically moved over at the same time, which stopped him from voting.

> Disruptive voter unhappy at not being on electoral roll.

> Good turn out from younger people but I was surprised at how many didn't realise you need to be registered to vote.

Qualitative comments suggested that the problem was also that they had attended the wrong polling station, perhaps because the location had changed. As one poll worker explained:

> People complained they couldn't find the polling station after a small change of location despite a letter telling them it changed, being notified on their poll card and many fluorescent signs outside. We were probably only about 200 yards away.

Others had no election to vote in:

> We explained that there was no poll where they live and thanked them for making the efforts to try and vote.[10]

It was noticeable that problems, though significant because they involved voters being turned away from the polls, were less frequently reported than they were at the 2015

Table 3. Voters turned away from polling stations (%).

	None	1	2–5	6–10	10+	N
People asking to vote, who were not on the electoral register	52.7	23.4	20.1	1.6	.5	4022

Note: Author's and Electoral Commission data combined.

general election where a similar survey was run and 69% reported at least one problem (Clark and James 2017), at the 2016 Brexit referendum where there were some angry citizens unable to vote (Clark and James 2016) or at the 2019 European elections a few weeks after the 2019 local elections described here (James 2019). One explanation for the difference against a general election might be that voters in local elections are more aware of their registration status because they are better informed and more motivated about politics at all levels.[11] It might also be that the move to individual electoral registration between 2014 and 2015 had created confusion at previous electoral events, and this confusion had subsided over time.

Accessibility

The surveys asked whether disabled voters experienced any problems with access to the polling stations and completing ballot papers. Table 4 illustrates that some problems with accessibility were experienced, especially for wheelchair users. Problems were more likely to be found in the London Boroughs ($\beta = .135$, $p < 0.01$). Poll workers gave many examples, including:

> Difficult access due to scaffolding outside building slightly obstructing the entrance especially for buggies and wheelchairs

> Venue had steep and uneven step which made access difficult

> We did not have any disabled voters in the polling station but this could have been because there was no availability of disabled parking directly outside the entrance to the station.

> exiting the station … they were not able to turn their mobility scooter until we moved tables to make a larger space.

In some cases, this seemed to mean that the usual processes that ensured ballot security such as the provision of private booths appeared to be compromised:

> No wheelchair access, as the presiding officer I took ballot papers to people in wheelchairs to complete.

> Disabled person … had a sight problem and I assisted in marking their paper and completing associated form.

Some problems were responded to with aids provided for the purpose:

> Two people struggled to read the papers, but this was quickly handled with the provided magnifying glass and aids

In each of these cases however, the poll worker was simply complying with the recommendations and procedures contained in their training, although these procedures have been criticized by sight-loss charities.[12]

Table 4. Accessibility problems at polling stations (%).

	None	1	2–5	6–10	10+	N
Disabled voters having problems with access to the polling station	91.4	5.9	2.4	.3	.1	2576
Disabled voters having problems completing ballot papers	85.7	10.2	3.8	.3	.0	2578

Note: Author's data only.

Language also posed a problem in some areas:

Dealing with voters where their first language is not English. A list of general questions and answers in a selection of languages relevant to the area. In my locality Slovak, Lithuanian, Russian, Polish etc

This meant that poll workers were unable to communicate the process to voter in some instances, but also raises questions about those voters' awareness of the parties and candidates.

Voter intimidation and ballot secrecy

Table 5 suggests that problems with voter intimidation are rare with the vast majority reporting no problems. Isolated cases were described in the qualitative comments, including one case in a London borough where: A person seemed to exercise undue influence on another voter. Other cases were gender (rather than ethnicity) based:

[M]en try to tell their partners how to vote.

Men telling women who were standing in polling booths how to vote, and in loud voices.

Some ladies handing their ballot paper to a man so we had to intervene. They then tried to go in the booth together, again intervened. I am not sure some of the ladies knew who to vote for and were relying on

Some forms of intimidation came through the party agents, whose behaviour was sometimes described as inappropriate. Examples cited in the qualitative comments were mostly about the behaviour of tellers, or party workers, who were sometimes reported as off-putting to voters:

Voters felt they were obliged to give information to the tellers outside the station due to the words used by the tellers

Even if they were not necessarily doing anything legally wrong, some citizens were concerned about their presence:

One voter vociferously complained about the teller's presence. The tellers were acting reasonably simply asking for the numbers

Tellers were also sometimes inexperienced, "didn't know what they were meant to do and expected polling station staff to advise them." Other forms of inappropriate activity cited by poll workers included the candidate entering the polling station and the display of party flags in cars parked close to polling stations.

Poll workers were also asked whether they experienced problems with ballot secrecy. The vast majority "agreed" or "strongly agreed" that there were no problems maintaining

Table 5. Behaviour of political parties inside polling stations (%).

	None	1	2–5	6–10	10+	N
Members of political parties intimidating the public[a]	92.7	3.7	2.8	.4	.4	5560
Members of political parties being where they should not be[b]	91.6	5.9	2.4	.1	.1	5677

Note: Author's and Electoral Commission data combined.
[a]The wording in the Electoral Commission surveys was "Intimidation of voters."
[b]The wording in the Electoral Commission survey was "Campaigners or tellers being where they should not be."

the secrecy of the ballot in polling stations – but 7.0% "disagreed" or "strongly disagreed." Ballot secrecy was undermined for a number of reasons. One reason was related to disability and accessibility. Another was poor equipment and location:

> The polling booths have no curtains across them so it is difficult to stop family members looking at each other's ballot papers and consulting on who to vote for or checking who the other(s) have voted for.

Conversely, some electors questioned whether their ballot secrecy would be guaranteed:

> when they realised their elector number was being written on the "Corresponding Number List."

Impersonation and fraud

Respondents were asked whether they were suspicious that any electoral fraud had taken place and whether they had confidence in the stated identity of the elector that they were presenting ballot papers to. Combining the data from the pilot and non-pilot areas, Table 6 shows that electoral fraud in polling stations was thought to be very rare. Suspicions about the identity of the elector were also very rare.

Qualitative comments revealed that the problems posed by the public in polling stations were much more varied. These included taking photos:

> An individual attempted to take a photo however was advised to take this outside of the polling station, the individual complied with the instruction.

Questions were asked by the public about why pencils and not pens were provided. This was a problem reported in 2016, where some campaigners claimed that electoral officials would rub-off votes marked in pencil (Clark and James 2016). One respondent claimed that:

> at least 3 people challenged why we used pencils and we offered them pens and tried to explain it was just because pencils don't run out and that we could not access their ballot paper after they put it in the box anyway

Voters could also be challenging in other ways, such as being intoxicated:

> A drunk male arrived around lunch time, he did have his poll card and was entitled to vote at my polling station, quickly realising that he was drunk he was ushered through the process, this was because he was shouting out that there were only three parties and no Green Party. He was given time to vote and left without incident.

Or in another experience:

> A man with mental health issues who wouldn't stop talking after he voted. He wanted to know our blood group; star sign; domestic arrangements; etc. But at least he came to vote.

Table 6. Concerns about electoral fraud (%).

	None	1	2–5	6–10	10+	N
Suspected cases of electoral fraud	99.3	0.6	0.1	0	0	5672
People asking to vote whose identity I was unsure of	94.0	3.9	1.9	0.1	0.1	5649

Note: Author's and Electoral Commission data combined.

Table 7. Correlations and partial correlations between British Pakistani-Bangladeshi community size and electoral integrity problems.

	Correlation with percentage of the population that are British Pakistani /Bangladeshi	Partial correlation controlling for population density
Members of political parties intimidating the public	.033	.002
Members of political parties being where they should not be	.068**	0.06**
People asking to vote whose identity I was unsure of	.046**	0.16
Suspected cases of electoral fraud	0.03*	0.13

$**p < 0.01$, $*p < 0.05$.

In short, impersonation was not a problem and poll workers experienced a greater variety of other challenges.

An earlier claim has been that Pakistani- and Bangladeshi-origin communities in England share a wide range of vulnerabilities, which may make them susceptible to becoming victims of electoral fraud (Sobolewska et al. 2015). This research has been used to claim that electoral fraud is therefore more likely to occur within these communities "clan-based voting that has entered this country from Pakistan and Bangladesh" (Golds 2015). Table 7 provides bivariate correlations in the first column of the relationship between different problems in polling stations and the percentage of the combined Pakistani and Bangladeshi community (measured by ethnicity from Table KS201UK of the 2011 census). Partial correlations are shown in the second column controlling for population density. Correlations are low in all cases and usually not significant after population density has been controlled for. There is therefore little statistical or qualitative evidence based on these surveys to suggest that problems with fraud is higher in these communities than any others.

The impact of voter identification requirements

Did the piloting of voter identification have any effect on the running of the poll? There was virtually no difference between the pilot and non-pilot areas in terms of whether electoral fraud was suspected. We might imply from this that the scheme had no effect – but a difference was probably never likely given that suspected fraud was so infrequent in the first place. Interestingly, a *higher* proportion of respondents in the pilot areas reported encountering electors whose identity they were unsure of. In the pilot areas 7.2% of poll workers encountered electors whose identity they were suspicious about. In the non-pilot areas, the figure was 4.7%. An ANOVA crosstab table Chi-square tests were run to see whether this different was statistically significant. It was significant at the $p < .001$ level. Voter ID requirements therefore seemed to make poll workers slightly *less* confident. When ID was requested, more stringent forms such as photographic ID generated more confidence (Table 8).

Table 8. Concerns about voter identity, by identity requirements (%).

Identity requirements	Poll workers reporting at least one person asking to vote whose identity they were unsure of
None	4.7
Poll Card	8.6
Mixed	6.7
Photo	6.5

Note: Electoral Commission data only.

Table 9. The effects of the ID pilots on voter turnout (%).

	None	1	2–5	6–10	10+	N
People being turned away because they did not have the appropriate identification	47.6	22.2	24.5	4.3	1.3	3155
People coming to the polling station but deciding not to vote as they did not want to comply with the ID verification requirements	76.7	18.6	3.7	0.8	0.2	3145

Note: Electoral Commission data only.

In the pilot areas poll workers were also directly asked about the impact of the pilots as part of the survey organized by the Electoral Commission. Approximately two-thirds of poll workers (65.3%) agreed that the ID requirements made voting more secure. But a third (31.3%) neither agreed or disagreed and this was the modal response for the photo ID pilots (Table 10).

Was this a new bureaucratic hurdle which led to some citizens not voting? This was a heavily contested question in the aftermath of the pilots. In 2018, estimates established by different methods ranged from 340 to 4,000, a figure later suggested to have been considerably overestimated (Dempsey 2018). In 2019, between 7 and 800 were estimated to not have returned to vote in the ten pilot councils after having been turned away for not having ID (Dempsey 2018; Uberoi 2019). Table 9 illustrates that over half of poll workers reported turning away at least one voter for not having the required form of identification in the Electoral Commission data. A small proportion of 1.3% of poll workers turned more than 10 voters away. This was a more frequently experienced problem than citizens being turned away because of incomplete electoral registers discussed above and does therefore represent a considerable bureaucratic hurdle. Meanwhile, a quarter of poll workers experienced a voter who was able to provide voter identification but refused to comply. This suggests that voter ID might be a burden for logistical convenience reasons – but also a barrier on philosophical and ethical reasons for voters. While some are able to provide ID, they might decide not to present it in protest.

Comments from the non-pilot areas provided mixed views about whether they wished to have voter ID implemented more broadly. Some were openly resistant and thought that some groups would be adversely affected:

> Although I enjoy working as a poll worker I would be much less willing to work if compulsory identity checks were introduced.

> Some identification would be a good idea, but disenfranchisement of vulnerable people will be inevitable if the currently experiment is extended: there are many people in the

Table 10. The effects of the pilots on other aspects of the election (%).

	Strongly disagree	Disagree	Neither agree or disagree	Agree	Strongly agree	N
Had little impact on our work	0.9	8.7	8.4	43.3	38.8	3179
The majority of voters were able to provide an acceptable form of identification	0.1	0.1	0.7	29.0	70.1	3150
Voting was more secure because voters had to prove their identity	0.4	3.1	31.3	25.7	39.6	2969
In my polling station we were successful in delivering the voter ID requirements	0.1	0.1	0.9	17.4	81.5	3174

Note: Electoral Commission data only.

community without photo id (e.g. driving licence or passport). Furtherance of identification at the poll can only take place if a national identity card is issued if we are to see a true democratic process still.

In my experience the new voter id rules seek to solve a problem which simply doesn't exist … .in my experience voting at the polling station is remarkable for the trust paid to the electorate and that they repay it by vanishingly low levels of fraud. The delight of many voters in being able to vote without id or a polling card is palpable and I cannot see the need to put up any further barriers.

In contrast, some others argued that:

I think that an identification process should be introduced as part of the voting. Some form of ID should be required to prove that the voter is who they say they are as I feel that this part of the process is open to fraud. Lots of voters who come into the Polling Station do question this with us and there is no answer that we can give them. I just feel that asking for a name and their address is not sufficient and photo ID of some sort is needed.

Conclusions

Polling stations play a pivotal role in the democratic process, but are often the site where claims of electoral malpractices are made, in both older and transitional democracies. This article has made an important contribution in rectifying some of these claims by providing the most extensive available data on the frequency and nature of problems at contemporary English polling stations. It has done so through a rich description using a mix of qualitative and quantitative data. The experiences of poll workers on the ground, conceptualized as street-level bureaucrats, provide a deep insight how elections function in practice.

Elections were found to be broadly well run, with fewer problems than are experienced at general elections. There are, however, persistent problems with people failing to register and therefore being eligible to vote in any given election, polling station accessibility requirements and inappropriate behaviour from party agents/candidates. Attempted impersonation was exceptionally rare. This reinforces findings from earlier studies (Clark and James 2016, 2017), but with a much larger dataset than was previously used. The data provides no evidence to suggest that electoral fraud is more prevalent in Pakistani and Bangladeshi communities counter to earlier research and public debate (Sobolewska et al. 2015).

The article provides additional evidence that identification requirements can lead some voters not to vote, as the evidence was that some voters were unable to present the necessary form of ID on the day. The frequency of this problem was more common than those turned away for registration reasons. Moreover, some voters did not vote or present voter ID out of ideological reasons. This presents an important new link between voter identification requirements and turnout which has not been discussed in the literature to date. Importantly, the introduction of voter identification in polling stations reduced the confidence of poll workers that the citizens asking to vote were who they said they were.

There are therefore important lessons for academic research, but also policy. Recent UK government focus on targeting electoral fraud, often with a focus on Pakistani and Bangladeshi communities, seems to be misjudged, and out of line with the most prevalent problems in polling stations. Voter ID does not seem to be a necessary reform and may affect other aspects of the electoral process. Reforms are instead needed to improve the completeness of the electoral register and improve accessibility for disabled citizens to make elections more inclusive.

Notes

1. The electorate was 1,107,904 (Northern Ireland Assembly 2007, 5). One percent of this figure is 11,090.
2. Bromley, Gosport, Watford, Swindon and Woking.
3. Braintree, Broxtowe, Craven, Derby, Mid-Sussex, North Kesteven, North-West Leicestershire, Pendle, Watford, and Woking councils took part.
4. The exception was Watford with a 72% seat share for the Liberal Democrats, a share the party maintained in 2019.
5. Local elections took place in 150 councils in 2018, and 248 in 2019 (Dempsey 2018; Uberoi 2019). Poll workers from 68 councils took part. Councils represented included 11 (16.2%) Metropolitan districts, 7 (10.2%) London boroughs, 7 (10.2%) Unitary authorities and 43 (63.3%) districts. This compares to a population of 319 local councils in England (excluding County Councils) of which 36 (11.1%) were Metropolitan districts, 32 (11.1%) were London boroughs, 55 (17.2%) were unitary authorities and 192 (60.1%) were district councils. The sample was therefore broadly representative of the population.
6. The evidence suggested that, depending on what model of ID was chosen, a national roll-out could cost anywhere between £4.3m and £20.4m in a UK general election (Cabinet Office 2018b). Interestingly, this written evidence, although published by parliament, was marked Official Sensitive by the Cabinet Office.
7. Pearson's correlations with population density (measured using data from Table QS102EW of the 2011 Census) were positive associated with "queues at the polling station" ($\beta = .114$, $p < 0.01$) and "queues at the polling station towards the end of polling day" ($\beta = .125$, $p < 0.01$).
8. The correlation was against population density measured using data from Table QS102EW of the 2011 Census.
9. Data available at: https://www.electoralcommission.org.uk/who-we-are-and-what-we-do/elections-and-referendums/past-elections-and-referendums/england-local-council-elections/results-and-turnout-2018-may-england-local-elections, accessed 16 September 2019.
10. Not all English local authorities are on the same election timetable. Some elect by thirds, and therefore have effectively annual elections. Others are all-out elections, held every four years. In any given round of English local elections, there are a sizeable number of councils not holding local elections in that particular year. Elections were held in 150 councils in 2018.
11. There is a suggestion from American research on local voting behaviour that lower turnouts in local contests mean that only the better informed and more motivated voters' turnout to vote in the first place. See Clark and Krebs (2012) for discussion.
12. See the Royal National Institute for the Blind's "Turned Out" series of reports https://www.rnib.org.uk/campaigning-policy-and-reports-hub-access-information/access-information-reports [16/9/2019].

Disclosure statement

No potential conflict of interest was reported by the authors.

References

Argersinger, Peter H. 1985. "New Perspectives on Election Fraud in the Gilded Age." *Political Science Quarterly* 100 (4): 669–687.
Atkeson, Lonna Rae, Lisa Ann Bryant, Thad E. Hall, Kyle Saunders, and Michael Alvarez. 2010. "A New Barrier to Participation: Heterogeneous Application of Voter Identification Policies." *Electoral Studies* 29 (1): 66–73.
Beetham, David. 1994. "Key Principles and Indicies for a Democratic Audit." In *Defining Democracy*, edited by David Beetham, 25–43. London: Sage.
Birch, Sarah. 2011. *Electoral Malpractice.* Oxford: Oxford University Press.
Birch, Sarah, and David Muchlinski. 2018. "Electoral Violence: Patterns and Trends." In *Electoral Integrity and Political Regimes: Actors, Strategies and Consequences*, edited by Holly Ann Garnett and Margarita Zavadskaya, 100–112. New York: Routledge.
Bite the Ballot, Toby S. James, and ClearView Research. 2016. *Getting the Missing Millions Back on the Electoral Register: A Vision for Voter Registration Reform in the UK.* London: All Parliamentary Party Group on Democratic Participation.
Burden, Barry C. 2018. "Disagreement Over ID Requirements and Minority Voter Turnout." *The Journal of Politics* 80 (3): 1060–1063.
Cabinet Office. 2018a. *Electoral Integrity Pilots Prospectus 2018.* London: Cabinet Office.
Cabinet Office. 2018b. *Public Adminstration and Constitutional Affairs Committee Voter ID and Electoral Intimidation.* London: Cabinet Office.
Cabinet Office. 2019. *Voter ID Pilots 2019: Pre-Pilot Equality Considerations.* London: Cabinet Office.
Clark, Alistair. 2015. "Public Administration and the Integrity of the Electoral Process in British Elections." *Public Administration* 93 (1): 86–102.
Clark, Alistair. 2017. "Identifying the Determinants of Electoral Integrity and Administration in Advanced Democracies: The Case of Britain." *European Political Science Review* 9 (03): 471–492.
Clark, Alistair, and Toby S. James. 2016. *An Evaluation of Electoral Administration at the EU Referendum.* London: Electoral Commission.
Clark, Alistair, and Toby S. James. 2017. "Poll Workers." In *Election Watchdogs*, edited by Pippa Norris and Alessandro Nai, 144–164. New York: Oxford University Press.
Clark, Alistair, and Timothy Krebs. 2012. "Elections and Policy Responsiveness." In *Oxford Handbook of Urban Politics*, edited by Karen Mossenberger, Susan E. Clarke, and Peter John, 87–113. Oxford: Oxford University Press.
Coleman, Stephen. 2013. *How Voters Feel.* Cambridge: Cambridge University Press.
Dahl, R. 1971. *Polyarchy: Participation and Opposition.* New Haven: Yale University Press.
Dempsey, Noel. 2018. *Local Elections 2018.* London: House of Commons Library.
Durose, Catherine. 2009. "Front-line Workers and Local Knowledge: Neighbourhood Stories in Contemporary UK Local Governance." *Public Administration* 87 (1): 35–49.
Electoral Commission. 2014. *Electoral Fraud in the UK: Final Report and Recommendations.* London: Electoral Commission.
Electoral Commission. 2015. *The May 2015 UK Elections: Report on the Administration of the 7 May 2015 Elections.* London: Electoral Commission.
Electoral Commission. 2018. *May 2018 Voter Identification Pilot Schemes.* London: Electoral Commission.

Electoral Commission. 2019. "Timetable for local elections in England: 2 May 2019."

Electoral Reform Society. 2019. "Voter ID: Undermining Your Right to Vote." https://www. electoral-reform.org.uk/campaigns/upgrading-our-democracy/voter-id/.

Erikson, Robert S, and Lorraine C Minnite. 2009. "Modeling Problems in the Voter Identification— Voter Turnout Debate." *Election Law Journal: Rules, Politics, and Policy* 8 (2): 85–101.

Frye, Timothy, Ora John Reuter, and David Szakonyi. 2019. "Hitting Them with Carrots: Voter Intimidation and Vote Buying in Russia." *British Journal of Political Science* 49 (3): 857–881.

Fund, John. 2008. *Stealing Elections: How Voter Fraud Threatens our Democracy*. New York and London: Encounter Books.

Gelb, Alan, and Anna Diofasi. 2016. "Biometric Elections in Poor Countries: Wasteful or a Worthwhile Investment?"

Gimpel, J. G., and J. E. Schuknecht. 2003. "Political Participation and the Accessibility of the Ballot Box." *Political Geography* 22 (5): 471–488.

Golds, Peter. 2015. "An Urgently Needed Plan of Action to Stop Electoral Fraud." *Conservative Home*. https://www.conservativehome.com/platform/2015/05/peter-golds-an-urgently-needed-plan-of-action-to-stop-electoral-fraud.html.

Green, Heather Dawn. 2019. "The Voter ID Pilots: An Unlawful Electoral Experiment." *Public Law* 2019: 242–250.

Grimmer, Justin, Eitan Hersh, Marc Meredith, Jonathan Mummolo, and Clayton Nall. 2018. "Obstacles to Estimating Voter ID Laws' Effect on Turnout." *The Journal of Politics* 80 (3): 1045–1051.

Hajnal, Zoltan, Nazita Lajevardi, and Lindsay Nielson. 2017. "Voter Identification Laws and the Suppression of Minority Votes." *The Journal of Politics* 79 (2): 363–379.

Hall, Thad E. 2013. "US Voter Registration Reform." *Electoral Studies* 32 (4): 589–596.

Hasen, Richard L. 2012. *The Voting Wars: From Florida 2000 to the Next Election Meltdown*. Grand Rapids, MI: Yale University Press.

Highton, Benjamin. 2017. "Voter Identification Laws and Turnout in the United States." *Annual Review of Political Science* 20 (1): 149–167.

Hood III, M. V., and Charles S. Bullock III. 2008. "Worth a Thousand Words? An Analysis of Georgia's Voter Identification Statute." *American Politics Research* 36 (4): 555–579.

James, Toby S. 2011. "Fewer 'Costs,' More Votes? UK Innovations in Electoral Administration 2000–2007 and Their Effect on Voter Turnout." *Election Law Journal: Rules, Politics, and Policy* 10 (1): 37–52.

James, Toby S. 2012. *Elite Statecraft and Election Administration: Bending the Rules of the Game*. Basingstoke: Palgrave Macmillan.

James, T. S. 2014a. "The Spill-over and Displacement Effects of Implementing Election Administration Reforms: Introducing Individual Electoral Registration in Britain." *Parliamentary Affairs* 67: 281–305.

James, Toby S. 2014b. "Electoral Management in Britain." In *Advancing Electoral Integrity*, edited by Pippa Norris, Richard Frank, and Ferran Matinez I Coma, 135–164. New York: Oxford University Press.

James, Toby S. 2019. "#DeniedMyVote – Why Many EU Citizens Were Unable to Vote in the European Parliament Elections." *Democratic Audit*, May 30. http://www.democraticaudit.com/2019/05/30/deniedmyvote-why-many-eu-citizens-were-unable-to-vote-in-the-european-parliament-elections/.

James, Toby S. 2020a. *Comparative Electoral Management: Performance, Networks and Instruments*. London and New York: Routledge.

James, Toby S., and Garnett. 2020b. "Introduction: The Case for Inclusive Voting Practices." *Policy Studies*. doi:10.1080/01442872.2019.1694657.

James, Toby S., Holly Ann Garnett, Leontine Loeber, and Carolien van Ham. 2019. "Electoral Management and Organizational Determinants of Electoral Integrity." *International Political Science Review* 40 (3): 295–312.

King, Bridgett A. 2020. "Administrative Irregularities and Voter Confidence." *Policy Studies*.

Law Commissions. 2016. *Electoral Law: An Interim Report*. London: Law Commissions.

Lehoucq, F. E. 2003. "Electoral Fraud: Causes, Types and Consequences." *Annual Review of Political Science* 6: 233–256.

Lehoucq, F. E., and I. Molina. 2002. *Stuffing the Ballot Box*. Cambridge and New York: Cambridge University Press.

Lipsky, Michael. 1980. *Street Level Bureaucracy*. New York: Russell Sage Foundation.

Martínez i Coma, Ferran, and Carolien van Ham. 2015. "Can Experts Judge Elections? Testing the Validity of Expert Judgments for Measuring Election Integrity." *European Journal of Political Research* 54 (2): 305–325.

Mawrey, Richard. 2015. "Andrew Erlam v. Mohammed Luther Rahman." In *M/350/14*, edited by High Court of Justice.

Miller, Peter, and Sierra Powell. 2016. "Overcoming Voting Obstacles: The Use of Convenience Voting by Voters With Disabilities." *American Politics Research* 44 (1): 28–55.

Minnite, Lorraine C. 2010. *The Myth of Voter Fraud*. Ithaca, NY: Cornell University Press.

Norris, Pippa. 2014. *Why Electoral Integrity Matters*. New York: Cambridge University Press.

Norris, Pippa, Ferran Martinez i Coma, and Max Gromping. 2016. *The Year in Elections, 2015*. Sydney and Harvard Universities: Electoral Integrity Project.

Northern Ireland Assembly. 2007. *Research Paper 01/07: Northern Ireland Assembly 2007*.

Orford, S., C. Rallings, M. Thrasher, and G. Borisyuk. 2011. "Changes in the Probability of Voter Turnout When Resiting Polling Stations: A Case Study in Brent, UK." *Environment and Planning C: Government and Policy* 29 (1): 149–169.

Orr, Graeme. 2016. *Ritual and Rhythm in Electoral Systems: A Comparative Legal Account*. Abingdon and New York: Routledge.

Pallister, Kevin. 2017. *Election Administration and the Politics of Voter Access*. New York: Routledge.

Pickles, Eric. 2016. *Securing the Ballot: Report of Sir Eric Pickles' Review into Electoral Fraud*. London: Cabinet Office.

Piven, Frances Fox, L. Minnite, and M. Groarke. 2009. *Keeping Down the Black Vote*. London and New York: The New Press.

Przeworski, Adam. 2018. *Why Bother with Elections?*. Medford, MA: Polity.

Schedler, Andreas. 2002. "The Menu of Manipulation." *Journal of Democracy* 13 (2): 36–50.

Schur, Lisa, Mason Ameri, and Meera Adya. 2017. "Disability, Voter Turnout, and Polling Place Accessibility." *Social Science Quarterly* 98 (5): 1374–1390.

Sobolewska, Maria, Stuart Wilks-Heeg, Eleanor Hill, and Magna Borkowska. 2015. *Understanding Electoral Fraud Vulnerability in Pakistani and Bangladeshi Origin Communities in England. A View of Local Political Activists*. Manchester and Liverpool: Centre on Dynamics of Ethnicity.

Stanford, Ben. 2018. "Compulsory Voter Identification, Disenfranchisement and Human Rights: Electoral Reform in Great Britain." *European Human Rights Law Review* 23 (1): 57–66.

Stewart, John. 2006. "A Banana Republic? The Investigation into Electoral Fraud by the Birmingham Election Court." *Parliamentary Affairs* 59 (4): 654–667.

Uberoi, Elise. 2019. *Local Elections 2019*. London: House of Commons Library.

van Hees, Suzanne G. M., Hennie R. Boeije, and Iris de Putter. 2019. "Voting Barriers and Solutions: the Experiences of People with Disabilities During the Dutch National Election in 2017." *Disability & Society* 34 (5): 819–836.

Walker, Peter. 2019. "Voter ID Trial at Local Elections is a Waste of Time, Say Campaigners." *Guardian*, April 30. https://www.theguardian.com/politics/2019/apr/30/voter-id-trial-local-elections.

Wilks-Heeg, Stuart. 2008. *Purity of Elections in the UK: Causes for Concern*. York: Joseph Rowntree Trust.

Wolfinger, Raymond E., and Steven J. Rosenstone. 1980. *Who Votes?* New Haven, CT: Yale University Press.

Implementing voter ID: lessons from Missouri, USA

Joseph Anthony and David C. Kimball

ABSTRACT

Many states have adopted laws requiring voters to present photo identification on Election Day. How are these laws implemented in a highly decentralized system of election administration? We report on a study of photo ID implementation in Missouri, focusing on the number of voters who check in at a polling place without photo identification during local and special elections held under the new law. These elections serve as early tests of the photo ID law and offer support for some hypotheses derived from implementation theory. We find evidence of uneven implementation of the photo ID requirement in Missouri. Local jurisdictions using electronic poll books checked in a much larger volume of voters without photo ID than jurisdictions using traditional paper poll books. Interviews with local officials suggest that voter and poll worker behaviour contribute to this pattern. Furthermore, other features, particularly jurisdiction size and the administrative and partisan structure of local officials, are associated with the number of voters who check in without photo identification. Therefore, the use of electronic poll books might overstate the number of voters lacking photo identification. In a decentralized system of election administration, it can be challenging to uniformly implement new voting requirements.

Many American states have adopted laws requiring people to present photo identification when they vote. How are these laws implemented in a highly decentralized system of election administration? This study examines initial implementation of a new photo identification (ID) requirement for voters in Missouri. In 2017 and 2018, the photo ID law was enforced in over 200 municipal, special and primary elections administered by local jurisdictions around the state. In this study we examine data on the number of voters who were checked in at polling places without photo identification as an indicator of how the law was implemented in local jurisdictions. Some jurisdictions may have gone to great lengths to educate voters about the new law, thereby helping voters comply with the law and cast a regular ballot. Other jurisdictions may have strictly enforced the law without providing much additional assistance to voters. We use implementation theory to test whether features of local election administration are associated with higher rates of voters checking in without photo ID.

We find evidence that the photo ID requirement was not enforced uniformly across Missouri jurisdictions in 2017 and 2018 elections. For example, we observe higher rates of voters who checked in without photo ID in more populous jurisdictions and especially in jurisdictions using electronic poll books. The learned behaviour of some poll workers and voters suggest that the numbers reported by local jurisdictions may overstate the number of voters lacking photo identification in places using electronic poll books. We also find fewer voters checking in without photo identification in urban jurisdictions with bipartisan appointed administrators than in jurisdictions with elected partisan administrators. This study highlights uneven implementation of voter eligibility rules in a decentralized system of election administration. Even clearly written laws like the Missouri voter identification requirement may not be implemented uniformly by local jurisdictions. Missouri voters who checked in without photo identification needed to provide additional documentation and fill out another form in order to vote, delaying the voting process and potentially preventing some from casting a valid ballot. Uneven implementation of the voter identification law is important because it indicates that voters had different experiences with the voter ID law across jurisdictions in Missouri. If the administrative burden in elections is higher for some voters than others, this could disproportionately affect voter turnout and the voter experience.

Background

Proposals to require more rigorous forms of voter identification have ignited contentious policy debates in the United States. Many states have passed new laws that require people to show photo identification to vote, particularly in ethnically diverse states with Republican Party control of state government (Hale and McNeal 2010; Bentele and O'Brien 2013; Rocha and Matsubayashi 2014; Biggers and Hanmer 2017). In state legislatures, support for new voting restrictions tends to divide neatly along partisan lines, with support coming almost exclusively from Republican lawmakers (McKee 2015; Hicks, McKee, and Smith 2016). Furthermore, photo ID laws have been the subject of extensive litigation in many states (Hasen 2012; Pitts 2015). Missouri shares these characteristics. For example, support for photo ID legislation has split sharply along party lines in the Missouri General Assembly (McKee 2015, 2). Furthermore, the state has played an outsized role in the development of voter ID policies in the United States.

A strict voter ID requirement has been a Republican policy priority in Missouri since the 2000 presidential election. Missouri adopted a voter ID requirement as part of an election reform package adopted in 2002. Because of partisan disagreements over voter ID proposals (Republicans wanted a stricter ID requirement than Democrats), and due to the presence of an active coalition of interest group stakeholders resisting a strict photo ID requirement, the compromise passed in 2002 allowed several non-photo forms of identification, such as a county-issued voter identification card or a utility bill (Kropf 2005, 166). Voters without acceptable identification could only cast a ballot if two supervising poll workers (one from each major party) vouched for the voter. This voter identification requirement remained in place until the photo ID law took effect in 2017. Meanwhile, U.S Senator Kit Bond (R-MO) was one of the leading GOP legislators involved in the passage of the Help America Vote Act of 2002 (HAVA). As a member of the Senate-

House conference committee, Senator Bond inserted a photo ID requirement for new voters who registered by mail into HAVA (Minnite 2010, 95; Hasen 2012, 47).

The legislative skirmishes in 2002 were just the beginning. In 2006 Republican Governor Matt Blunt and a GOP-majority General Assembly passed a new law requiring voters to show a non-expired photo ID. The 2006 law was overturned by the Missouri Supreme Court (Weinschenk v. Missouri, 2006) on the grounds that it violated Missouri's equal protection clause and the constitutional right to vote. The Missouri Constitution includes an explicit guarantee of the right to vote: "no power, civil or military, shall at any time interfere to prevent the free exercise of the right of suffrage" (Article I, section 25). As it happens, a majority of the judges on the Missouri Supreme Court in 2006 were appointed by Democratic governors.

Since 2006 the Republican majority in the state legislature has attempted to pass strict photo ID legislation on many occasions, but those bills failed to pass both chambers or were vetoed by Democratic Governor Jay Nixon. In 2016 the GOP legislative majority succeeded by placing on the November ballot a constitutional amendment allowing for a photo ID requirement for "a person seeking to vote in person" (Amendment 6). The joint resolution placing the proposed amendment on the ballot did not need to be signed by the governor. Amendment 6 passed with the support of 63% of Missouri voters.

In Missouri there are strong party differences in support for a photo identification requirement. Figure 1 plots voter support for the photo ID amendment by Donald Trump's share of the two-party presidential vote in Missouri local jurisdictions (the data symbols are sized in proportion to the number of votes cast in each jurisdiction). As the graph shows, there was a strong partisan component to the vote on Amendment 6 (the correlation between support for Trump and the photo ID amendment is .95).[1] The photo ID amendment received a majority Yes vote in all local jurisdictions except Kansas City and St. Louis City. The "No" votes tended to concentrate in the more populous urban jurisdictions. In 2016 the General Assembly also passed legislation (HB 1631) laying out procedures for the new photo ID requirement, overriding Gov. Nixon's veto.

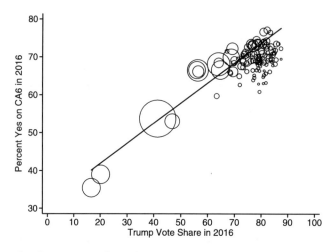

Figure 1. Support for photo ID amendment by trump support in Missouri counties 2016 election. Note: Circles are sized in proportion to the number of votes cast in each county.

Legislation associated with the photo ID requirement (a resolution to place the constitutional amendment on the ballot and the implementing law) passed on party line votes in both chambers, with Republicans in support and Democrats in opposition. As a result, the new photo ID requirement went into effect on 1 June 2017. Civil rights groups filed two lawsuits in state court to block implementation of the law, but one of the lawsuits was dismissed in January of 2018.

Missouri has adopted what some observers label as a "non-strict" photo ID requirement (e.g. NCSL 2018). The photo identification requirement applies to polling place voters but not to absentee voters. The enabling legislation creates three paths to casting a ballot for registered in-person voters, depending on the type of identification they provide: (1) those who provide a valid photo ID vote a regular ballot (regular voters); (2) those who provide a valid non-photo ID and sign a statement attesting to their lack of a photo ID also vote a regular ballot (affidavit or "statement" voters, using the vernacular of the enabling legislation); and (3) those without any acceptable identification cast a provisional ballot (provisional voters). Thus, voters without photo identification had to traverse an additional layer of bureaucracy to check in at a polling place. The provisional voters had their ballots counted if they returned to the polling place later on Election Day with a valid photo ID or if their signature at the polling place matched their signature in the voter registration file. The legislation also tasks the Secretary of State's office with helping voters without a photo ID obtain a Missouri non-driver license for free (including paying the cost of securing underlying documents, like a birth certificate, that are needed to procure a state photo ID).[2] Finally, the Department of Revenue is supposed to provide an annual report to the General Assembly on the cost to the state of providing these free documents to voters.

Decentralization is a defining feature of election administration in the United States, and Missouri elections are highly decentralized. Missouri has 116 local jurisdictions that administer elections, more than most states. Elections are managed by bipartisan boards in six large urban jurisdictions (Clay County, Jackson County, Kansas City, Platte County, St. Louis City, and St. Louis County). In each of these jurisdictions four board members (two from each major political party) are appointed by the governor, subject to confirmation by the state senate. The board members then appoint a bipartisan pair of directors to manage the operations of the office. The bipartisan structure in these jurisdictions extends to the staff, so that each component of election administration (such as checking in voters, overseeing poll workers, or counting ballots) is conducted by a bipartisan team. The election boards in these six jurisdictions are solely tasked with administering elections – they do not have any other responsibilities. In the remaining Missouri jurisdictions local officials are county clerks chosen in partisan elections, and roughly two-thirds of the county clerks in Missouri are Republicans.[3] In addition to managing elections, county clerks in Missouri have many other responsibilities, including record-keeping, tax administration, and licensing.

Some states have uniform technology and processes for many election functions, while other states have a lot of local variation in election administration (GAO 2007; Hale, Montjoy, and Brown 2015). Missouri is positioned toward the local variation end of the spectrum, as local election officials have considerable discretion. Part of this is due to the fact that local jurisdictions bear the cost of election administration in Missouri. For example, local jurisdictions in Missouri select and purchase their own voting equipment and design and print their own ballots. More importantly for the purposes of enforcing voter identification requirements, there is variation in polling place technology across the state. In the 2016 election 64 Missouri jurisdictions deployed electronic poll books to check in voters, while the remaining 52 jurisdictions used paper poll books (EAC 2017).

Finally, in Missouri there is also tremendous variation in jurisdiction size. A handful of metropolitan jurisdictions each serve over 100,000 voters in a general election while a majority of Missouri jurisdictions serve less than 10,000 voters in an election. The vast disparities in jurisdiction size likely mean different needs and priorities in election administration (Alvarez and Hall 2005; Kimball and Baybeck 2013). For example, the adoption of electronic poll books in Missouri is a function of jurisdiction size. Eleven of the twelve largest jurisdictions in the state, including the six jurisdictions overseen by bipartisan boards, have adopted electronic poll books. Our interviews indicate that jurisdictions which purchased the technology did so with the goal of making polling place operations more efficient. Small counties tend to lack the resources to afford electronic poll books and do not serve an electorate large enough to justify such a purchase.

Explaining photo ID implementation in Missouri

In this section we use policy implementation theory to develop hypotheses about the roll out of the photo ID requirement in Missouri. There is a well-developed framework in public administration for understanding policy implementation that considers the law, relationships between officials at different levels of government, and characteristics of local officials and the jurisdictions they serve. In applying these ideas, we consider the state and local election officials in Missouri and their response to the new law.

One important element of policy implementation is the clarity of the new law. Successful implementation depends, in part, on a new law containing unambiguous policy directives and decision rules for implementing officials to follow (Sabatier and Mazmanian 1980). While there is strong disagreement about the need for a photo ID law in Missouri, the new procedures for voters lacking a photo ID in Missouri (described above) are fairly clear in enumerating the acceptable forms of photo identification and the procedures for voters who appear at their polling place without photo identification. However, the Secretary of State's voter education campaign caused some confusion. The title of the campaign ("Show It 2 Vote") led some to believe that voters needed photo identification in order to vote, when that was not the case. This is one reason why state courts stopped implementation of some parts of the law in the fall of 2018.

Implementation also hinges on assignment of the new policy to agencies or officials who are committed to its objectives (Sabatier and Mazmanian 1980). In Missouri the Secretary of State is the official charged with administering elections in the state. As it happens, Republican Secretary of State Jay Ashcroft was first elected in November 2016, the same election in which Amendment 6 passed. Ashcroft made his support for the photo ID amendment a principal feature of his campaign. In recent congressional testimony Ashcroft claimed that "voter fraud is an exponentially greater threat than hacking of our election equipment" (Wise 2018). It is fair to say that Secretary of State Ashcroft is highly committed to implementing the new photo ID law in Missouri.

After passage of the photo ID requirement, Secretary of State Ashcroft led a public education effort to inform voters about the new requirement, including opportunities for state assistance in acquiring photo ID for voting (https://www.sos.mo.gov/showit2vote). The implementing legislation in Missouri includes boilerplate language for voter identification statements that voters with acceptable non-photo identification must sign before casting a ballot. The Secretary of State's office produced special blue provisional ballot envelopes for local jurisdictions to use for voters who lack any identification (in contrast to yellow envelopes used for other types of provisional ballots). The Secretary of State's office also created forms for jurisdictions to use to report the number of non-photo provisional ballots cast in an election. It appears that local jurisdictions are using all of these documents.

Hypotheses

Turning to the local level, the principal-agent problems associated with polling place voting are well known. It can be a challenge for election officials to train and monitor poll workers to ensure that voting laws are enforced uniformly and fairly (Montjoy and Slaton 2002; Alvarez and Hall 2006). Adopting a photo ID requirement creates another principal-agent predicament for local election officials, since research in other states finds that poll workers do not enforce voter identification requirements uniformly (Atkeson et al. 2009, 2014; Cobb, Greiner, and Quinn 2012). We believe that principal-agent theory also applies to the relationship between the Secretary of State and local election officials. There is variation in how local election officials respond to constituent requests for voting information, including voter identification requirements (White, Nathan, and Faller 2015; Porter and Rogowski 2018). Given extensive local variation and a history of local discretion in election administration in Missouri, it is possible that different jurisdictions will implement aspects of the new photo ID requirement in different ways, given their relationship with or partisan affiliation to the GOP Secretary of State.

Principal-agent theory and implementation theory suggest that agreement between principals and agents on the importance of the problem a new law addresses reduces resistance to implementation (Sabatier and Mazmanian 1980). Support for the goals of a new law may yield more enthusiastic local enforcement of the law (Moynihan and Silva 2008). Partisanship is a major source of disagreement over beliefs about the frequency of voter fraud and the need for voter ID requirements, and there is much stronger support for photo ID laws from Republicans than Democrats (Hicks, McKee, and Smith 2016; Stewart, Ansolabehere, and Persily 2016). The adoption of the photo identification requirement in Missouri revealed sharp partisan divisions in support for the new law. Thus, we hypothesize that GOP county clerks in Missouri are more committed to the photo ID law and will more closely adhere to directives from the Secretary of State on the photo ID policy. This should lead Republican county clerks to more vigorously enforce the photo identification requirements than Democratic clerks. At the same time, Democratic clerks may do more to educate voters about the new requirements and to help constituents acquire the needed identification. For example, Bright and Lynch (2017) find that after the adoption of a photo ID law in Kansas a Democratic county clerk increased voter turnout by providing free photo IDs to voters and by informing constituents how to comply with the new law.

The personal characteristics of local officials may also determine how they respond to new policies. One important characteristic is job experience. As local officials become more confident in their role and abilities, they may be less favourably disposed toward additional mandates from higher levels of government (Lipsky 1980; Moynihan and

Silva 2008). Thus, we hypothesize that more experienced local election officials may prefer their prior polling place practices and be more resistant to new photo ID requirements than novice local officials. We measure local official experience as a dummy variable indicating whether, at the start of 2018, the clerk or election director has been in that position for at least five years. In Missouri, 68% of the local officials have five or more years of experience, while the remainder are relatively new to the position.

Another important local factor is an administrator's organizational capacity, or ability to carry out its functions. The absence of administrative capacity or resources can produce implementation failures and fuel local opposition to policy innovations (Sabatier and Mazmanian 1980), particularly in the election field (Hale and Slaton 2008; Moynihan and Silva 2008; Burden et al. 2012). Thus, local election officials concerned about resource or administrative shortages may have a less favourable view of enforcing new voter identification requirements. This concern may be strong in Missouri, where county clerks have many other responsibilities in addition to election administration.

Furthermore, a lack of technology or a change in technology can influence the implementation of new policies (Sabatier and Mazmanian 1980). Local officials who have sunk costs in their current technology may resist policy changes that mandate new technology (Montjoy and O'Toole 1979). This may be especially important in election administration. Technology used for checking in voters deserves careful examination in the implementation of photo ID requirements for voters. As noted above, in Missouri many counties employed electronic poll books before passage of the photo ID requirement.

Some jurisdictions programmed their electronic poll books to scan county-issued voter identification cards to speed up the check-in process. As a result, voters and poll workers may have grown accustomed to scanning identification cards. In addition, officials and poll workers indicated that some electronic poll books had difficulty scanning driver's licenses. However, voter identification cards have no photograph and are not valid photo IDs under the new law in Missouri. Thus, checking in with an identification card may force the voter to sign the non-photo ID statement. We hypothesize that jurisdictions with electronic poll books will process a higher share of non-photo ID "statement" voters than jurisdictions using paper poll books. In summary, implementation theory and prior studies in other states lead us to expect uneven implementation of the new photo identification requirement across Missouri jurisdictions given the learned behaviour of election authorities and glitches in the technology of electronic poll books.

Finally, some characteristics of the local constituents may influence how many voters check in without valid photo identification in an election. For example, jurisdiction size may be an important related factor for implementation. Regardless of election administration features, densely populated urban jurisdictions have a disproportionate share of young, mobile and minority residents (Kimball and Baybeck 2013) and thus may serve a larger share of registered voters lacking a valid photo ID (Barreto, Nuno, and Sanchez 2009; Hershey 2009; Hood and Bullock 2012; Hopkins et al. 2017). Thus, larger urban jurisdictions may have a larger share of voters checking in without photo identification, regardless of election administration features. Since we will be controlling for several important election administration features we expect larger jurisdictions in Missouri to process a higher share of voters via the non-photo procedures (voter statements or provisional ballots) than less populous jurisdictions.

We also examine several demographic variables that are correlates of people who lack a driver's license at higher rates than the overall adult population. These control variables include the percentage of a county's residents who are non-white, median age, and residential mobility, all obtained from the Census Bureau. People who have moved recently may not have an updated and valid driver's license when the next election occurs. Thus, we expect counties with higher rates of residential mobility to process a higher number of voters through one of the non-photo identification methods. Similarly, non-white and elderly voters are less likely than other voters to possess a valid driver's license. As a result, we expect that Missouri counties with a higher median age and larger percentage of non-white residents will check in more voters via one of the non-photo identification methods.

Data and methods

As of the fall of 2018, local jurisdictions in Missouri had held over 200 elections since the photo ID requirement took effect on 1 June 2017.[4] Many of these were municipal elections held in April of 2018 and primary elections held in August of 2018, while the rest were special elections to fill state or local offices or decide local ballot measures. These were relatively low turnout elections – the median number of voters in these elections was 1860. The highest turnout was 60% of registered voters, while median turnout was 15.5%. As a result, within a year of the law taking effect every jurisdiction in the state had administered at least one election with the photo ID requirement. We examine early Missouri elections under the new photo identification requirement as a test of implementation theory.

Critical questions associated with the implementation of photo ID laws include (1) how many voters lack a valid photo ID and (2) who are they? There is disagreement about the impact of photo ID laws on voter turnout, particularly among racial and ethnic subgroups (Erikson and Minnite 2009; Hajnal, Lajevardi, and Nielson 2017; Burden 2018; Grimmer et al. 2018; Pryor, Herrick, and Davis 2019), but several studies find that white voters are more likely to possess valid photo ID than non-white voters (Hopkins et al. 2017, 83). This paper does find some evidence that the photo ID law in Missouri may have a disproportionate impact on communities with higher non-white populations. While this finding is important, the primary focus of the paper here establishes evidence for a more foundational question, that photo ID laws can be implemented in an uneven fashion within the same state.

To obtain information about Missouri voters who lack photo ID, after each election we sent a public records request via email to the top county election official. Public records requests are governed by Missouri's Sunshine Law. We used the same language for each request, modifying sample language for a sunshine request provided by the Missouri Attorney General.[5] In each public records request we asked for the names and addresses of each registered voter who cast a provisional ballot or affidavit ballot without a photo ID in the election (a copy of our request is included in the appendix). Some counties complied with our request but other counties declined, citing an opinion from the Secretary of State that the data we requested did not quality as public records under state law. We also gathered other information from each jurisdiction, including the number of registered voters eligible to vote and the number of ballots cast in each election.

The Secretary of State's office also collects data from each jurisdiction on the number of non-photo statements and provisional ballots signed by voters in an election. They have shared those data with us. Between the data provided by the Secretary of State and the public records requests we have complete voter totals for 177 elections held in 2017 and 2018 under the photo ID requirement in Missouri.[6] This is a panel dataset – each observation is a county-election pair, since some counties held more than one election during this period. In those elections 33,832 voters were recorded as lacking a valid photo ID (roughly 1.9% of ballots cast). The vast majority of the non-photo ballots (33,446) were cast by voters who signed an affidavit after showing non-photo identification, while the remaining (386) were provisional ballots cast by voters who lacked acceptable identification. Among the provisional ballots, 289 (75%) were counted, mostly because of a signature match.

We also gathered census data to measure features of the local electorate in each Missouri jurisdiction. We measure jurisdiction size by the number of ballots cast in each election. We also compute the natural log of the number of ballots cast to deal with the heavy positive skew in the distribution of jurisdiction size. Additional control variables include the percentage of a county's residents who are non-white, median age, and the percentage of residents who have moved within the past year. These demographic measures come from the 2017 American Community Survey five-year estimates, produced by the Census Bureau.

Finally, we interviewed some with local election officials by email and phone about photo ID implementation in Missouri. Interviews were conducted with four separate local election officials dispersed throughout the state; two participants were from rural jurisdictions, one was from a mid-sized jurisdiction, and the fourth represented a major metropolitan jurisdiction. The authors had prior working relationships with two of the participants, and the remaining two participants contacted the authors to provide more information about their experiences. These local election officials described their overall experiences implementing the photo ID law, and two officials specifically discussed issues with poll workers and electronic poll books in implementing the new law.

Our dependent variable is the number of voters who check in without photo identification (using the affidavit or provisional method described above). We focus on this measure because it is an important piece of evidence in evaluating photo ID laws, particularly in lawsuits challenging these laws. In theory, this measure simply counts the number of voters who lack valid photo identification at the time of an election. However, as we describe above, we suspect that this measure is also influenced by local administrative factors. For example, if voters are not fully informed about the law they may not know to bring photo ID even when they have it. Similarly, the interaction of polling place technology and past practices may lead some poll workers to ask voters to show an ID that does not have a photo, thus landing an unsuspecting voter in our measure. We focus on this measure because we think it may be influenced by factors reflecting the implementation of the new voter identification law in Missouri.

There appears to be substantial variation in implementing the photo ID requirement in Missouri elections. The histogram in Figure 2 summarizes the share of voters checking in without valid photo identification in each of the Missouri elections where we have complete data. The distribution is highly skewed. In most elections, very few voters checked in without photo ID. In roughly one quarter of elections the local jurisdictions reported zero voters checking in without photo Id. However, in the top quartile of elections more than

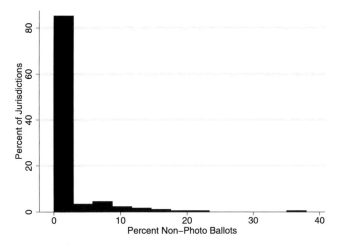

Figure 2. Distribution of non-photo ballots in Missouri elections.

1% of voters appeared without a valid photo ID, and among the top decile of elections more than 7% of voters checked in without valid photo identification. In a few unusual elections more than 20% of voters were recorded as not having photo identification.

We next test some of the hypotheses described above in explaining local variation in the share of ballots cast by voters who check in without photo identification. The most robust finding is that the share of voters checking in without photo ID is substantially higher in jurisdictions using electronic poll books to check in voters. Notably, the electronic poll books used by local jurisdictions were purchased and programmed for the 2016 election cycle, before the photo ID law was adopted. In other words, the technology was not origi-nally established to read traditional forms of photo ID such as a driver's license.

As noted above, large urban jurisdictions with substantial resources are more likely to use electronic poll books than smaller rural jurisdictions in Missouri. We classify each Missouri county based on the U.S. Office of Management and Budget designations of metropolitan and rural counties, updated in 2016. Metropolitan areas include counties that have a high degree of economic and social integration with an urban area of at least 50,000 people. Any county not part of a metropolitan area is considered rural. By this measure, 81 local jurisdictions in Missouri are rural while 35 local jurisdictions are metropolitan.

As Figure 3 shows, the share of voters checking in without photo identification is about 2.5 percentage points higher, on average, in jurisdictions using electronic poll books than in jurisdictions using paper poll books. This same basic pattern holds in the more popu-lous metropolitan jurisdictions and in smaller rural Missouri jurisdictions, although the differences are more pronounced in metropolitan jurisdictions. This provides initial support for our hypothesis that jurisdictions with electronic poll books are likely to check in more voters without photo ID due to poll workers' learned behaviour and tech-nological issues posed by electronic poll books.

To provide a more rigorous test of our hypotheses we estimate a regression function with multiple predictors. The dependent variable is the number of voters in each election that checked in using one of the non-photo ID methods described above (either by signing an affidavit or by casting a provisional ballot). There are concerns that OLS regression does

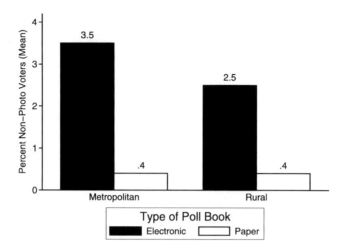

Figure 3. Mean percent of non-photo ballots in Missouri elections by polling place technology and county location.

not adequately capture the data-generating process in this application. First, the number of voters checking in without photo ID has a lower bound of 0, but least squares regression models do not constrain the expected value to be greater than or equal to 0. Second, counts of voters checking in without photo ID produce a heavily skewed distribution, as Figure 2 indicates.

As a result, we estimate a negative binomial regression model more appropriate where the dependent variable is a count.[7] The negative binomial model is used when there is "overdispersion" in count data (Long 1997), meaning that there is higher than expected variation in the dependent variable. Overdispersion can occur in count data if events are clustered in particular locations or time periods. For example, a voter checking in without photo identification in a particular precinct or county may be linked to other voters without photo ID in the same place (because of local poll worker practices or the technology used to check in voters, for example). The negative binomial regression model estimates an extra parameter (alpha) to test for overdispersion: positive alpha scores statistically different than zero indicate overdispersion in the data.

In this application we also modify the generic negative binomial regression model. Since the number of voters in each election varies dramatically, we weight each election by the number of ballots cast, which has the effect of counting each voter equally. In other words, it prevents the results from being overly influenced by the many small counties that have relatively few voters. It is also possible that observations within the same county are not independent, due to unobserved county-level factors (such as training of poll workers or local efforts to educate voters about the new voter identification law). Thus, we estimate standard errors that are corrected for the clustering of elections within the same county (Williams 2000).[8]

The results of our negative binomial regression analysis are presented in Table 1. The first column provides the results of a model that includes election administration features and county size as independent variables. The second model in Table 1 includes several demographic characteristics that are associated with people who lack a driver's license or valid photo identification. To assess the substantive impact of each independent variable,

Table 1. Predictors of the number of non-photo ID voters in Missouri elections.

Independent variable	Model 1 coef. (s.e.)	Model 2 coef. (s.e.)
Electronic poll book	2.2*	2.6*
	(0.5)	(0.6)
Republican clerk	2.0*	2.2*
	(0.8)	(0.7)
Democratic clerk	2.3*	2.4*
	(1.0)	(0.9)
Clerk experience	−0.9	−0.8
	(0.5)	(0.6)
Ballots in 2016 (natural log)	0.4*	0.4*
	(0.2)	(0.2)
County residential mobility		−0.1
		(0.1)
County non-white percent		0.01
		(0.02)
County median age		0.1
		(0.1)
Constant	−10.9*	−13.3*
	(2.4)	(5.7)
Alpha	2.7*	2.6*
	(0.7)	(0.7)
N	177	177
Model Chi-Square	53.2*	145.9*

Note: The dependent variable is the number of voters recorded as checking in without a photo ID. Cell entries are negative binomial regression coefficients with standard errors in parentheses. Standard errors are corrected for non-independence of errors within counties. Observations (counties) are weighted by the number of ballots cast in the election.
*$p < .05$, two-tailed.

negative binomial coefficients do not yield straightforward interpretation. As a result, we use the model estimates to compute the percent change in the expected number of voters checking in without photo identification given a change in particular variables.[9]

Consistent with Figure 3, our most reliable result is that the number of voters checking in without photo identification is substantially higher in jurisdictions using electronic poll books. In both models, in counties using electronic poll books the expected number of voters checking in without photo ID is roughly 8 times higher than in counties using paper poll books. Based on the estimates of model 2, the expected probability of checking in zero voters without photo identification is .20 in counties using paper poll books but just .07 in counties using electronic poll books. Even after controlling for other factors, electronic poll books seem to check in many more voters without photo identification than paper poll books. Below we describe interviews with local officials in counties with unusually high rates of voters checking in without valid photo identification. In those interviews the county clerks indicate that the use of electronic poll books contributed to relatively high rates of voters checking in without photo ID.

We also find that larger jurisdictions tend to produce higher rates of voters checking in without photo identification. Doubling the size of a jurisdiction's electorate increases the expected number of voters checking in without photo ID by about 50%. We also find a moderate but positive correlation between turnout (as a percent of registered voters) and the number of voters checking in via one of the non-photo methods ($r = .33$). The estimated impact of jurisdiction size does not change when we control for age, race, and residential mobility of county residents (model 2). In addition, none of these demographic control variables are statistically associated with the number of voters checking in without photo identification.[10] This suggests that the higher number of voters checking in without photo ID in larger jurisdictions has more to do with the volume of voters being served in those jurisdictions than with the demographic profile of the local electorate. While some other studies raise concerns about the disproportionate impact of a photo identification requirement on minority voters, we do not find higher rates of voters checking in without photo ID in Missouri counties with large non-white populations. Overall, our hypothesis about the disproportionate concentration of voters without photo identification in heavily populated urban counties is supported in these early elections.

Contrary to our second hypothesis, we find no significant difference between Republican and Democratic county clerks.[11] When we test for a statistical difference between the model coefficients for Republican clerks and Democratic clerks we fail to reject the null hypothesis ($p = 0.6$ in model 1, and $p = 0.8$ in model 2). However, after controlling for jurisdiction size and poll book technology, jurisdictions with elected partisan clerks tend to have substantially higher rates of voter checking in without photo ID than the six urban jurisdictions with bipartisan election management. In either model the expected number of voters checking in without photo ID is roughly 7 times higher in counties with elected partisan clerks than in jurisdictions with a bipartisan appointed board of elections.

The local structure of election administration seems to make a big difference. We are unable to isolate the specific causal mechanism, but these results may be due to several factors. As noted above, the six most urban jurisdictions in Missouri have a bipartisan administrative and staff structure, they tend to be relatively well-resourced, and they focus solely on elections (unlike the county clerks). Furthermore, in recent years the appointed commissioners and directors in the urban jurisdictions have been experienced administrators. The largest urban jurisdictions may have a more developed administrative capacity (particularly in staff and poll worker recruitment and training) to adapt to new voter identification requirements. The net result of these factors seems to mean that the urban jurisdictions, despite serving a large volume of voters, are in a better position to educate poll workers and voters to ensure that voters with photo ID can check in without additional paperwork. Finally, our results suggest that experienced local officials (measured as whether the local election official has served in that position for at least five years) tend to produce lower rates of voters without photo identification, although the estimated coefficients fall short of statistical significance.

Uneven implementation of the law

While quantitative data indicates that some jurisdiction features are not related to the volume of voters checked in without photo identification, we also uncovered some qualitative evidence of difficulties in uniformly enforcing the new law. After the sunshine requests were sent to election authorities for the April municipal elections, we talked with several election authorities who explained some challenges with implementation; one election authority called the lead author to explain her jurisdiction's implementation issues. Based on these conversations, it appears that challenges with implementing the photo ID requirement fall primarily into two categories: (1) technology, and (2) poll worker training.

In one mid-sized, non-urban jurisdiction, the local election authority was reticent to send us the copies of the signed affidavits for the April municipal election, because as she stated,

[a]fter speaking with some of the Election Judges after the April 3rd election, I feel strongly these numbers ... are skewed, and we will have a true depiction of the number of voters without a photo ID in the upcoming August and November elections. (Personal and email communication, May 30, 2018)

This county clerk also stated that election judges had been trained "extensively" before the April 3 election, which was the first election held in that jurisdiction since the new photo ID law had been passed. Even with this heightened training, the county clerk explained that

some election judges did not understand that they could not use the voter's voter identification card to scan [into] the [electronic] poll pad after seeing the voter's photo ID. And even though every registered voter was sent information from our office regarding the new photo voter ID law ... it was routine for the voters to have their voter identification card out and ready for the judges to scan [italics original]. (Personal communication May 30, 2018)

In other words, if voters presented poll workers with both their voter ID card and their photo ID, some poll workers would scan the voter identification card and not the photo ID, which automatically prompted the voter affidavit to be brought up onto the screen of their electronic poll pad. Poll workers would then turn the poll pad around and ask voters to sign the affidavit, regardless of whether that person had a photo ID. The county clerk seemed almost embarrassed that these mistakes had occurred, and she explained that her office is committed to additional poll worker trainings before both the upcoming August and November elections.

A second county clerk in a smaller, more rural jurisdiction talked about similar implementation issues when he was called as a follow-up to our sunshine request. This county clerk was also hesitant to share affidavit information because he said it would be an "inaccurate" measure of how many voters came to the poll without the proper photo ID. He indicated that most voters came to polls with both a photo ID and their voter ID card, however the bar code on many drivers' licenses did not scan as easily into the electronic poll pad. Therefore, many poll workers would scan the voter ID card when the photo ID failed to scan, and still other poll workers chose to scan the voter ID card by default, even when a voter presented a photo ID. Thus, many voters signed affidavits even though they had a photo ID with them; in fact the county clerk believes that "almost all" voters who signed affidavits did have some form of photo ID (Personal communication, June 27, 2018). This election authority also stated that he had trained poll workers to scan voters' photo ID, however they often scanned voter identification cards "out of habit" (personal communication, June 27, 2018).

In these cases, and perhaps others, poll workers seem to fall back on habitual practices of scanning county-issued voter ID cards instead of the voter's photo ID, and voters also seem to be in the habit of presenting their voter ID cards to poll workers for this scan. In addition, the technology employed by some jurisdictions in administering an electronic poll pad seems to lack (until recently) a way to distinguish voters who sign an affidavit and whom also possess a photo ID. These initial conversations with election authorities indicate that there are still some bugs to work out from both a technological and a poll worker training perspective to ensure that the new photo ID law is accurately and consistently applied across all Missouri jurisdictions in future elections.

Conclusion

Election reform proposals have received a lot of attention in the United States. Voter identification proposals, in particular, have been a source of longstanding partisan debate in many state legislatures. Once voter identification laws are adopted, and upheld by courts, some tend to view that as the end of the debate. However, laws still need to be enforced. Voter identification laws and other election reforms often provide a good test of theories of policy implementation. Election laws are enforced by local officials and poll workers who may not share the same understanding of new laws. Local jurisdictions may use different technology or different practices that need to be adapted to new voting laws in different ways. In a decentralized system of election administration, laws that impose new requirements for registering or checking in voters invite uneven implementation. Uneven implementation of the law may mean that some people face more barriers to voting than others. In this study, we find evidence that Missouri's photo identification law has not been implemented uniformly across jurisdictions, largely related to polling place technology and the administrative structure of local election offices.

One of our consistent findings in Missouri is that jurisdictions using electronic poll books checked in substantially more voters without photo identification than jurisdictions using paper poll books. The estimated impact of polling place technology does not diminish when we control for other factors. This appears to be an unintended consequence of the technology, since electronic poll books were adopted in order to improve the speed and convenience of the check-in process. Our interviews with election officials indicate that in some locations voters and poll workers got used to scanning voter identification cards (which lack a photo), perhaps not realizing that it would trigger an additional layer of bureaucracy to check in voters. The way electronic poll books are used to sign in voters may determine how many voters are flagged as lacking valid photo identification. Based on elections held under the new voter identification law in Missouri, poll worker behaviour and the use of check-in technology deserve careful scrutiny when implementing photo ID laws.

We also find that counties with partisan elected clerks check in significantly more voters without photo identification than jurisdictions with an appointed bipartisan structure. This effect is somewhat unexpected, given that Missouri jurisdictions with bipartisan election boards are the largest localities in the state and likely serve a disproportionate number of voters that lack a valid driver's license. We are not sure of the exact causal mechanism producing this effect, but the urban jurisdictions in Missouri are unique in having a bipartisan staff structure and a sole focus on elections. The result appears to be a more professional election office that is better able to ensure that voters and poll workers are aware of new voting laws. The administrative structure of local election offices deserves more attention in studies of election implementation.

Finally, this study suggests that counting the number of voters who check in without photo identification may not be a valid or reliable measure of the number of voters who do not possess a valid photo ID. In particular, local jurisdictions using electronic poll books may overstate the number of voters who lack a valid photo ID. It is fortunate that small-scale local elections have provided the first run for new photo ID requirements in Missouri, to help work out the kinks before large major elections take place. As we show, there can be serious challenges in enforcing registration and voting requirements uniformly in a decentralized system of election administration.[12]

Notes

1. If we remove the four large urban counties at the left side of Figure 1 we observe a correlation of .65 between voter support for Trump and voter support for Amendment 6.
2. The state reported issuing 1390 non-driver licenses for voting in the first year after the photo ID requirement took effect. More than half of those non-driver licenses were issued in the city of St. Louis (Priorities USA v. State of Missouri 2018).
3. The one exception is St. Charles County, which chooses an election administrator in partisan elections.
4. St. Louis County held a special election by mail for the Robinwood West Community Improvement District on 13 June 2018. Since mail ballots are not subject to the photo ID requirement we exclude this election from our analysis. We also excluded a November 2017 special election in Randolph County where nobody voted.
5. Sample language for a Missouri record request can be found at https://ago.mo.gov/missouri-law/sunshinelaw/sample-language-forms/records-request-form.
6. In cases where we received data directly from local jurisdictions they always matched the numbers the Secretary of State reported to us.
7. Sinclair and Alvarez (2004) and Kimball and Kropf (2005) also estimate negative binomial models to examine election administration outputs.
8. We use the nbreg command in Stata version 15 to estimate the model. The corrected standard errors are specified by the "vce(cluster)" option. The total number of ballots cast in an election is used to standardize the counts with the "exposure" option. This simply accounts for the fact that there are more opportunities to have voters check in without photo ID in larger counties than in smaller counties. Long and Freese (2014, 504–14) describe the negative binomial model, overdispersion, corrected standard errors, and the exposure concept. Some might prefer using ordinary least squares regression to model the dependent variable. OLS regression analyses (available from the authors) produce similar results to the ones reported here.
9. The percent change and predicted probabilities reported throughout the paper are "as observed" – calculated while holding other independent variables at observed values and then averaging over all cases in the sample (see Hanmer and Kalkan 2013).
10. We tested some other control variables. One was median household income (the 2017 ACS five-year estimate), to account for the fact that wealthier counties were more likely to purchase electronic poll books. We also measured mean poll worker age and whether the county reported difficulty in finding enough poll workers. The latter two measures are from the 2016 EAVS survey (EAC 2017). When added to either model in Table 1 these variables were not statistically significant and did not substantially change the other results.
11. We also tested whether the party affiliation of the election clerk interacts with characteristics of the county electorate (partisanship and minority population). If officials are looking to gain an advantage for their political party then they might enforce rules more strictly in places where supporters of the opposite party are concentrated (e.g. Kimball, Kropf, and Battles 2006). For example, Republican officials might implement the photo identification requirement more vigorous in counties with a larger share of Democratic voters. However, when we interact clerk partisanship with the non-white share of the population or county partisanship (as measured by the vote for president in 2016) we find no significant differences in the share of non-photo ID voters. In addition to professional norms and oversight mitigating against partisan enforcement of the law, there are two additional reasons for the absence of large partisan differences in the implementation of Missouri's photo ID law. First, minority voters (and Democrats) in Missouri are concentrated in the metropolitan

counties served by bipartisan teams of election directors. Second, partisanship tends to be muted in the local, special, and primary elections examined in this study.

12. Missouri courts are also imposing some uniformity in photo identification enforcement. As noted above, opponents of the photo ID law filed two lawsuits to block its implementation. On 9 October 2018 (a month before the midterm elections) a Missouri judge granted part of their request, and the court decision was upheld by the Missouri Supreme Court (Priorities USA v. State of Missouri 2018). The court decision does not repeal the basic photo ID requirement passed by Missouri voters, but it blocks certain provisions of the implementing legislation. Most significantly, the court ruling prevents state and local election authorities from requiring voters without photo identification to sign the affidavit form, provided that those voters have another acceptable form of non-photo identification. The court ruling also prohibits state election officials from disseminating promotional materials that state that voters must have a photo ID in order to vote. The judge's decision noted the uneven implementation of Missouri's photo identification legislation.

Disclosure statement

No potential conflict of interest was reported by the authors.

Funding

This research is supported by a New Initiatives Grant in Election Science through the MIT Elections Lab.

References

Alvarez, R. Michael, and Thad E. Hall. 2005. "Rational and Pluralistic Approaches to HAVA Implementation: The Cases of Georgia and California." *Publius* 35: 559–577.

Alvarez, R. Michael, and Thad E. Hall. 2006. "Controlling Democracy: The Principal-agent Problems in Election Administration." *Policy Studies Journal* 34: 491–510.

Atkeson, Lonna Rae, Lisa Ann Bryant, Thad E. Hall, Kyle Saunders, and Michael Alvarez. 2009. "A New Barrier to Participation: Heterogeneous Application of Voter Identification Policies." *Electoral Studies* 29: 66–73.

Atkeson, Lonna Rae, Yann Kerevel, R. Michael Alvarez, and Thad E. Hall. 2014. "Who Asks for Voter ID? Explaining Poll Worker Discretion." *The Journal of Politics* 76: 944–957.

Barreto, Matt A., Stephen A. Nuno, and Gabriel R. Sanchez. 2009. "The Disproportionate Impact of Voter ID Requirements on the Electorate–New Evidence from Indiana." *PS: Political Science and Politics* 42 (1): 111–116.

Bentele, Keith G., and Erin E. O'Brien. 2013. "Jim Crow 2.0? Why States Consider and Adopt Restrictive Voter Access Policies." *Perspectives on Politics* 11: 1088–1116.

Biggers, Daniel R., and Michael J. Hanmer. 2017. "Understanding the Adoption of Voter Identification Laws in the American States." *American Politics Research* 45: 560–588.

Bright, Chelsea L. M., and Michael S. Lynch. 2017. "Kansas Voter ID Laws: Advertising and its Effects on Turnout." *Political Research Quarterly* 70 (2): 340–347.

Burden, Barry C. 2018. "Disagreement Over ID Requirements and Minority Voter Turnout." *The Journal of Politics* 80: 1060–1063.

Burden, Barry C., David T. Canon, Kenneth R. Mayer, and Donald P. Moynihan. 2012. "The Effect of Administrative Burden on Bureaucratic Perception of Policies: Evidence from Election Administration." *Public Administration Review* 72: 741–751.

Cobb, Rachael V., D. James Greiner, and Kevin M. Quinn. 2012. "Can Voter ID Laws Be Administered in a Race-Neutral Manner? Evidence from the City of Boston in 2008." *Quarterly Journal of Political Science* 7: 1–33.

EAC (U.S. Election Assistance Commission). 2017. *2016 Election Administration and Voting Survey*. Washington, DC.

Erikson, Robert S., and Lorraine Minnite. 2009. "Modeling Problems in the Voter Identification – Voter Turnout Debate." *Election Law Journal: Rules, Politics, and Policy* 8: 85.

GAO (U.S. Government Accountability Office). 2007. *Elections: All Levels of Government Are Needed to Address Electronic Voting System Challenges*. GAO 07-741T. Washington, DC.

Grimmer, Justin, Eitan Hersh, Marc Meredith, Jonathan Mummolo, and Clayton Nall. 2018. "Obstacles to Estimating Voter ID Laws' Effect on Turnout." *The Journal of Politics* 80: 1045–1051.

Hajnal, Zoltan, Nazita Lajevardi, and Lindsay Nielson. 2017. "Voter Identification Laws and the Suppression of Minority Votes." *The Journal of Politics* 79: 363–379.

Hale, Kathleen, and Ramona McNeal. 2010. "Election Administration Reform and State Choice: Voter Identification Requirements and HAVA." *Policy Studies Journal* 38: 281–302.

Hale, Kathleen, Robert Montjoy, and Mitchell Brown. 2015. *Administering Elections: How American Elections Work*. New York: Palgrave Macmillan.

Hale, Kathleen, and Christa Daryl Slaton. 2008. "Building Capacity in Election Administration: Local Responses to Complexity and Interdependence." *Public Administration Review* 68: 839849.

Hanmer, Michael J., and Kerem Ozan Kalkan. 2013. "Behind the Curve: Clarifying the Best Approach to Calculating Predicted Probabilities and Marginal Effects from Limited Dependent Variable Models." *American Journal of Political Science* 57: 263–277.

Hasen, Richard L. 2012. *The Voting Wars*. New Haven, CT: Yale University Press.

Hershey, Marjorie Randon. 2009. "What We Know about Voter-ID Laws, Registration, and Turnout." *PS: Political Science & Politics* 42 (1): 87–91.

Hicks, William D., Seth C. McKee, and Danial A. Smith. 2016. "The Determinants of State Legislator Support for Restrictive Voter ID Laws." *State Politics & Policy Quarterly* 16: 411431.

Hood III, M. V., and Charles S. Bullock III. 2012. "Much Ado about Nothing? An Empirical Assessment of the Georgia Voter Identification Statute." *State Politics and Policy Quarterly* 12 (4): 394–414.

Hopkins, Daniel J., Marc Meredith, Michael Morse, Sarah Smith, and Jesse Yoder. 2017. "Voting but for the Law: Evidence From Virginia on Photo Identification Requirements." *Journal of Empirical Legal Studies* 14: 79–128.

Kimball, David C., and Brady Baybeck. 2013. "Are all Jurisdictions Equal? Size Disparity in Election Administration." *Election Law Journal: Rules, Politics, and Policy* 12: 130–145.

Kimball, David C., and Martha Kropf. 2005. "Ballot Design and Unrecorded Votes on Paper Based Ballots." *Public Opinion Quarterly* 69: 508–529.

Kimball, David C., Martha Kropf, and Lindsay Battles. 2006. "Helping America Vote? Election Administration, Partisanship, and Provisional Voting in the 2004 Election." *Election Law Journal: Rules, Politics, and Policy* 5: 447–461.

Kropf, Martha. 2005. "Dogs and Dead People: Incremental Election Reform in Missouri." In *Election Reform: Politics and Policy*, edited by Daniel J. Palazzolo and James W. Ceaser, 157–176. Lanham, MD: Lexington Books.

Lipsky, Michael. 1980. *Street-Level Bureaucracy*. New York: Russell Sage Foundation.

Long, J. Scott. 1997. *Regression Models for Categorical and Limited Dependent Variables*. Thousand Oaks, CA: Sage.

Long, J. Scott, and Jeremy Freese. 2014. *Regression Models for Categorical Dependent Variables Using Stata*. 3rd ed. College Station, TX: Stata Press.

McKee, Seth C. 2015. "Politics is Local: State Legislator Voting on Restrictive Voter Identification Legislation." *Research and Politics* 2 (3). doi:10.1177/2053168015589804.

Minnite, Lorraine C. 2010. *The Myth of Voter Fraud*. Ithaca: Cornell University Press.

Montjoy, Robert, and Lawrence J. O'Toole. 1979. "Toward a Theory of Policy Implementation: An Organizational Perspective." *Public Administration Review* 39: 465–476.

Montjoy, Robert, and Christa Daryl Slaton. 2002. "Interdependence and Ethic in Election Systems: The Case of the Butterfly Ballot." *Public Integrity* 4: 195–210.

Moynihan, Donald P., and Carol L. Silva. 2008. "The Administrators of Democracy: A Research Note on Local Election Officials." *Public Administration Review* 68: 816–827.

NCSL (National Conference of State Legislatures). 2018. "Voter Identification Requirements." May 15. http://www.ncsl.org/research/elections-and-campaigns/voter-id.aspx.

Pitts, Michael J. 2015. "Empirically Measuring the Impact of Photo ID Over Time and Its Impact on Women." *Indiana Law Review* 48: 605–630.

Porter, Ethan, and Jon C. Rogowski. 2018. "Partisanship, Bureaucratic Responsiveness, and Election Administration: Evidence from a Field Experiment." *Journal of Public Administration Research and Theory* 28: 602–617.

Priorities USA v. State of Missouri. Case No. 18AC-CC00226. Cole County Circuit Court. 2018.

Pryor, Ben, Rebekah Herrick, and James A. Davis. 2019. "Voter ID Laws: The Disenfranchisement of Minority Voters?" *Political Research Quarterly* 134 (1): 63–83.

Rocha, Rene R., and Tetsuya Matsubayashi. 2014. "The Politics of Race and Voter ID Laws in the States: The Return of Jim Crow?" *Political Research Quarterly* 67: 666–679.

Sabatier, Paul, and Daniel Mazmanian. 1980. "The Implementation of Public Policy: A Framework of Analysis." *Policy Studies Journal* 8: 538–560.

Sinclair, D. E. "Betsy", and R. Michael Alvarez. 2004. "Who Overvotes, Who Undervotes, Using Punchcards? Evidence from Los Angeles County." *Political Research Quarterly* 57: 1525.

Stewart III, Charles, Stephen Ansolabehere, and Nathaniel Persily. 2016. "Revisiting Public Opinion on Voter Identification and Voter Fraud in an Era of Increasing Partisan Polarization." *Stanford Law Review* 68: 1455–1489.

White, Ariel R., Noah L. Nathan, and Julie K. Faller. 2015. "What Do I Need to Vote? Bureaucratic Discretion and Discrimination by Local Election Officials." *American Political Science Review* 109: 129–142.

Williams, Rick L. 2000. "A Note on Robust Variance Estimation for Cluster-Correlated Data." *Biometrics* 56: 645–646.

Wise, Lindsay. 2018. "Voter Fraud Much Greater Threat than Election Hacking, Missouri's Jay Ashcroft Says." Kansas City Star, June 20. https://www.kansascity.com/news/politicsgovernment/article213550254.html.

Appendix

Public records request

Dear _____:

This is a request for records under the Missouri Sunshine Law, Chapter 610, Revised Statutes of Missouri, to you as the election authority for _____ County.

We are requesting that you make available to us the following records:

Documentation of all voters who did not bring photo identification to vote in the election held on 3 April 2018 in _____ County. This request is specifically for (1) all copies of provisional ballot envelopes cast by voters without photo identification, and (2) copies of affidavits signed by voters without photo identification.

We request that all fees for locating and copying the records be waived. The information obtained through this request will be used to determine how many voters have been impacted by photo identification laws and procedures across the state of Missouri.

Please let us know in advance of any search or copying if the fees will exceed $5.00. If portions of the requested records are closed, please segregate the closed portions and provide us with the rest of the records.

Please email these documents to Joseph Anthony at josephanthony@mail.umsl.edu. For a mailing address, please contact Joseph at this email address, or by calling (314) 608–2043. We will also be requesting this type of information after the August primary and November general elections later this year. Thank you for your time and work.

Best,

Joseph Anthony   David Kimball
PhD Candidate in Political Science   Professor of Political Science
University of Missouri–St. Louis   University of Missouri–St. Louis

Waiting to vote: the effect of administrative irregularities at polling locations and voter confidence

Bridgett A. King ⓘ

ABSTRACT

When citizens experience an irregularity while voting, their confidence in elections is diminished, and they are more likely to perceive the results of the election as illegitimate. Although there are many irregularities that a voter may experience, this article evaluates the consequence of extensive wait times to vote on citizen confidence in the United States. Utilizing the 2008–2016 Survey on the Performance of American Elections (SPAE) the analysis finds that wait times have a negative effect on confidence as do challenges with the voting equipment and voter registration. The effect of negative experiences extends beyond lowered confidence that a voter's ballot is counted as intended to lower confidence that ballots at the local, state, and national level are counted as intended by voters as well. While extended wait times have a limited effect, negatively effecting the confidence in a voter's personal ballot and ballots across the local jurisdiction, negative experiences with registration or ballots and voting equipment affect evaluations of confidence at the personal level and across the local jurisdiction, state, and nation.

Electoral irregularities and democracy

Election Day involves an extensive set of rules and procedures that are administered by state and local election officials and poll workers. Their collective efforts not only make voting possible for eligible citizens but also the collection, aggregation, and certification of election results. The procedures and officials that facilitate elections are rarely acknowledged unless problems arise. In such instances, perceived problems can result in increased public distrust in election administration (Hale, Brown, and Montjoy 2015, p xxiii). Citizens perceiving elections and the results they generate as legitimate is essential for democracy. The functioning of a democracy requires citizen trust in the administrative rules and procedures that determine who wins and who loses, the belief that electoral contests are legitimate, acceptance of the outcome as fair, and deference to elected officials (Norris 2014; James et al. 2019).

Focusing on the United States, this article evaluates the relationship between citizens experiencing in-person administrative irregularities when casting a ballot and confidence that ballots are counted as intended by voters. Specifically, the analysis addresses the relationship between voter wait time, problems with the voting equipment or ballot, and problems with voter registration and confidence. While there is scholarship that investigates the relationship between voter registration and problems with the voting equipment and confidence in the United States, there has yet to be an investigation that asks, how do extended wait times affect voter confidence? In addressing this question, the article considers the effect of polling location irregularities on voter confidence that their personal ballot is counted as intended and confidence that ballots across the local jurisdiction, state, and the nation are counted as intended. Although the focus of this article is the United States, the consequences of procedural and administrative irregularities experienced by voters on confidence are not limited to this country. Kerr (2013) finds that during the 2007 Nigerian election, voters who experienced irregularities related to intimidation or violence had less confidence in the quality of the election than voters who did not. In a recent cross-national study of 121 elections in 109 countries, Frank and Martínez i Coma (2017) survey election experts and report similar findings; noting the important role that election administration plays in contributing to the overall integrity of elections. This article therefore contributes to the growing body of literature that evaluates the role of election and administrative irregularities on citizen confidence in elections (Frank and Martínez i Coma 2017; Hall, Monson, and Patterson 2007, 2009; Claassen et al. 2008; Kerr 2013; King 2017).

The article proceeds as follows. First, a discussion of administrative irregularities and the scholarship that has addressed the consequences of polling location irregularities for voters is presented. This is followed by an explanation of the importance and role of confidence in election administration. The third section provides the data and methodology that is used to address the relationship between irregularities and confidence and a discussion of the findings. The article concludes with a presentation local and federal innovations and responses to administrative challenges and recommendations for the field.

Irregularities and in-Person voting

In recent elections, voter wait time has received considerable attention. However, citizens waiting to vote and the presence of long lines is not new to the political landscape in the United States.

Following the passage of the 1964 Civil Rights Act and 1965 Voting Rights Act, when newly enfranchised African Americans tried to register to vote and cast a ballot, they often experienced intentionally long lines and wait times (Lewis and Allen 1972). Delaying tactics such as registrars opening registration offices late and closing early, taking prolonged lunch breaks, and keeping blacks waiting in line [were] commonly reported (Lewis and Allen 1972, 121).

> After registering to vote, black voters continue[d] to face other barriers. Commonly reported problems include[d] the omission of black voters' names from registration lists, crowded lines of voters in predominantly black precincts, harassment of voters, refusal to assist illiterate black voters, intimidation and exclusion of poll watchers, and the furnishing of incomplete or erroneous instructions to black voters (Lewis and Allen 1972, 124).

The lines experienced by black Americans in the mid-twentieth century were the result of direct and overt discrimination; however extended wait times can occur for a variety of reasons including technology challenges, voter turnout that is higher than expected, and an insufficient distribution of resources. Voters in Pennington County, Kentucky, for example, experienced lines and delays on Election Day because the e-poll books were unable to connect to the server (Vondracek 2018). In Maricopa County, Arizona voters experienced long wait times during the 2018 midterm election because of turnout that was higher than expected.[1] Extended wait times may also occur as a consequence of an insufficient distribution of resources (poll workers and voting machines) (Spencer and Markovits 2010; Pettigrew 2017).

Scholars who have investigated voting wait time in recent American elections find that there is a relationship between wait time and evaluations of poll worker quality (Burden and Milyo 2015) and the decision to vote (Highton 2006; Stewart and Ansolabehere 2013; Pettigrew 2016; Harris 2018).[2] Additionally, neighbourhood composition is strongly associated with how long a voter will wait on Election Day. Neighbourhoods that are more population dense and non-white experience longer wait times (Kimball 2013; Stewart and Ansolabehere 2013; Pettigrew 2017). Beyond understanding where extended waits occur, scholars from a broad variety of disciplines have worked to identify models that facilitate the most optimal flow and processing of voters at polling locations on Election Day. In many instances this scholarship has focused on determining the best way to organize a polling location while maximizing the quality of the voter experience and minimizing administrative problems (Grant 1980; Allen, Bernshteyn, and Rockwell 2009; Edelstein and Edelstein 2010; Stewart and Ansolabehere 2013; Yang et al. 2013; Herron and Smith 2017).

Although the primary focus of this analysis is wait time, other administrative irregularities or negative experiences can also contribute to voters reporting less confidence that ballots are counted as intended. Such experiences might include the voter's name being absent from the voter list, voting provisionally, and the ease of the voting method (Atkeson and Saunders 2007). Problems with the voting equipment and the type of equipment can also affect confidence (Claassen et al. 2013; King 2017). Outside of the United States, scholars report similar findings. Kerr (2018) finds that voters in Nigeria who experience challenges with the voting equipment are less likely to consider national elections free and fair and less likely to be confident in the vote count. Other scholars who have focused on more established democracies also find that in-person voting experiences contribute to evaluations of confidence and trust in elections generally and broadly (Sances and Stewart 2015; King 2017; Karp, Nai, and Norris 2018).

Although extended wait time and other irregularities that voters experience are not common and may not be the result of an intentional, systematic attempt to disenfranchise voters, the consequences for confidence and trust in government and election administration specifically may be the same. The wait time before casting a ballot, similar to problems with the voting equipment or low-quality poll workers, may lead voters to believe that something is wrong and that they should not trust the administrative procedures that determine the results of an election.

Citizen confidence in election administration

Scholars have argued that confidence in election administration, elections, or electoral processes is unique and different from trust in government. When assessing trust in government, citizens are often asked about individual elected officials and their policy decisions. Evaluations of trust that focus on elected officials and their decisions do not capture the nuance of citizen evaluation. For example, a voter may not be confident in the machines but may trust their elected officials. Alternatively, voters may trust electoral processes and procedures while believing that all elected officials are corrupt (Alvarez, Hall, and Llewellyn 2008, 755). These differences are not captured by general measures of confidence or trust in government.

Measures of trust in election administration are distinct because they require the voter to assert their confidence in the processes and procedures as opposed to government or individuals in government (Citrin and Luks 2001). Measures of confidence are also unique because they ask voters about a "very specific additive component (confidence) and a very specific objective component (whether a voter's ballot was counted correctly)" (Atkeson, Alvarez, and Hall 2015, 209). Additionally, measures of trust or confidence in election administration serve as a measure of electoral system performance (Atkeson and Saunders 2007; Alvarez, Hall, and Llewellyn 2008; Hall, Monson, and Patterson 2009; Atkeson, Alvarez, and Hall 2015).

Given that elections are the primary way that citizens express their preferences for representation and policy (Montjoy and Slayton 2002), understanding how in-person voting experiences, particularly system irregularities, contribute to confidence in election administration is important. It is important not only for elections and democratic functioning but also because if voters do not believe that ballots are counted accurately and outcomes are legitimate, they may also have lower levels of trust in other government institutions (Atkeson, Alvarez, and Hall 2015, 210).

Data and Methods

The relationship between voting wait time and confidence is evaluated using a series of ordered logistic regression models with data from the 2008, 2012, 2014, and 2016 Survey of the Performance of American Elections (SPAE). [3] The SPAE is designed to gauge the quality of the election experience from the perspective of voters. In the survey, interviews were conducted with 10,200 registered voters nationwide biannually. The interviews were conducted to represent the nation on several demographic characteristics- including education, income, race, and partisanship. Given the nature of the research question, respondents are limited to those who voted in-person (Election Day or early). Before the analysis, the surveys for the election years were merged. As the context in which elections occur can affect citizen confidence in ways that are beyond the scope of election administration, election year and state fixed effects are included in the models to account for conditions of the state and electoral environment in a given election year that may positively or negatively affect confidence.[4] The primary dependent variable, confidence in elections is evaluated using a question in the SPAE that asks voters to evaluate confidence that their ballot was counted as intended. The confidence measure is coded on a four-point scale where very confident = 4, somewhat confident = 3, not too confident = 2, and not confident at all = 1.

The key explanatory variable, "wait time" is a dichotomous variable that is used to capture the number of minutes voters waited before voting. In the 2008–2016 SPAE, respondents were asked how long they had to wait in line to vote. Possible responses included: no wait, less than 10 min, 10–30 , 31 min to an hour, and more than one hour. Respondents who replied "I don't know" are excluded from the analysis. The key explanatory variable, "wait time" is coded as a dichotomous variable that differentiates between voters who waited from 0 to 30 min (coded as zero) and voters who waited for 31 min or more (coded as one).

Although there is no formal consensus regarding how long a voter should wait (Government Accountability Office 2014), a 30-minute wait is often used a benchmark by those studying elections as the maximum (Bipartisan Policy Center 2018; United States Presidential Commission on Election Administration 2014). A wait of 30 min or less is also the most frequent wait time reported by voters (Stewart 2013a, 2013b, 2015, 2017).[5] A wait that is longer than 30 min is not only contrary to best practices but also exceeds the "normal" wait time experienced by voters (Stewart 2013a, 2013b, 2015, 2017). Given this, it is hypothesized that voters who wait more than 30 min will have less confidence than those who wait less than 30 min prior to casting an in-person ballot.

In addition to wait time, the analysis takes into consideration other components of the in-person voting experience that have a demonstrable negative effect on confidence (Hall, Monson, and Patterson 2007, 2009; Claassen et al. 2008; King 2017). In the SPAE voters are asked if they experienced problems with their registration when they went to vote and if they experienced problems with the voting equipment or with the ballot that interfered with their ability to cast a ballot as intended. Dichotomous variables to account for these are included in the analysis with one indicating the voter did experience a problem with the voting equipment or ballot or their registration and zero indicating the voter did not experience any of the above problems.

Whether voters choose to cast a ballot early or on Election Day can also affect confidence. Citizens who vote absentee or early are further removed from the election process and feel less confident that their ballot is likely to be counted (Atkeson and Saunders 2007). Given this, a dichotomous variable for early voting is included. Voters who cast their ballot in-person early are coded as one; those who did not and voted on Election Day are coded as zero. Because partisan affiliation with the party in power or the winning party in highly salient electoral contests can affect confidence, (Bullock, Hood, and Clark 2005; Atkeson, Alvarez, and Hall 2009; Beaulieu 2014; Sances and Stewart 2015), a measure of party affiliation is included.

Lastly, individual variables to account for voter age, sex, income, and education are also included (See Appendix Table A1 for complete question wording and variable coding).

The analysis proceeds as follows. First, the relationship between confidence, wait time, problems with the equipment, and voter registration are considered. Following this, an analysis of the effect of the variables above on broad measures of confidence is presented. This includes confidence in ballots being counted as intended by voters at the local, state, and federal level. The analysis concludes with discussion and recommendations.

Analysis and findings

The distribution of the primary independent variable, wait times reflects what we tend to know about wait times. As noted in Figure 1, the overwhelming majority of voters wait less than 30 min. The figure also displays the percent of voters who report experiencing problems with voter registration and the voting equipment or ballot. Like extended wait times,

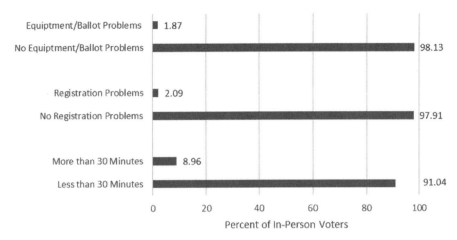

Figure 1. Voter reported irregularities.

the majority of voters do not report registration or equipment and ballot problems. Although the percent of voters that report waiting more than 30 min is less than 10%, extended wait times are a more frequent occurrence than problems with voter registration and the equipment or ballot.

In addition to the distribution of general experiences with irregularities, we might also consider the distribution of irregularities across racial/ethnic groups. Figure 2 displays the distribution of irregularities across racial/ethnic groups. Compared to white, Hispanic, and Asian voters, African American voters are most likely to report waiting more than 30 min or experiencing a problem with the voting machine or their voter registration. This observation is similar to those of other scholars (Kimball 2013; Stewart and Ansolabehere 2013;

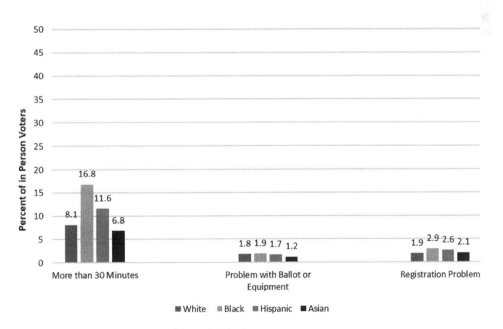

Figure 2. In-person voter reported irregularities by race.

Pettigrew 2017). Although the percent of voters across racial/ethnic groups who experience these irregularities when compared to the total number of voters included in the survey, is limited, the distribution further demonstrates that racial minorities, most notably African Americans continue to experience challenges when voting in person at rates that are higher than voters from different racial/ethnic groups.

Irregularities and individual ballot confidence

Table 1 presents a series of Ordered Logistic Regression Models. Model 1 investigates the relationship between wait times and confidence, without consideration of other administrative components of the in-person voting experience that may affect confidence in elections. The model suggests that waiting matters. Compared to a wait of 30 min or less, voters who wait longer are less confident that their ballot is counted as intended ($-.229$, $P < 0.001$). Model 2 incorporates variables that account for problems with voter registration and the voting equipment or ballot. Once included, wait time remains negative and statistically significant, although the magnitude of the effect decreases ($-.153$; $P = 0.002$). Problems with the ballot or voting equipment (-1.342, $P < 0.001$) and problems with voters' registration ($-.857$, $P < 0.001$) both have a negative and significant effect on confidence. Of these, problems with the voting equipment or ballot have the greatest impact. In many ways, this should not be surprising. The ballot and voting equipment are the tools that voters use to express their preferences for candidates and policies. While challenges with voter registration can be addressed utilizing a provisional ballot[6]

Table 1. Ordered logistic regression models of factors affecting individual confidence.

	Model 1	Model 2
Variable		
Wait	−.229 (.049)***	−.153 (.050)**
Registration Problems		−.857 (.090)***
Equipment and Ballot Problems		−1.342 (.093)***
Early Voter	−.073 (.039)‡	−.081 (.039)*
Black	−064 (.052)	−.069 (.052)
Hispanic	.152 (.096)	.140 (.096)
Asian	−.101 (.122)	−.107 (.123)
Age	.017 (.000)***	.016 (.001)***
Income	.027 (.004)***	.024 (.004)***
Education	.082 (.011)***	.086 (.011)***
Male	.108 (.029)***	.116 (.029)***
Democrat	.230 (.037)***	.232 (.037)***
Independent	−.178 (.036)***	−.170 (.036)***
Year 2008	.173 (.041)***	.170 (.041)***
Year 2012	−.228 (.041)***	−.224 (.041)***
Year 2014	.088 (.044)*	.095 (.045)*
Cut Point 1	−2.777 (.134)	−2.898 (.136)
Cut Point 2	−1.800 (.129)	−1.909 (.131)
Cut Point 3	.143 (.128)	.065 (.129)
N	25,440	25,343
Log likelihood	−18371.856	−18198.625
Psuedo R2	.0274	.0353
χ^2	1034.30, 64 df, $p > .000$	1323.57, 66 df, $p > .000$

Note: Ordered logistic regression coefficients with standard errors in parentheses.
***$p < .001$.
**$p < .01$.
*$p < .05$.
‡$p < .10$.

or through technology (e-poll books for example)[7] when a voter has a problem with the ballot or voting equipment there may or may not be an onsite remedy to address the problem to the voter's satisfaction. For example, in jurisdictions that utilize optical scanners, when the machines fail, voters are often instructed to continue voting with the paper ballots. The ballots can then be counted after the machines are repaired or replaced. (Norden and Famighetti 2015). A voter may not perceive this practice to be secure or legitimate and may not believe the ballot will be counted. In an electoral environment where problems experienced by individual voters are shared broadly, this may especially be true.[8]

Similar to Model 1, Model 2 suggests that there is no relationship between race and confidence that one's personal ballot is counted as expected. Similar findings are reported by King (2017) and Atkeson and Saunders (2007) who find that there is no significant relationship between voter race and confidence in one's ballot being or vote counted as intended.

To better understand the way that voting irregularities can impact evaluations of confidence, marginal effects were estimated using Table 1, Model 2. All else being equal the probability of a voter being very confident that their ballot is counted as intended decreases by three percentage points when the voter waits more than 30 min (Table 2). While wait time that extends beyond 30 min may be the exception and not the rule when experienced by voters, it diminishes confidence in elections; even when controlling for other potential irregularities. Given that the model also includes variables for problems with the ballot or voting equipment and voter registration, estimates were also generated to evaluate their effect on confidence. The estimates suggest that when a voter experiences a challenge with the voting equipment or ballot, they are 30 percentage points less likely to be very confident and when a voter has a problem with their registration, they are 18 percentage points less likely to report being very confident. Interestingly while problems with registration and problems with the voting equipment or ballot occur less frequently, the magnitude of their effect on confidence is considerably greater than that of an extended wait time.

Irregularities and local, state, and national confidence

As demonstrated by Table 1, voter wait time that extends beyond 30 min negatively affects the confidence that voters have in their ballot being counted as intended. The effect of this experience, however, may extend beyond confidence in the personal ballot. To evaluate the diffuse consequences of negative in-person voting experiences on confidence, the effect of irregularities on confidence that ballots are counted as intended by voters across the local jurisdiction (city or county), state, and nation are considered. Similar to the question that served as the

Table 2. Marginal effect of irregularities on measures of confidence.

	Wait time	Registration problem	Voting equipment or Ballot problem
Personal	−.029 [−.048, −.009]	−.182 [−.223, −.141]	−.297 [−.339, −.254]
Local	−.036 [−.063, −.008]	−.150 [−.197, −.103]	−.313 [−.360, −.267]
State		−.135 [−.179, −.091]	−.232 [−.274, −.190]
National		−.045 [−.076, −.015]	−.113 [−.137, −.088]

Note: Predicted probabilities and associated 95% confidence intervals generated using the Margins Command in STATA. Margins calculates marginal probabilities based on changes in significant variables of interest (here the presence or absence of irregularities) while holding values for all other variables constant. Statistical uncertainty for these predictions is calculated using the delta method. Confidence intervals in brackets.

dependent variable in Table 1, the SPAE includes questions that ask voters to evaluate their confidence that ballots across their local jurisdiction, state, and nation were counted as intended by voters. Each confidence measure is coded on a four-point scale where very confident = 4, somewhat confident = 3, not too confident = 2, and not confident at all = 1.[9]

Looking at the full model (Table 3) which includes, wait time, registration and machine or ballot problems, the experience of extended wait times for voters negatively effects confidence that ballots are counted as intended by voters across their city/county ($-.162$, $p = .008$) but not across their state ($-.094$; $p = .115$) and the nation ($-.032$; $p = .573$). The effect of a wait of more than 30 min on local confidence is a 3.6% decrease in the probability of being very confident (Table 2).

Although there is no relationship between wait time and confidence across the United States, the effect of waiting does matter for voters in unconsolidated democracies. As an example, Kerr (2018) who focuses on the 2015 Nigerian election finds that when voters spend more time at the polling location, they are less likely to believe that national elections are free and fair. Unlike wait time which does not affect the state and national level confidence measures, the negative effect of both voter registration and equipment or ballot problems on confidence extends beyond voter confidence in their individual ballot (Table 3) to voter confidence across their county or city, state, and the nation.

The marginal effects of registration problems and problems with the equipment or ballot on the probability of being very confident across the local jurisdiction, state, and nation are displayed in Table 2. It is notable that as evaluations of confidence move to more distant levels of governance there is a decrease in size of the negative effect of the in-person administrative irregularity on confidence.[10] Compared to (national)

Table 3. Ordered logistic regression models of factors affecting confidence.

	Local	State	Nation
Variable			
Wait	−.162 (.061)**	−.094 (.059)	−.032 (.058)
Registration problems	−.648 (.101)***	−.584 (.100)***	−.271 (.097)**
Equipment and Ballot Problems	−1.634 (.112)***	−1.046 (.111)***	−.762 (.106)***
Early voter	−.074 (.043) ǂ	−.071 (.040) ǂ	−.145 (.038)***
Black	−.265 (.056)***	−.251 (.055)***	−.023 (.054)
Hispanic	.028 (.121)	.121 (.118)	.116 (.115)
Asian	.094 (.134)	.158 (.129)	.126 (.123)
Age	.010 (.001)***	.000 (.001)	−.014 (.000)***
Income	.017 (.002)**	.013 (.004)**	−.000 (.004)
Education	.084 (.012)***	.048 (.011)***	.037 (.010)**
Male	.094 (.032)**	.044 (.030)	.052 (.029) ǂ
Democrat	.135 (.040)**	.190 (.038)**	.438 (.036)***
Independent	−.179 (.040)***	−.121 (.038)**	.054 (.036)
Year 2012	−.358 (.039) ***	−.281 (.037)***	−.613 (.035)***
Year 2014	−.115 (.041)**	−.226 (.038)***	−.339 (.036)***
Cut Point 1	−3.644 (.147)	−4.261 (.137)	−2.692 (.118)
Cut Point 2	−2.490 (.141)	−2.890 (.132)	−1.299 (.117)
Cut Point 3	−.334 (.139)	−.771 (.130)	.735(.116)
N	17,245	17,245	17,131
Log likelihood	−14785.583	−17070.965	−21073.52
Psuedo R^2	.0320	.0323	.0220
χ^2	978.10, 65 df, $p > .000$	1138.43, 65 df, $p > .000$	948.49, 65 df, $p > .000$

Note: Ordered logistic regression coefficients with standard errors in parentheses.
***$p < .001$.
**$p < .01$.
*$p < .05$.
ǂ$p < .10$.

institutions, voters are more confident in local institutions (Mutz and Flemming 1999) and find it more difficult to convince themselves that votes are not fairly counted at the state and local level compared to the national level (Sances and Stewart 2015). The present analysis, however, not only indicates that in-person voting irregularities negatively affect voter confidence that ballots are counted fairly but also that the levels of government where voters typically exhibit the most trust are the most heavily affected.

Demographics and confidence

The models in Table 3 identify race effects for African Americans. Compared to whites, black voters are less confident that ballots across their local jurisdiction (−.265, p < .001) and state (−.251, p < .001) are counted as intended by voters. While many studies rely on one election to assess the relationship between race and confidence, the present analysis builds on this literature in a particular way by demonstrating that across elections, African Americans demonstrate markedly less confidence in the accuracy of election outcomes in their local jurisdiction and states than their white counterparts.[11] Alvarez, Hall, and Llewellyn (2008) suggest the difference in the rates of confidence between black and white voters may be the result of the historical efforts by whites to disenfranchise black voters through Jim Crow Laws (literacy tests, poll taxes, constitutional interpretation tests, etc. See Keyssar 2000). They also suggest that the environment and events surrounding an election may contribute to perceptions that there is an intentional effort to disenfranchise African American voters; an assertion that is also supported by Nunnally (2011) and Avery (2009). With few exceptions, the rules that govern voting and registration are determined by states, elections are administered at the local level, and states and local jurisdictions continue to be at the centre of court challenges about access to voting and registration. The negative relationship between race and confidence for African Americans at those levels of government may then be an artifact of contemporary issues surrounding voting access in the United States.[12]

Across the models in Tables 1 and 3, party affiliation is a statistically significant predictor of voter confidence. Voters who are affiliated with the Democratic party report higher rates of confidence that their ballot and ballots across their local jurisdiction, state, and the nation are counted as intended by voters. The positive and significant relationship for Democrats is what one might expect. With the exception of the 2016 presidential election, the presidential elections included in the analysis resulted in a Democrat president-elect of the United States. Although the 2014 election concluded with Republicans gaining control of the Senate, the "loser" effect is less pronounced among those who are affiliated with the party in control of the White House (Doherty 2018).[13] Given this, Democrats were political winners more often than not. The positive effect on confidence may then be the result of party successes from the 2008 and 2012 presidential elections that offset the negative effect of Democratic party losses. Lastly, the models (Tables 1 and 3) also support the previous scholarship, which identifies a negative relationship between early voting and confidence (Atkeson and Saunders 2007).

Overall, the findings suggest that the effect of extended wait time on confidence is limited. While wait time affects the confidence that the individual voter has in their personal ballot and votes across their local jurisdiction being counted as voters intend, wait times that exceed 30 min, do not affect the way voters perceive the process across their state or the nation. Problems with registration and the equipment or ballot however as irregularities are pervasive and not only affect voter confidence personally but also across the local jurisdiction, state, and the nation.

Discussion

If we think of polling locations as a system, there are various points at which one abnormality can create a chain reaction and extend the time required to vote. As noted by Grant (1980, 20), "the system is composed of serial queues, each representing a component of the process." Efficient component management, which can be affected by the accuracy of voter registration records, an insufficient number of voting machines, voting machines that are not functioning properly, an inadequate number of poll workers, inadequately trained poll workers, or an unusually long ballot, can create extended queues on Election Day, queues that increase the amount of time required to vote, thus increasing the cost for voters (Haspell and Knotts 2005).[14]

Given that the majority of voters attribute their wait time to the check-in portion of in-person voting, resources might be shifted to check-in, whether it be with more poll workers or the use of e-poll books to expedite the process of voter check-in and reduce administrative error.[15][16] Although technology can be used to expedite administrative processes and procedures, it is not always a perfect solution. Technology can have disparate effects among voters. Stein et al. (2019) for example find that in majority white polling locations, scanning a voter's driver license speeds up the check-in process. In majority-minority polling locations, the same process increases check-in time. Further, the type of equipment, usability, and the voter's prior knowledge of the voting equipment (Claassen et al. 2013) can affect citizen evaluations of the election experience.

Of the three irregularities included in the analysis, two of them have been directly addressed by recent pieces of federal legislation. Voting technology and voter registration records were both addressed by the Help America Vote Act (HAVA) in 2002 and the Consolidated Appropriations Act of 2018. HAVA established minimum federal election administration standards. These include standards for voter identification, poll workers training, updated and upgraded voting equipment, provisional voting, statewide voter registration databases, and administrative complaint procedures. Additionally, through HAVA the Election Assistance Commission (EAC) was established as "an independent, bipartisan commission charged with developing guidance to meet HAVA requirements, adopting voluntary voting system guidelines, and serving as a national clearinghouse of information on election administration" (www.eac.gov). The EAC was then responsible for distributing $650,000,000 in grants to states to make improvements to election administration (Public Law 107-252).

Most recently, through the Consolidated Appropriations Act of 2018, the United States Congress allocated $380 million in additional HAVA grant funds. The grants were made available to states to improve the administration of elections for Federal office in the areas of voting equipment, post-election auditing, voter registration systems, cybersecurity, training, and communication (Election Assistance Commission 2018).[17] It is clear the two most recent efforts on the part of the federal government to address the administration of elections directly address those areas that, according to this analysis significantly impact the confidence that citizens have in elections when voting in-person.

Conclusion

In 2001, the National Commission on Federal Election Reform wrote,

> ... it is critical that all Americans have confidence in our electoral system, and we should strive to eliminate any reasonable perception that the basic mechanisms of democratic participation favor some citizens over others. No voter should ever feel that the process of voting was intimidating or that there were improper barriers, either intentional or unintentional, that prevented the exercise of their right to vote (46).

While one might argue that the irregularities included in the analysis are idiosyncratic and infrequent, their effect on citizen confidence in elections is undeniable and affect voter confidence across the electoral system. In the 2016 SPAE, the percent of voters who reported waiting more than 30 min was 8.43%. The percent of voters who reported waiting more than 60 min was 2.17. Although both percentages reflect a small fraction of the total voters who participated in the presidential election, it is still several million voters. In 2016 there were approximately 138, 846,571 ballots cast (McDonald 2018). Given this, approximately 11,704,765 voters waited more than 30 min, and 3,012,970 waited more than 60 min. Similar estimates suggest that in a given election, millions of voters have negative experiences with voter registration and problems with the ballot or voting machine.[18]

Election administrators work in environments of increasing demand with finite resources. They are not in a position to address all the factors that may contribute to voter confidence, particularly those that lie outside the scope of election administration. However, as the field of individuals who study election administration in the United States and countries around the globe continues to expand, the continued integration of the knowledge, skills, and abilities from a variety of disciplines, professions, nations, and regions can be utilized to develop resources. Resources, which can assist in administrative decision-making and facilitate citizen participation and confidence.[19]

Notes

1. Voter turnout rivaled that of a presidential election. There were more than 260,000 ballots cast in-person on Election Day and more than 1.1 million early votes cast during the 2018 midterm election. Turnout in the 2016 presidential election was 1,608,875 (Maricopa County Recorder 2016, 2018).
2. An estimated 200,000 people did not vote in 2014 because of the lines they encountered in 2012 (Pettigrew 2016).
3. A nationwide SPAE was not conducted in 2010 and thus is not included in the analysis.
4. Although included in the models the state fixed effects are not presented.
5. Data from the 2013 Cooperative Congressional Election Survey-MIT Module, suggests that the typical American places the threshold of acceptable wait time to vote between 30 and 60 min (Pettigrew 2016).
6. Following the presidential election in 2000, the Help America Vote Act (HAVA) was passed in 2002. HAVA provided states with limited administrative clarity regarding accessibility to provisional ballots across the 50 states. HAVA mandated that, a potential voter has the right to utilize a provisional ballot in the event their name does not appear on the registration list or the voter's eligibility is challenged by an election official (Section 302 of the Help America Vote Act (HAVA) (42 U.S.C. §15482)).
7. Many jurisdictions use paper poll books that contain a list of eligible voters. These books have to be printed before each election and delivered to individual voting sites/polling locations.

Electronic poll books or e-poll books are electronic version of the traditional poll book that often come in the form of a laptop or tablet.

8. For example, voters may share their experiences on social media. A tween from the 2016 presidential election demonstrates this point. The tweet reads, "The voting machine in Oakland is broken, so we put our ballots in a box, which falls open exposing the ballots #yourtaxdollarsatwork." November 8, 2016, 8:22 AM. Tweet. The tweet and accompanying photograph were subsequently reported by national news outlets (See Brewster 2016).

9. The 2008 election is not included in the analysis; questions regarding confidence at the local, state, and federal level were not included until 2012.

10. As an exception there is a slight increase in the effect problems with the equipment or ballot, when moving from personal to local levels of confidence.

11. King (2017) for example uses data from the 2012 election and Atkeson and Saunders (2007) utilize data from the 2006 midterm election.

12. Because racial/ethnic minorities are more likely to experience each individual irregularity and black was significant in the local and state models reported in Table 3, models that include black * irregularity interactions were generated to determine if the effect of irregularities on confidence for African American voters was different compared to white voters. The models suggest that while racial and ethnic minorities may be more likely to experience irregularities, the effect on confidence is not unique (For Models See Appendix B and C).

13. Stewart (2018) finds that following the 2014 midterm election, Republican victories in federal and state elections nationwide were followed by a 14-point increase in Republican confidence and a slight decrease in confidence among Democrats.

14. Famighetti, Melillo, and Perez (2014) found that during the 2012 presidential election, polling locations that had more voters (those who had not voted early or absentee) per machine and more voters per poll worker experienced longer Election Day delays than those that had a lower number of voter per poll worker and machine.

15. Of voters who report waiting more than 30 min, 72 percent report that the wait occurred before check in with 14.6 percent reporting the wait occurred while waiting for the voting machine.

16. "E-poll books allow poll workers to look up voters across the entire county or state. This can reduce time spent checking in votes. E-poll books also allow poll workers to easily direct voters to the correct polling place if they are at the wrong one, scan a driver's license to pull up a voter's information, avoiding data entry errors, notify a poll worker if a voter has already voted early" (National Conference of State Legislatures 2017).

17. The election assistance commission also provided states with the opportunity to request that the funds be used for categories other than those specified above (Election Assistance Commission 2018).

18. In the 2016 election, 2.08 percent or 2.8 million voters had registration problems. In the same election year, 1.77 percent or 2.45 million voters had problems with the ballot or voting equipment (Stewart 2017).

19. For example, there are resources accessible to some voters in the United States that allow them to track the location of their absentee ballot. As an example ballottrax in Arapahoe County, Colorado and Ballot Tracking, Reporting, and Communication Engine (TRACE) in Denver, Colorado. A similar resource exists in Estonia. Voters have access to a tool that allows them to track their ballot, verify that it was received, see how the vote was recorded, and verify that it is correct.

Disclosure statement

No potential conflict of interest was reported by the author.

ORCID

Bridgett A. King ⓘ http://orcid.org/0000-0002-6562-0126

References

Allen, T., Mikhail Bernshteyn, and Chris Rockwell. 2009. "Helping Franklin County vote in 2008: Waiting Lines. Report to Michael Stinziano and Matthew DamShroeder and The Franklin County Board of Elections." (ND). http://vote.franklincountyohio.gov/assets/pdf/press-releases/PR-07302008.pdf.

Alvarez, R. Michael, Thad E. Hall, and Morgan H. Llewellyn. 2008. "Are Americans Confident Their Ballots are Counted?" *The Journal of Politics* 70 (3): 754–766.

Atkeson, Lonna Rae, R. Michael Alvarez, and Thad E. Hall. 2009. "Provisional Voting in New Mexico." Pew Charitable Trusts, The Center for the States, Provisional Ballots: An Imperfect Solution. http://www.pewcenteronthestates.org/initiatives_detail.aspx?initiativeID=54789.

Atkeson, Lonna Rae, R. Michael Alvarez, and Thad E. Hall. 2015. "Trust in Elections and Trust in Government: Why Voter Confidence Differs from Other Measures of System Support." *Election Law Journal* 14 (3): 207–219.

Atkeson, Lonna Rae, and Kyle L. Saunders. 2007. "The Effect of Election Administration on Voter Confidence: a Local Matter?" *PS: Political Science & Politics* 40 (4): 655–660.

Avery, James M. 2009. "Political Mistrust among African Americans and Support for the Political System." *Political Research Quarterly* 62 (1): 132–145.

Beaulieu, Emily. 2014. "From Voter ID to Party ID: How Political Parties Affect Perceptions of Election Fraud in the US." *Electoral Studies* 35: 24–32.

Bipartisan Policy Center. 2018. "Improving the Voter Experiences: Reducing Polling Place Wait Times by Measuring Lines and Managing Polling Place Resources." https://bipartisanpolicy.org/library/improving-the-voter-experience-reducing-polling-place-wait-times-by-measuring-lines-and-managing-polling-place-resources/.

Brewster, Thomas. 2016. "A Lot of Voting Machines are Broke across America (But' it's Totally Normal)." *Forbes Magazine*, November 8. https://www.forbes.com/sites/thomasbrewster/2016/11/08/broken-voting-machines-election-2016-not-rigged-or-russian-hackers/#3e434fa5c541.

Bullock III, Charles S., M. V. Hood III, and Richard Clark. 2005. "Punch Cards, Jim Crow, and Al Gore: Explaining Voter Trust in the Electoral System in Georgia, 2000." *State Politics & Policy Quarterly* 5 (3): 283–294.

Burden, Barry, and Jeffrey Milyo. 2015. "The Quantities and Qualities of Poll Workers." *Election Law Journal: Rules, Politics, and Policy* 14 (1): 38–46.

Citrin, Jack, and Samantha Luks. 2001. "Political Trust Revisited: Deji Vu All Over Again?" In *What Is It about Government That Americans Dislike?* edited by Hibbing John R. and Theiss-Morse Elizabeth, 9–27. New York: Cambridge University Press.

Claassen, Ryan L., David B. Magleby, J. Quinn Monson, and Kelly D. Patterson. 2013. "Voter Confidence and The Election-Day Voting Experience." *Political Behavior* 35 (2): 215–235.

Claassen, Ryan L., David B. Magleby, J. Quin Monson, and Kelly D. Patterson. 2008. "At Your Service" Voter Evaluations of Poll Worker Performance." *American Politics Research* 36 (4): 612–634.

Doherty, Carroll. 2018. "Key findings on Americans' views of the U.S. Political System and Democracy." *Pew Research Center.* https://www.pewresearch.org/fact-tank/2018/04/26/key-findings-on-americans-views-of-the-u-s-political-system-and-democracy/.

Edelstein, William A., and Arthur D. Edelstein. 2010. "Queuing and Elections: Long Lines, DREs, and Paper Ballots." Proceedings of EVT/WOTE. Washington, D.C., August 9–10.

Election Assistance Commission. 2018. Help America Vote Act Election Security Grants Award Packet.   https://www.eac.gov/assets/1/6/HAVA_Election_Security_Final_Award_Packet_041718.pdf.

Famighetti, C., A. Melillo, and Myrna Perez. 2014. "Election Day Long Lines: Resource Allocation," Brennan Center for Justice at New York University School of Law. https://www.brennancenter.org/publication/election-day-long-lines-resource-allocation.

Frank, R., and F. Martínez i Coma. 2017. "How Election Dynamics Shape Perceptions of Electoral Integrity." *Electoral Studies* 48: 153–165.

Government Accountability Office. 2014. "Elections: Observations on Wait Times for Voters on Election Day 2012." https://www.gao.gov/products/GAO-14-850.

Grant III, F. 1980. "Reducing Voter Waiting Time." *Interfaces* 10: 18–25.

Hale, Kathleen, Mitchell Brown, and Robert Montjoy. 2015. *Administering Elections: How American Elections Work*. New York, NY: Palgrave.

Hall, Thad, J. Quin Monson, and Kelly D. Patterson. 2007. "Poll Workers and the Vitality of Democracy: An Early Assessment." *PS: Political Science & Politics* 40 (4): 647–654.

Hall, Thad E., J. Quin Monson, and Kelly D. Patterson. 2009. "The Human Dimension of Elections." *Political Research Quarterly* 62 (3): 507–522.

Harris, Andy. 2018. "Lines." Paper presented at the Pre-APSA Workshop: Building Better Election: New Challenges in Electoral Management, Cambridge, MA, August 2018.

Haspell, M., and H. Gibbs Knotts. 2005. "Location, Location, Location: Precinct Placement and the Costs of Voting." *The Journal of Politics* 67: 560–573.

Herron, D. Michael, and Daniel A. Smith. 2017. "Race, Shelby County, and the Voter Information Verification Act in North Carolina." *Florida State University Law Review* 43: 465–475.

Highton, Benjamin. 2006. "Long Lines, Voting Machine Availability, and Turnout: The Case of Franklin County, Ohio in the 2004 Presidential Election." *PS: Political Science and Politics* 39 (1): 65–68.

James, T. S., H. A. Garnett, L. Loeber, and C. van Ham. 2019. "Electoral Management and the Organisational Determinants of Electoral Integrity: Introduction." *International Political Science Review* 40 (3): 295–312.

Karp, N., Alessandro Nai, and Pippa Norris. 2018. "Dial 'F' for Fraud: Explaining Citizens Suspicions About Elections." *Electoral Studies* 53: 11–19.

Kerr, N. 2013. "Popular Evaluations of Election Quality in Africa: Evidence From Nigeria." *Electoral Studies* 32 (4): 819–837.

Kerr, N. 2018. "Election-Day Experiences and Evaluations of Electoral Integrity in Unconsolidated Democracies: Evidence From Nigeria." *Political Studies* 66: 667–686.

Keyssar, Alexander. 2000. *The Right to Vote: The Contested History of Democracy in the United States*. New York, NY: Basic Book.

Kimball, D. 2013. "Why are Voting Lines Longer for Urban Voters?" In *Paper Presented at the Southwestern Social Science Association Conference*, 1–26. New Orleans, LA.http://www.umsl.edu/.

King, Bridgett A. 2017. "Policy and Precinct: Citizen Evaluations and Electoral Confidence." *Social Science Quarterly* 98 (2): 672–689.

Lewis, John, and Archie E. Allen. 1972. "Black Voter Registration Efforts in the South." *Notre Dame Law Review* 48 (1): 105–132.

Maricopa County Recorder. 2016. "Summary Election Report: Final results." https://recorder.maricopa.gov/electionarchives/2016/11-08-2016%20Final%20Summary%20Report.pdf.

Maricopa County Recorder. 2018. "Summary Election Report: Final results." https://recorder.maricopa.gov/electionarchives/2018/11-06-2018%20Final%20Official%20Summary%20Report%20NOV%202018.pdf.

McDonald, Michael P. 2018. "2016 November General Election Turnout Rates " United States Elections Project. Accessed May 31, 2019.

Montjoy, Robert S., and Crista D. Slayton. 2002. "Interdependence and Ethics in Election Administration." *Public Integrity* 4 (3): 195–210.

Mutz, Diana C., and Gregory N. Flemming. 1999. "How Good People Make Bad Collectives: A Social-Psychological Perspective on Public Attitudes Toward Congress." In *Congress and the Decline of Public Trust*, edited by Joseph Cooper, 79–100. Boulder: Westview Press.

National Conference of State Legislatures. 2017. "Electronic Poll Books: E-Poll Books." http://www.ncsl.org/research/elections-and-campaigns/electronic-pollbooks.aspx#What20can20e-pollbooks%20do?

Norden, Lawrence, and Famighetti Christoper. 2015. *America's voting machines at risk*. New York: Brennan Center for Justice. https://www.brennancenter.org/sites/default/files/2019-08/Report_Americas_Voting_Machines_At_Risk.pdf.

Norris, Pippa. 2014. "Why mass perceptions of electoral integrity matter." The Election Integrity Project. Retrieved from file:///C:/Users/bak0020/Downloads/haa-2014-why-electoral-integrity-matters-norris1%20(1).pdf.

Nunnally, Shayla C. 2011. "(Dis)Counting On Democracy To Work: Perceptions of Electoral Fairness in The 2008 Presidential Election." *Journal of Black Studies* 42 (6): 923–942.

Pettigrew, Stephen. 2016. "The Downstream Consequences Of Long Waits: How Lines at The Precinct Reduce Future Turnout." In *Poster Presentation at the 33rd Annual Meeting of the Society for Political Methodology*, 1–42. Houston, TX.

Pettigrew, Stephen. 2017. "The Racial Gap In Wait Times: Why Minority Precincts Are Underserved By Local Election Officials." *Political Science Quarterly* 132: 527–547.

Sances, Michael W., and Charles Stewart III. 2015. "Partisanship and Confidence in the Vote Count: Evidence From U.S. National Elections Since 2000." *Electoral Studies* 40: 176–188.

Spencer, Douglas M., and Zachary S. Markovits. 2010. "Long Lines at Polling Stations? Observations From an Election Day Field Study." *Election Law Journal: Rules, Politics, and Policy* 9 (1): 3–17.

Stein, Robert, Christopher Mann, Charles Stewart, Zachary Birenbaum, Anson Fung, Jed Greenberg, Farhan Kawsar, et al. 2019. "Waiting to Vote in the 2016 Presidential Election: Evidence From a Multi-County Study." *Political Research Quarterly*. early release doi:10.1177/1065912919832374.

Stewart, Charles. 2013a. "2012 Survey of the Performance of American Elections. Harvard Dataverse." https://dataverse.harvard.edu/dataset.xhtml?persistentId=hdl:1902.1/21624.

Stewart, Charles. 2013b. "2008 Survey of the Performance of American Elections." Harvard Dataverse. https://dataverse.harvard.edu/file.xhtml?fileId=2433003&version=1.0.

Stewart, Charles. 2015. "2014 Survey of the Performance of American Elections. Harvard Dataverse." https://dataverse.harvard.edu/dataset.xhtml?persistentId=doi:10.7910/DVN/28979.

Stewart, Charles. 2017. "2016 Survey of the Performance of American Elections." Harvard Dataverse. https://dataverse.harvard.edu/dataset.xhtml?persistentId=doi:10.7910/DVN/Y38VIQ.

Stewart, Charles. 2018. "Voter Confidence in the 2018 Election: So Long to the Winner's Effect?" *Election Updates*. https://electionupdates.caltech.edu/2018/12/19/voter-confidence-in-the-2018-election-so-long-to-the-winners-effect/.

Stewart III, C., and S. Ansolabehere. 2013. "Waiting in line to vote." White paper. https://www.eac.gov/documents/2017/02/24/waiting-in-line-to-vote-white-paper-stewart-ansolabehere/.

United States Presidential Commission on Election Administration. 2014. The American Voting Experience: Report and Recommendations of the Presidential Commission on Election Administration. https://www.eac.gov/election-officials/pcea/.

Vondracek, Christopher. 2018. "Auditor Says Internet Connection Caused Voting Delays." *Rapid City Journal*, June 6. https://rapidcityjournal.com/news/auditor-says-internet-connection-issues-caused-voting-delays/article_d69d7936-956e-58c4-849d-28dbb9a9bd26.html.

Yang, M., Theodore Allen, Michael Fry, and David Kelton. 2013. "The Call for Equity: Simulation Optimization Models to Minimize the Range of Waiting Times." *IIE Transactions* 45: 781–795.

Appendices

Table A1. SPAE questions and coding for election administration variables.

Variable name	Survey question	Responses and coding
Individual confidence	How confident are you that your vote in the General Election was counted as you intended?	4-Very Confident 3-Somewhat Confident 2-Not too Confident 1-Not at all Confident
Local confidence	How confident are you that votes in your county or city were counted as voters intended?	4-Very Confident 3-Somewhat Confident 2-Not too Confident 1-Not at all Confident
State confidence	Now, think about vote counting throughout. How confident are you that votes in were counted as voters intended?	4-Very Confident 3-Somewhat Confident 2-Not too Confident 1-Not at all Confident
National confidence	Finally, think about vote counting throughout the country. How confident are you that votes nationwide were counted as voters intended?	4-Very Confident 3-Somewhat Confident 2-Not too Confident 1-Not at all Confident
Wait	How long did you wait to vote before casting your ballot	1-none 2–0 to 10 3-10-30 4-31-60 5-more than 60 Recode 0-no wait to 30 min 1-more than 30 min
Registration problems	Was there a problem with your voter registration when you tried to vote?	1-Yes 0-No
Equipment or Ballot problems	Did you encounter any problems with the voting equipment or the ballot that may have interfered with your ability to cast your vote as intended?	1-Yes 0-No
Early voting	How did you vote this election?	1-Early 0-Election Day
Gender	Are you male or female?	1-Male 0-Female
Age	In what year were you born?Note: Age was calculated by subtracting the election year from the year reported.	1-18-24 2-25-34 3-35-44 4-45-54 5-55-64 6-65+
Income	Thinking back over the last year, what was your family's annual income?	1-Less than $25,000 2-$25,000-$39,999 3-$40,000-$59,999 4-$60,000-$79,999 5-$80,000-$99,999 6-$100,00 or greater
Educational attainment	What is the highest level of education you have completed?	1-No High School 2-High School Graduate 3-Some College 4–2 Year Degree 5-4Year Degree 6-Post-Graduate Degree
Race	What racial or ethnic group best describes you?	White, non-Hispanic Black, non-Hispanic Hispanic, alone or in combination Asian

(Continued)

Table A1. Continued.

Variable name	Survey question	Responses and coding
Party Identification	Generally speaking, do you think of yourself as a … ?	Republican Democrat Independent

Note: All "I don't know" and "I don't remember" responses were coded as missing.

Table B1. Ordered logistic regression models of factors affecting local confidence.

Variable	Model 1	Model 2	Model 3
Wait	−.177 (.067)**	−.162 (.061)**	−.162 (.061)**
Wait * Black	.084 (.154)		
Registration Problems	−.649 (.101)***	−.654 (.101)***	−.660 (.109)***
Registration Problem * Black			.074 (.272)
Equipment and Ballot Problems	−1.364 (.112)***	−1.394 (.118)***	−.660 (.109)***
Equipment and Ballot Problems * Black		.325 (.378)	
Early Voter	−.074 (.043) ‡	−.074 (.043) ‡	−.074 (.043) ‡
Black	−.276 (.060)***	−.271 (.057)***	−.268 (.057)***
Hispanic	.030 (.121)	.030 (.121)	.029 (.121)
Asian	.096 (.134)	.095 (.134)	.094 (.134)
Age	.010 (.001)	−.010 (.001)***	.010 (.001)***
Income	.017 (.005)**	.017 (.005)**	.017 (.005)**
Education	.048 (.012)***	.084 (.012)***	.084 (.012)***
Male	.094 (.032)**	.094 (.032)**	.094 (.032)**
Democrat	.135 (.040)**	.135 (.040)**	.135 (.040)**
Independent	−.179 (.040)***	−.179 (.040)***	−.179 (.040)***
Year 2012	−.359 (.039)***	−.358 (.039)***	−.358 (.039)***
Year 2014	−.115 (.041)**	−.115 (.041)**	−.115 (.041)**
Cut Point 1	−3.645 (.147)	−3.645 (.147)	−3.644 (.147)
Cut Point 2	2.491 (.141)	−2.491 (.141)	−2.490 (.141)
Cut Point 3	−.333 (.139)	−.335 (.139)	−.334 (.139)
N	17,341	17,341	17,341
Log Likelihood	−14785.433	−14785.213	−14785.546
Psuedo R^2	.0320	.0320	.0320
χ^2	978.41, 66 df, $p > .000$	978.85, 66 df, $p > .000$	978.18, 66 df, $p > .000$

Note: Ordered logistic regression coefficients with standard errors in parentheses.
***$p < .001$.
**$p < .01$.
*$p < .05$.
‡$p < .10$.

Table C1. Ordered logistic regression models of factors affecting state confidence.

Variable	Model 1	Model 2
Wait	−.094 (.059)	−.094 (.060)
Registration Problems	−.587 (.100)***	−.589 (.108)***
Registration Problems * Black		.033 (.276)
Equipment and Ballot Problems	−1.059 (.116)***	−1.047 (.111)***
Equipment and Ballot Problems * Black	.148 (.381)	
Early Voter	−.071 (.040) ‡	−.071 (.040) ‡
Black	−.254 (.055)***	−.252 (.056)***
Hispanic	.122 (.118)	.121 (.118)
Asian	.159 (.129)	.158 (.129)
Age	.000 (.001)	.000 (.001)
Income	.013 (.004)**	.013 (.004)**
Education	.048 (.011)***	.048 (.011)***
Male	.044 (.030)	.044 (.030)
Democrat	.190 (.038)***	.190 (.038)***
Independent	−.120 (.038)**	−.121 (.038)**
Year 2012	−.281 (.037)***	−.281 (.037)***
Year 2014	−.226 (.038)***	−.266 (.038)***
Cut Point 1	−4.262 (.137)	−4.261 (.137)
Cut Point 2	−2.891 (.132)	−2.890 (.132)
Cut Point 3	−.772 (.130)	−.771 (.130)
N	17,245	17,245
Log Likelihood	−17070.899	−17070.958
Psuedo R^2	.0323	.0323
χ^2	1138.58, 66 df, $p > .000$	1138.44, 66 df, $p > .000$

Note: Ordered logistic regression coefficients with standard errors in parentheses.
***$p < .001$.
**$p < .01$.
*$p < .05$.
‡$p < .10$.

Disability and election administration in the United States: barriers and improvements

April A. Johnson and Sierra Powell

ABSTRACT
Although people with disabilities are considerably less likely to vote than those without a disability, empirical explanations as to why remain underdeveloped. The present study investigates whether this discrepancy in turnout rates is directly related to voting procedures. Analyzing data from the Cooperative Congressional Election Study, we assess the ways in which people with disabilities are disenfranchised by election administration barriers. Specifically, we identify how experiences with voter registration, voter identification regulations, and methods of ballot submission impact those with and without disabilities. Also considered is the degree to which disability affects one's own political competence and political interest. Reflecting on these findings, we offer recommendations for reducing such electoral hurdles and providing pathways by which comprehensive political incorporation of all individuals with disabilities might be achieved.

Exercising the right to vote cuts to the core of what it means to participate in a democratic system of government. Indeed, the extent to which the populace successfully casts a ballot in a duly constituted election provides a measure of the health of that democratic system. Here we examine the health of American democracy through the lens of citizens with disabilities. Many people with disabilities experience barriers as they work to complete daily life activities, nevertheless voting. Whether or not people with disabilities are able to participate in politics in the United States provides a strict test for how well American democracy is functioning in practice. Further, as Michelle Bishop of the National Disability Rights Network has noted, "our vote is a big part of making sure that we continue to move forward and that we're respecting the civil and human rights of people with disabilities" (Haelle 2018).

In any election, drivers of turnout include contextual factors, such as the candidates and salient issues of that year and also administrative factors, such as how easy or hard it is for potential voters to access the franchise. Consider one notable example from 2016. Roughly one year before the 2016 election, candidate Donald Trump came under fire for mocking Serge Kovaleski, a *New York Times* reporter who has joint condition arthrogryposis. This event placed a spotlight on disability politics during what would eventually be a race between Republican nominee Donald Trump and Democratic nominee Hillary Clinton. Former President Bill Clinton would reference Trump's Kovaleski event in his convention speech and the Clinton campaign would later capitalize on the sound bite in their advertising (Carmon 2016). Administratively, from the Voting Rights Act in 1965 to the Help America Vote Act in 2002, national legislation has sought to reduce procedural barriers to the participation of people with disabilities in U.S. elections.[1] Yet despite these efforts, such barriers remain. In a small, qualitative study of focus group participants who identified as having an intellectual or developmental disability, one participant suggested of the 2016 General Election that "[m]aybe if they had more places with wheelchair ramps that would make it easier for people with disabilities" (Friedman 2018).

Beyond national pieces of legislation that have attempted to aid people with disabilities, there are many aspects of election administration that may adversely affect voter turnout of both people with and people without a disability. From voter registration in advance of an election, to voter identification requirements at the polls, to the many available methods of ballot submission, this project considers whether election procedures in and of themselves impose differential effects on persons with and without disabilities. Our present analysis of administrative impediments are further expounded by examining the role of these barriers on individual perceptions of the voting process and of their own political competence.

Prior literature

The 2010 U.S. Census estimates that nearly 1 in 5 Americans live with a disability (Brault 2012). Indeed, a more recent report of the Annual Disability Statistics Compendium shows that the size of the civilian disability population in the United States has been slowly increasing since 2008, the earliest year shown (Kraus et al. 2018). The aging of the baby boomer generation is swelling the population of people with disabilities in the United States, as are longer life spans relative to previous decades (Predit 2009). There is also evidence to suggest that measures of impairment and the conceptualization of disabilities by governmental agencies, such as the U.S. Social Security Administration, have become more nuanced over time.[2] Thus, the rise in individuals reporting disabilities may additionally relate to improved measurement and reporting practices. With these demographic changes, people with disabilities are becoming a much larger and more visible portion of the electorate than in decades past. Although proportionally the ranks of people with disabilities are expanding, this group's political clout may not be, as the political behaviour literature has firmly established that voting levels among people with disabilities are dismal in both the United States and in other countries.

Studies examining American elections over the past several decades have consistently documented the gap in voting participation between people with various types of disabilities and those without them (Schur and Kruse 2000; Schur et al. 2002; Schur, Shields, and Schriner 2005; Hall and Alvarez 2012; Schur and Adya 2013; Miller and Powell 2016). Schur, Ameri, and Adya (2017) present data from the 2012 U.S. General Election, documenting an overall disability gap of 5.7%. Even higher gaps were observed for particular types of disabilities, such as those with cognitive disabilities who experienced a gap of 17.7% relative to those without a cognitive disability (2017). In the 2014 midterm election, the Pew Research Center found a 5% turnout gap between people with a disability as compared to people with no disability (Igielnik 2016). Further, Pew found that "[a]mong those who did not turn up to vote on Election Day 2014, 20% of those with disabilities pointed to an illness or disability that 'made it too difficult to vote'" (Igielnik 2016). Perhaps even more startling, data from the most recent 2016 U.S. General Election suggests a 12% voting gap between those reporting and not reporting a disability (Powell and Johnson 2019). While a clear pattern exists here, it should be noted that the degree to which disability affects political behaviour more broadly depends on what aspects of political incorporation are examined (e.g. voting, displaying a political sticker, making a political comment online) and how disability is measured (e.g. physical impairment, mental difficulties, disability benefits, employment status). We discuss the difficult task of operationalizing disability in the subsequent methodology section.

While much of the research on disability has stemmed from American electoral con-texts, hosts of global researchers have begun to publish on the subject as well. Data from the Netherlands, where nearly one in eight citizens have long-term disabilities (Van Hees, Boeije, and de Putter 2019), documented that people with physical and learn-ing impairments experienced particularly low turnout. Administrative barriers related to information gathering, using one's cognitive capabilities to understand and process this information, and arriving at one's polling location were particularly influential factors in such dampened engagement (Van Hees, Boeije, and de Putter 2019). Data from the European Social Survey (ESS) again confirms people with disabilities to be less likely to vote than people without disabilities but specifically indicates that people with disabilities who felt discriminated against were even less likely to turn out to vote than those who did not feel discriminated against (Mattila and Papageorgio 2016; Reher 2018). Curiously, evi-dence has indicated that some European election administration measures adopted in order to boost turnout, such as advanced voting and mail-in ballots, instead depressed turnout amongst those with poor functional ability (Wass et al. 2017). Contemporary scholars clearly demonstrate that having a disability affects one's approach towards the political system. Yet, despite these observed effects and the rich political science literature related to election administration, these lines of research have existed largely parallel to one another. Clearly more empirical research is needed on the interplay between election administration and people with disabilities in both the United States and internationally (Priestley et al. 2016).

Relevant election administration measures which affect voting include provisions such as same-day voter registration, opportunities to vote (in-person) in advance of Election Day, opportunities to vote by mail, and voter identification requirements. With regard to same day voter registration, also called Election Day registration, only 16 states[3] and the District of Columbia have such legislation (National Conference of State Legislatures 2019a). The United States is not necessarily unique in requiring voters to register prior to voting, but it is exceptional in that the responsibility to do so falls solely on the individual. Indeed, scholars have long known state registration laws to depress turnout, particularly for citizens of lower socioeconomic status (Rosenstone and Wolfinger 1978; Highton 1997; Hershey 2009). Along these lines, one study examining the 2012 election found that roughly 1 in 4 unregistered people with disabilities cited disability or illness as the reason for their lack of registration (Schur, Adya, and Kruse 2013).

To be fair, significant strides have been made to enfranchise those with disabilities. Initiatives such as curbside voting in Texas (Broadway 2018) and "fast pass" procedures in Georgia (Georgia Secretary of State 2018) and other areas aim to expedite the voting process for those with limited capabilities. Nevertheless, research shows people with disabilities to experience greater levels of polling place difficulties than those without a disability, especially with regard to reading or seeing the ballot, figuring out how to vote or operating voting machinery, getting inside the polling place, finding or getting to the polling place, and waiting in line (Schur, Ameri, and Adya 2017). Because of these and other difficulties, "[t]he anticipation of issues, based on prior experience, can create a 'chilling effect' for potential voters who may not want to face an inaccessible polling place or hostile poll workers again" (Belt 2016, 1496). The present state of research, then, examines the extent to which people with disabilities may be likely to take advantage of various convenience voting measures. Several studies have suggested mail-in or absentee voting to be a particularly promising avenue, as states work toward closing the disability turnout gap (Miller and Powell 2016; Schur, Ameri, and Adya 2017).

Regarding voter identification requirements, 35 states have laws requiring voters to show identification in advance of voting (National Conference of State Legislatures 2019b) Because some individuals lack the identification required in these states, political behaviour scholars have found voter identification requirements to be associated with modest levels of depressed turnout (Muhlhausen and Sikich 2007; Alvarez, Bailey, and Katz 2008; Erikson and Minnite 2009). Recently, the literature has argued these depressive effects to be particularly pronounced among racial and ethnic minorities (Hajnal, Lajevardi, and Nielson 2017; Barreto et al. 2018). Like many racial and ethnic minority groups, the ranks of people with disabilities are concentrated among lower socioeconomic classes (Ross and Bateman 2018). More pointed research is needed to examine whether people with disabilities, in particular, are disproportionally affected by voter identification laws (Hershey 2009).

Predictors of one's participation in politics is, of course, not limited to contextual factors or election administration procedures. One's own attachment to politics has a role to play as well. Canonical work by Campbell et al. (1960) and subsequently replicated by Lewis-Beck et al. (2008) documented a positive relationship between political interest and voting. In later years, Verba, Scholzman, and Brady highlight psychological resources a part of their civic voluntarism model, noting political interest as a measure of "*wanting* to take part … is also related to *being able* to take part" (Verba, Schlozman, and Brady 1995, 494, emphasis in original). Relatedly, the literature has shown that people with greater resources tend to be more politically engaged and also more politically knowledgeable (Verba, Schlozman, and Brady 1995; Carpini and Keeter 1996). While research regarding individual-level motivations to participate in politics is abundant, work specifically dedicated to investigating such motivations among persons with disabilities is scant. Perhaps due to its infancy, conclusive findings related to disability status, political interest, knowledge of government, and political efficacy have remained opaque (Schur and Adya 2013; Powell and Johnson 2019).

Hypotheses

Globally, those with disabilities represent a large and growing population, making the lack of empirical insight into their experiences with voting and with the political system quite perplexing. The present study approaches documented voting gaps between individuals with and without disabilities by probing the extent to which administrative barriers depress participatory behaviours. Accordingly, we present four hypotheses. *H1* speaks to the role of disability status across various forms of political involvement.

> H1: Individuals with disabilities are less participatory in the American political system than are individuals without disabilities. Those with disabilities are less likely to vote, less likely to be registered to vote, and less likely to engage in election-related activities, both in-person and online, than those without disabilities.

In the United States, one of the greatest barriers to casting a vote is first getting registered. Unlike in Great Britain and other countries (Chen and Rosenberg 2009), registration is not an automatic process once an individual reaches voting age. To reduce some of the information costs associated with registration Congress passed the Motor Voter Act in 1994. This Act allows one to register to vote at a local Department of Motor Vehicles agency, most often during the procurement of a driver's license. While this method of voter registration remains extremely popular (Knack 1995; Naifeh 2015), it is clear that those with disabilities, whose limited mobility, vision, hearing, cognitive functioning, or otherwise might prevent them from driving (Marshall et al. 2005), might not take advantage of this administrative shortcut.

Furthermore, if voting and involvement with politics is habitual (Campbell et al. 1960; Fowler 2006), we speculate that distance from the political system early on should carry reciprocal effects for those with disabilities. Political behaviourists have generally found that those who are disengaged from the voting process are also likely to disengage with other political activities, such as attending to political news, displaying a campaign sign, or discussing political news (Norris 2004; Lewis-Beck et al. 2008). We expect to observe these same patterns for those with disabilities. Consider, for example, if one experiences problems physically accessing the polling place or accessing political news due to disability we might also expect for these individuals to experience low levels of political efficacy, furthering their distance from the political system (Schur, Shields, and Schriner 2003).

> H2: Individuals with disabilities are more likely than individuals without disabilities to make use of convenience voting procedures. Specifically, disability status should be positively associated with same-day registration, early voting, and voting by mail.

Significant strides have been made by election officials to reduce the barriers to voting, particularly as it affects disadvantaged populations (Root and Kennedy 2018). One of these measures, same-day registration, allows constituents to register to vote on Election Day at one's polling location. If those with disabilities are in fact less likely to be previously registered to vote (*H1*), then we may expect this group to instead see higher rates of same-day registration. After clearing the primary hurdle of voter registration, submission of one's ballot remains an additional task. To individuals with physical or mental limitations, whose chronic conditions may require frequent doctor's visits, the simple act of day-to-day self-care presents difficulties (Dunlop, Hughes, and Manheim 1997). On top of these ever-present barriers, the act of voting itself can require considerable physical and mental challenges as one secures transportation, waits in line at the polls, and works to navigate voting technology. Because of the barriers they face, those with disabilities, more so than other populations, should find it easier to submit a ballot on their own time, according to their schedule, and potentially from the convenience of their own home. For this reason, voting via mail and voting early (i.e. before Election Day) are expected to be especially popular for those with disabilities.

> H3: Individuals with disabilities are more likely than individuals without disabilities to encounter negative experiences at the polls. Those with disabilities are more likely to report problems when attempting to vote, problems related to voter identification requirements, lengthier voting times, and perceptions of intimidation within the voting process than those without disabilities.

As noted in *HI*, we argue that individuals with disabilities may find it more difficult to obtain a government-issued form of identification, such as a driver's license. Indeed, Curry et al. (2017) find that only 33% of adolescents with autism spectrum disorder obtain a driver's license, as compared with 83.5% of their peers. This is problematic for an increasing number of disabled voters whose state election laws require such government-issued documentation. In addition to the potential for problems at the polls, particularly that of voter identification, people with and without disabilities may experience problems with lengthy wait times. Even minimal to moderate waiting times could be problematic for people with disabilities as they may, for example, become discouraged that accessible machines are not up and running or that there are not available chairs for accommodation (Self Advocates Becoming Empowered 2017). For these reasons, we posit that those with disabilities may tend to experience more difficulties while voting relative to those without a disability.

Given physical immobility and other health-related issues, individuals with disabilities may struggle to negotiate the environment of their designated polling location. Parking lots with inadequate wheelchair ramps, polling queues that lack seating or hand rails, and complexities related to the digitized nature of many voting machines can present impediments to casting a vote (Schur, Ameri, and Adya 2017). Such struggles, we believe, are likely to impose a sense of self-consciousness or a heightened awareness of one's disability. Disability status therefore may predict feelings of incompetence and/or intimidation in such a public space.

> H4: Individuals with disabilities are more likely than individuals without disabilities to report detachment from the American political system. Disability status is expected to be negatively associated with political interest and political knowledge.

Similar to *HI*, it is believed that the pronounced voting gap between those with and without disabilities correlates with detachment from contemporary political actors and events. As noted by many philosophers, as well as political behaviourists (Dalton 2017), interest in politics and knowledge of government are the foundation of participation in civic life. We have suggested that formal administrative barriers to voting, such as those related to registration and voter identification, disenfranchise those with disabilities. Yet informal or latent barriers to participation, particularly a lack of motivation or provocation, may also play a role in political detachment. We propose that the established voting gap between those with and without disabilities may stem from lower levels of political interest and knowledge amongst this group. Although it is outside of the realm of this project to identify whether disinterest in the political system *causes* disengagement or vice versa, we do acknowledge the potential for reciprocal effects.

Sources of data and measures

In order to examine the influence of election administration on the political activities of people with disabilities, we draw on data from the 2012 and 2016 Cooperative Congressional Election Study (CCES). These two cross-sectional datasets are administered by YouGov/Polimetrix and represent a large, nationally stratified sample of individuals in the United States. In the quantitative analyses that follow, our independent variable is disability reported at the individual level. In accordance with our four main hypotheses, dependent variables include: voter turnout, registering to vote, same-day registration, campaign activity, online political engagement (2016 only), voting early, voting by mail/ absentee ballot, problems voting (including those with identification requirement), time spent voting, perceptions of intimidation at the polls, political interest, and political knowledge. All analyses were weighted by the CCES Common Content sample weight for that dataset and were limited to respondents 18 years of age or older and those reporting U.S. citizenship. Detailed question wording and coding of all variables can be found in Appendix A.

Disability status

Disability rights advocates, government agencies, medical practitioners, and scholarly researchers alike wrestle with the challenge of defining disability status, and the concept remains notoriously complex (Friedman and Owen 2017). To agencies like the World Health Organization (WHO) and the Centers for Disease Control and Prevention (CDC), disability status encompasses a broad range of conditions and states. Based largely on WHO standards, the CDC defines disability as any mental or physical impairment that complicates or impairs one's day-to-day activities and interactions (2017). More specifically, WHO notes three categories to which disability status can apply: impairments, activity limitations, and participation restrictions (2019). Implicit in the WHO standard is the belief that disability status is not solely a condition related to one's health, but an issue concerning one's interaction and connectedness within society (2019). Indeed, this definition lends itself well to the study of how disability status relates to voting and election administration. In the United States, the Americans with Disabilities Act (1990) has clarified further that those with disabilities include not only individuals with a "physical or mental impairment that substantially limits one or more major life activity" (1990), but those who have a prior *record* of such impairment, even if not current.

Perhaps due to the breadth and plasticity of disability status, many contemporary researchers (Igielnik 2016; Miller and Powell 2016; Schur, Ameri, and Adya 2017) have been inclined toward more simplified, binary operationalizations of the construct. We follow this practice- in part due to the nature of CCES data- in the measure of our independent variable. Those who indicated being "permanently disabled" were coded as 1 and all other employment statuses were coded as 0 (see Appendix A). Accordingly, we find that approximately 6% of the 2012 CCES sample ($N = 3,269$) and also 6% of the 2016 CCES sample report having a disability ($N = 3,829$).

Impeded by shortcomings in available data,[4] we acknowledge two limitations in the aforementioned measurement strategy. First, general disability status does not capture the nuanced nature types of disabilities such as physical mobility as compared to visual impairment, and so on. It is simply a binary variable. Second, disability is operationalized via self-reported employment status. Although the bulk of disability research in political science analyzes disability in the same manner (see Miller and Powell 2016; Powell and Johnson 2019), we recognize the need to tease out the effects of employment from disability status. As such, we include three additional comparison groups in the present project: 1) those working full-time 2) those who are retired and 3) those who fall into an "other" employment category. All were dummy coded such that a 1 indicates the respondent reported that employment status and a zero indicates any other response. Full-time individuals represent those who indicated their employment status as working "full-time" (N = 18,503 in 2012, N = 27,283 in 2016). Retired individuals indicated their current employment status as "retired" (N = 14,287 in 2012, N = 12,764 in 2016). The third category representing "other" are individuals who selected "unemployed," "temporarily laid off," "homemaker," working "part-time", "student", or "other" as their current employment status (N = 17,566 in 2012, N = 19,200 in 2016).

Dependent variables

Despite simplified legal definitions and binary measures, disability remains a broad construct. Not only are there varying types of disabilities, but varying manifestations and extents to which persons experience such disabilities. To gain some leverage on the complexity of disability identity, we employ a range of behavioural and attitudinal variables as dependent variables. To test *H1*, we examine the effect of disability status on voter turnout, registering to vote, campaign activity, and online political engagement. In terms of election administration, registering to vote signifies the first barrier to enfranchisement in the voting process. This variable was gauged in the CCES post-election wave and simply asked respondents whether they were registered (1) or not registered (0). While voter turnout remains the hallmark measure of political behaviour, we recognize that other forms of political engagement can be quite influential in affecting electoral outcomes and expressing one's beliefs about government. Specifically, we aggregate individual levels of campaign activity according to four indicators: attending local political meetings, displaying political signage, working for a candidate/campaign, and donating money to a candidate/campaign. Individual campaign activity totals ranged from 0 (engaging in none of these activities) to 4 (engaging in all 4 activities). We also assess online political engagement by aggregating five indicators: posting a story about politics, posting a comment about politics, reading/watching a political story/video, following a political event, and forwarding a story/photo/link about politics to friends (see Appendix A for full variable details and coding). Individual online engagement totals ranged from 0 (engaging in none of these activities) to 5 (engaging in all 5 activities). Although measures of online engagement are only available within the 2016 CCES, this variable provides an interesting contrast to more traditional forms of electoral behaviour.

    H2 relates to convenience voting measures, which we define here as same-day registration, early voting, and voting by mail. As suggested, convenience measures have been implemented in order to reduce the costs associated with voting, thus making the process more inclusive. It should be noted, however, that convenience measures vary according to state laws. All states allow for absentee ballots submitted by mail, many states have some form of early voting, and only a select few allow same-day registration.

CCES measures of same-day registration, early voting, and vote by mail are binary, meaning an individual either reported engaging in this form of convenience voting (1) or they did not (0).

Our third hypothesis examines the experience of disability status at the polls. For those who cast a vote in-person, we identify whether individuals with disabilities reported a general problem in voting (1 = yes, 0 = no). If a problem was indicated, CCES respondents could further indicate if the problem related to voter identification requirements (1 = yes, 0 = no). In *H3*, we also examine the length of time an individual spent voting (1 = none, 2 = less than 10 min, 3 = 10–30 min, 4 = 31 min to 1 h, 5 = more than 1 h) and perceptions of intimidation at the polls (1 = yes, 0 = no). While most of the administrative barriers we consider in this article are quite formal (e.g. registration, time spent voting), perceptions of intimidation provide a particularly subjective and intimate glimpse into one's (negative) interaction with the American voting system. This variable is informative in aiding our efforts, despite its availability solely within the 2016 CCES module.

The final hypothesis we test at present, *H4*, considers the potential for electoral barriers and/or disenfranchisement to impose an impact individual levels of political interest and political knowledge. Interest in politics ranges from following what's going on in government and public affairs "hardly at all" (1) to following what's going on in government and public affairs "most of the time" (4). In both 2012 and 2016, political knowledge is gauged by aggregating responses to two factual questions: Which party currently has a majority of seats in the House and which party currently has a majority of seats in the Senate? Individual knowledge totals range from 0 (both incorrect responses) to 2 (both correct responses).

Control variables

All inferential models within our results section employ standard demographic and political controls. Demographic control variables include: age, age-squared,[5] gender, marital status, race, ethnicity, education, income, religiosity, and geographic location (south). Besides their inclusion in most political behaviour models, age (Schur and Adya 2013), gender (Bureau of Labor Statistics 2018), race, and ethnicity (Ross and Bateman 2018) have all been shown to correlate with disability status itself. For instance, Native Americans and African-Americans tend to have the highest reported rates of disability (2018), as do women and older individuals (Bureau of Labor Statistics 2018). As such, we include dummy variables for female, white, black, and Hispanic.

The United States remains an outlier among developed nations in terms of its high levels of religiosity and religious affiliation (Fahmy 2018). Moreover, these factors play a continual role in shaping American political attitudes and electoral outcomes (Layman 1997; Wald and Calhoun-Brown 2014). Here we include a 4-category measure of religiosity within all models (see Appendix). Likewise, income and education have a longstanding positive relationship with political participation (Campbell et al. 1960; Schlozman, Verba, and Brady 2012) as well as a negative relationship with disability status (Ross and Bateman 2018). These factors are particularly relevant control variables at present, given our employment-based measure of disability. For these reasons we control for one's highest level of education completed and their family's annual income. We further include a dummy variable to capture whether an individual lives within the south[6] due to this region's concentration of individuals with disabilities (Powell and Johnson 2019), as well as its history of discriminatory voting practices and decreased levels of voter turnout more generally (Hajnal, Lajevardi, and Nielson 2017). In our two samples we observe that nearly 30% of individuals reporting a disability live in the south (see Table B1).

With regard to political controls, all models factor in an individual's partisan identification, ideological orientation, strength of partisan attachment, strength of ideological orientation, interest in politics, and level of political knowledge (see Appendix A for question wording). Party identification and political ideology are widely considered to not only affect participation, but also to help individuals conceptualize their relationship with politics (Campbell et al. 1960; Bartels 2000; Green, Palmquist, and Schickler 2004; Lewis-Beck et al. 2008; Huddy, Mason, and Aarøe 2015). Previously we noted political interest and political knowledge as important predecessors of political engagement. For these reasons, we treat political interest and political knowledge as both dependent variables (H4) and also as key control variables in our other models (H1, H2, and H3).

For models related to early voting and same day voter registration we acknowledge that these opportunities are not available in all states. Thus, for these analyses we include dummy variables which control for whether the state an individual resides in offered in-person early voting and/or same day registration (coded as a 1) or whether the state did not offer such opportunities (coded as 0). It is important to note that the CCES measure of early voting specifically asks individuals whether they voted early *in-person*, as opposed to voting early via absentee ballot. Therefore, our state-level control for early voting only captures in-person early voting opportunities. In 2012, 33 U.S. states offered in-person early voting and in 2016 37 U.S. states offered in-person early voting. Same day registration was available in 9 U.S. states in 2012 and in 12 U.S. states in 2016. No state-level control was included for models analyzing vote by mail. In the U.S., all states offer some form of absentee voting, thus there is no state-level variation to control for with regard to this dependent variable.

Results

Consistent with a long line of disability research, data from the CCES indicates that this group was markedly absent from the polls in both the 2012 and 2016 General Elections (Figure 1). While turnout was down in 2016 amongst all employment categories, individuals who reported having a permanent disability were on average 5.6% less likely to vote in the last two General Elections than those working full-time and on average 8.8% less likely to vote than those who were retired. Turnout among unemployed people reporting disabilities was also lower than that of those in the "other" employment category (e.g. homemakers, part-time workers, students), though the observed difference is quite small. Fully specified logistic regression models in which all demographic and political variables are controlled for find that disability exerts a significant, negative effect on voting in both 2012 ($p < 0.001$) and 2016 ($p < 0.001$). Among CCES respondents who reported not voting, a follow up question was asked to gauge one's main reason for failing to do so. A full 30% of persons with permanent disabilities in 2016 and 37% of persons with permanent disabilities in 2012 specifically cited "disability or illness" as the main reason why they did not cast a vote. Even when controlling for potential confounding individual-level

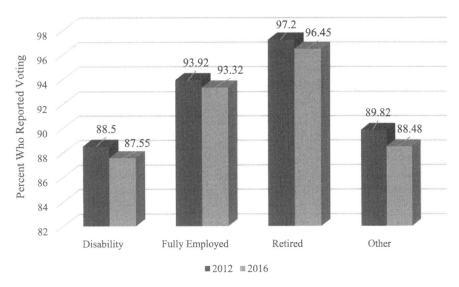

Figure 1. Voter Turnout by employment status.

variables such as income, age, education, and partisanship, individuals with disabilities were more likely to cite disability or illness as their main impediment to voting ($p < 0.001$ in both 2012 and 2016).

Registering oneself to vote before Election Day is a substantial hurdle to political enfranchisement, which, as Table 1 illustrates, appears to disproportionately affect those with disabilities. Compared with individuals working full-time (the excluded category), individuals citing permanent disabilities were less likely to be registered in both 2016 ($p = 0.051$) and in 2012 ($p = 0.000$). Our results reveal that among the 2012 CCES sample of those indicating permanent disability as their employment status, 92% were registered to vote, compared to 96% of those working full-time. The 2016 CCES sample indicates that 86% of disabled individuals were registered to vote, compared with 94% of those working full-time. See also Table B2 and Table B3 within the Appendix for full models of these analyses.

Table 1. Effect of employment status on political involvement.

Predictor	Registered to vote B (S. E.)	Campaign activity B (S. E.)	Online engagement B (S. E.)
2012			
Has disability	−0.372 (0.081)***	0.040 (0.054)	–
Retired	0.001 (0.094)	−0.088 (0.041)*	–
Other	−0.193 (0.054)***	0.143 (0.028)***	–
N	34940	35015	–
2016			
Has disability	−0.180 (0.092)	0.080 (0.049)	0.201 (0.047)***
Retired	−0.268 (0.109)*	−0.013 (0.039)	0.049 (0.045)
Other	−0.315 (0.057)***	0.094 (0.027)**	0.102 (0.026)***
N	42334	42568	29449

Note: A logistic regression was used to derive results for voter registration model. Two separate ordered logistic regressions were used to derive results for campaign activity (an aggregated 4-question scale) and online engagement (an aggregated 5-question scale). Models are weighted and include full demographic and political controls. All models include individuals working full-time as the excluded category. Significant at *$p < 0.05$, **$p < 0.01$, ***$p < 0.001$.

In contrast, however, persons with labour precluding disabilities are no less likely to engage in campaign activities than are those working full-time ($p = 0.101$ in 2016, $p = 0.459$ in 2012) (Table 1). Likewise, our analysis of disability status and online engagement reveal that unemployed persons with disabilities were even *more* likely than full-time workers to follow, post, share, and comment on political stories or videos online in 2016 ($p < 0.001$). Here, a full 20% of individuals with disabilities reported engaging in either four or five forms of online political activity. While the results within Table 1 identify those working full-time as the excluded category, re-specification of the model to include the "other" employment group as the excluded category (not shown) produces similar results. Compared with those in the "other" employment category (e.g. homemakers, students), those reporting disabilities were still more likely to engage in online political activity in 2016 ($p = 0.036$).

Our dependent variables of campaign activity and online engagement each represent scales composed of multiple questions. Figures 2 and 3 provide a breakdown of responses to these scaled questions according to employment category. Similar patterns of campaign involvement can be observed across activity type and across employment category (Figure 2). For brevity, Figure 2 only highlights 2016 campaign activities, though 2012 data produce nearly identical results. Working for a campaign or candidate along with attending a political meeting or rally remained the least popular forms of political involvement. In contrast, displaying a sign and donating money are perhaps more accessible, straightforward channels for political activism. Such reduced barriers to political enfranchisement are advantageous to individuals who experience issues of physical mobility and/or cognitive limitations. Indeed, 17% of unemployed persons with disabilities in 2016 reported donating money to a candidate or campaign and roughly 15% reported displaying a political sign or sticker.

Likewise, online engagement with political content is arguably one of the most obstacle-free methods by which disadvantaged or marginalized populations can express their

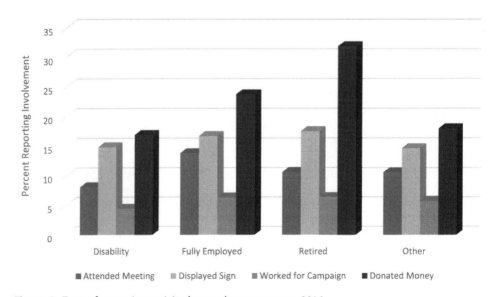

Figure 2. Type of campaign activity by employment status, 2016.

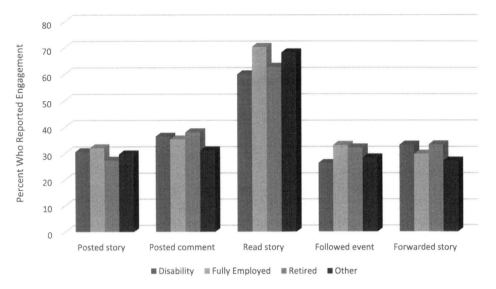

Figure 3. Type of online political engagement by employment status, 2016.

opinions. Figure 3 provides detailed summary statistics regarding employment status and types of online engagement. Across all groups, reading a political story was the most popular form of online engagement, followed by posting a comment about politics. While this data is only available within the 2016 CCES, we observe that nearly 31% of those who reported permanent disabilities also reported posting a story, video, or link about politics and 33% of the same group reported forwarding political content.

Results within Table 1 paint an incongruent picture of disability status and inclusion within the political process. Support for *HI*, therefore, is mixed. Unemployed persons with disabilities are statistically less likely to vote and are less likely to be registered to vote than are persons working full-time. Yet when considering other forms of political involvement, particularly those with lower costs of entry such as donating to a candidate or following a political story online, those who reported permanent disabilities are equally or in some cases *exceedingly* participatory than those without such disabilities. It is worth noting that, despite our reliance on an employment-based measure of disability, we do observe meaningful differences in political behaviour across groups. While critics may perceive those who are retired, those with disabilities, and those claiming other employment statuses to possess roughly equal amounts of "free time" (as compared to those who work full-time), we demonstrate that disability status and the experiences that accompany the possession of a disability have their own unique impact on political outcomes.

Clearly, for those citing disability in response to their employment status, one considerable barrier to voting appears to be registration. To what extent do convenience measures lessen such costs? The evidence related to disability status and convenience voting methods (*H2*) is illuminating, as some forms of voting appear to be utilized more often than others. In both samples, less than one fifth of CCES respondents with labour precluding disabilities reported same day registration (16% in 2016, 15% in 2012) or in-person early voting (18% in 2016, 17% in 2012). In regression models, permanent disability exhibited a negative effect on same day voter registration and early voting across both General

Election years, though these results were only significantly different from those working full-time in 2012 (Table 2). Importantly, we again note dissimilarities in the way individuals within each employment category approach politics and voting. Retired persons, for instance, appear to make use of early voting opportunities more so than those working full-time. When re-specified to include those in the "other" employment group as the excluded category, and controlling for state-level opportunities to engage in early voting in-person, we still find that those with disabilities were less likely to vote early ($p = 0.011$ in 2016, $p = 0.047$ in 2012).

One way to move beyond any physical or other barriers of the polling place has been through the apparent popularity of vote by mail systems. Results examining disability status and voting by mail (Table 2) are unmistakable: Unemployed individuals with disabilities are significantly more likely to make use of vote by mail procedures than are those working full-time ($p < 0.001$ in both years). Of all 2016 CCES respondents who indicated "permanently disabled" as their employment status, a full 30% reported voting by mail or absentee ballot.[7] This figure increased slightly from the 2012 General Election, where 27% of those with disabilities voted by mail. Results within Table 2 reveal that retired persons, disabled persons, and individuals in the "other" employment category are all more likely to vote by mail than are those working full-time. However, when the model is re-specified to include either retired or "other" individuals as the excluded category (not shown), those with disabilities remain significantly more likely than both retired persons ($p < 0.001$ in 2012 and 2016) and those in the "other" employment group ($p < 0.001$ in 2012 and 2016) to vote by mail. With regard to H2, our analyses illustrate that convenience measures can be beneficial for the political incorporation of individuals with labour precluding disabilities, though they do not appear to be used uniformly.

Table 3 considers one's experiences with administrative obstacles at the polls. Here, no evidence emerges with regard to differential effects of employment status on voting problems. In general, very few CCES respondents indicated problems at the polls and, in the event that they did, those with labour precluding disabilities were just as likely as all other individuals to experience such issues. Disability status is also unrelated to more specific problems related to voter identification requirements. In other words, for those reporting "permanently disabled" as their employment status, who both cleared the initial hurdle of registration and voted in-person, there were no significant differences in their propensity

Table 2. Relationship between employment status and convenience voting methods.

Predictor	Same day registration B (S. E.)	Voted early B (S. E.)	Voted by mail B (S. E.)
2012			
Has disability	−0.547 (0.231)*	−0.181 (0.079)*	0.496 (0.062)***
Retired	−0.016 (0.209)	0.075 (0.058)	0.258 (0.050)***
Other	−0.489 (0.119)***	−0.024 (0.041)	0.238 (0.035)***
N	3820	32074	32074
2016			
Has disability	−0.029 (0.196)	−0.053 (0.068)	0.634 (0.054)***
Retired	0.056 (0.214)	0.246 (0.052)***	0.351 (0.046)***
Other	0.115 (0.118)	0.124 (0.036)**	0.241 (0.033)***
N	4141	38272	38272

Note: Results reflect three separate logistic regression analyses. Models are weighted and include full demographic and political controls. Same Day Registration models also include a dummy variable capturing whether the state an individual lives in offered same day registration during that election year. Voted Early models include a dummy variable capturing whether the state an individual lives in offered in-person early voting during that election year. All models include individuals working full-time as the excluded category. Significant at *$p < 0.05$, **$p < 0.01$, ***$p < 0.001$.

Table 3. Election administration problems by employment status.

Predictor	Problem voting B (S. E.)	ID problem B (S. E.)	Time voting B (S. E.)	Intimidated B (S. E.)
2012				
Has disability	−0.156 (0.177)	−0.500 (0.507)	−0.275 (0.056)***	–
Retired	−0.389 (0.179)*	0.096 (0.484)	−0.138 (0.044)**	–
Other	−0.232 (0.089)**	0.118 (0.245)	−0.125 (0.029)***	–
N	32359	650	24322	–
2016				
Has disability	0.237 (0.144)	−0.364 (0.428)	−0.308 (0.051)***	0.467 (0.167)**
Retired	0.267 (0.157)	−0.080 (0.455)	−0.184 (0.042)***	0.142 (0.221)
Other	−0.0868 (0.078)	0.178 (0.207)	−0.240 (0.027)***	−0.057 (0.083)
N	38478	896	28927	28888

Note: Problem Voting, ID Problem, and Intimidated models reflect results from three separate logistic regression analyses. Time Voting results were derived from an ordered logistic regression. Models are weighted and include full demographic and political controls. All models include individuals working full-time as the excluded category. Significant at *$p < 0.05$, **$p < 0.01$, ***$p < 0.001$.

to experience voter identification problems. As compared with those working full-time, disability status, retired status, and "other" employment statuses saw shorter wait times at the polls ($p < 0.001$ in 2012 and in 2016). When the ordered logistic regression model is re-specified to include individuals with disabilities as the excluded category we observe longer wait times at the polls for those working full-time ($p = 0.000$ in 2012, $p = 0.000$ in 2016), for those who are retired ($p = 0.029$ in 2012, $p = 0.002$ in 2016), and for those falling into the "other" employment category ($p = 0.007$ in 2012, $p = 0.012$ in 2016). It appears that when unemployed people with disabilities do cast a vote in person they are more likely than those without such disabilities to experience an expedited process.

On the other hand, results within Table 3 highlight a significant and positive effect of disability status on perceptions of intimidation at one's polling location. Although this question was only asked in the 2016 CCES module, we observe here a clear difference in the voting experience of those reporting a disability. Unemployed persons with disabilities were more likely than full-time workers to report personally feeling intimidated at the place where they voted ($p = 0.005$). These results include controls for- among other things-age, education, political knowledge, partisanship, and race. Re-specification of the model again confirms these results. When disability status serves as the excluded category (not shown) we observe that those working full-time ($p = 0.000$), those who are retired ($p = 0.171$), and those in the "other" employment category ($p = 0.000$) were all *less* likely to report feeling intimidated than those with permanent disabilities. Although only 3% of those reporting labour precluding disabilities in the 2016 CCES sample indicated feeling intimidated at the polls, our results show that this 3% is in fact noteworthy when compared to other employment categories. In terms of our expectations stated within *H3*, we find that American polling locations within the last two General Elections contained both positive (shorter wait times) and negative (feelings of intimidation) attributes for individuals with disabilities.

Our final hypothesis (*H4*), examines individual levels of detachment from politics (Table 4). Results here suggest that those with disabilities are indeed interested in politics and government, though the statistical significance of this effect varies by election year. When compared with those working full-time, individuals reporting being "permanently disabled" as their employment status were more likely to be politically

Table 4. Effect of employment status on political attachment.

Predictor	Political knowledge B (S. E.)	Political interest B (S. E.)
2012		
Has disability	−0.123 (0.444)**	0.282 (0.044)***
Retired	0.123 (0.041)**	−0.004 (0.041)
Other	0.096 (0.025)***	0.068 (0.024)**
N	41748	41748
2016		
Has disability	0.143 (0.045)**	0.073 (0.045)
Retired	0.095 (0.041)**	−0.157 (0.041)***
Other	0.134 (0.026)***	0.029 (0.025)
N	42568	42568

Note: Models are weighted and include full demographic and political controls. All
    models include individuals working full-time as the excluded category. Significant
    at *$p < 0.05$, **$p < 0.01$, ***$p < 0.001$.

interested in 2012 ($p = 0.000$) and in 2016 ($p = 0.103$). Positive coefficients indicate that individuals within the "other" employment group were also more interested in politics than were those working full-time, whereas negative coefficients indicate that individuals within the retired employment category were less interested in politics than full-time workers. To clarify these results, we re-specified the ordered logistic regression model such that disability served as the excluded category. In doing so, we find that those with disabilities were in fact *less* politically interested than both retired persons ($p = 0.000$ in 2012 and in 2016) and those within the "other" employment category ($p = 0.000$ in 2012, $p = 0.278$ in 2016).

Results related to disability status and political knowledge are also muddled, as the coefficient direction flipped between the 2012 and 2016 CCES sample. With regard to individuals working full-time, those with disabilities were statistically less politically knowledgeable in 2012 and statistically more politically knowledgeable in 2016. Of those who indicated permanently disabled as their employment status, 44% within the 2016 CCES and 38% within the 2012 CCES exhibited the highest levels of political knowledge. We caution, however, that political knowledge was scaled using only two questions, both of which relate to present day partisan balances in government. Considering these measurement issues, along with volatility in our results across election years, support for *H4* is minimal. A significant, negative effect for disability status on political knowledge is the only evidence suggestive of a lack of political attachment among those reporting disabilities. Overall, unemployed people with disabilities appear just as or even *more* interested and knowledgeable of politics than those working full-time.

Conclusion

The present set of empirical analyses serve to broaden the discussion of disability, election administration, and participation in civic life. Although many of our findings are disheartening to disability advocates and political behaviour scholars alike, such examination allows us to identify areas in which both federal and state governments can improve political incorporation and the strength of American democracy. First, in highlighting discrepancies between voting and other forms of participation, such as online engagement, we show that individuals with labour precluding disabilities *do indeed* desire to engage with politics and regularly seek out easily accessible ways to do so, namely through web-based channels. Government officials might, therefore, take special care to attend to email correspondence or online petitions of people with disabilities and groups dedicated to representing these individuals.

Second, we demonstrate that registration requirements before Election Day pose a sizeable obstruction to voting. This is curious, given that individuals with disabilities appear to engage regularly with politics in an online setting and online registration methods (available in 37 states[8]) reduce administrative barriers. Regardless of the method, the fact that voter registration is incumbent upon individuals to initiate clearly imposes information costs and creates gaps in voting. Recent state legislative efforts to enact automatic or opt out (as opposed to opt in) voter registration (National Conference of State Legislature 2019c) could certainly be a boon for many disadvantages populations, including those with disabilities.

Third, our analyses suggest that voting by mail, rather than early voting or same-day registration opportunities, may be more preferable forms of political inclusion for those with disabilities. Should states and local municipalities follow the lead of Oregon, Washington, and Colorado, who mandate postal voting across all types of elections, political engagement among the American public may increase. Indeed, the recent introduction of vote by mail methods in city-level elections within Alaska and Nebraska suggest that voting by mail does indeed boost voter turnout and is generally a more positive experience for constituents (Roberts 2018) than traditional in-person voting procedures.

Because electoral laws, such as registration deadlines, voter identification requirements, and early voting windows, are at the discretion of individual states, future research may aim to investigate such state-level variation in an attempt to clarify how these differences impact the political behaviour of those with disabilities. Likewise, this line of research would benefit tremendously from wide-scale, comparative analyses. Although the specifics of each country's electoral laws and their citizenry make generalizability challenging, much insight is to be gained in the way of combating disenfranchisement, especially for policy-makers.

Additionally, it is clear that better measures are much needed in the field of disability politics. We remain hopeful that future datasets are able to incorporate questions about types of disability alongside standard political questions, such as partisanship. We also expect the effect of disability to manifest itself differently depending on when in one's life one became disabled. Thus we suggest future research which not only delves into the political ramifications of disability onset but also the extent to which one's disability affects their political identity. Finally, efforts to further refine how people with disabilities are identified in the United States are ongoing, particularly within the 2020 Census. We encourage academic researchers to take note of disability-related organizations, such as the National Disability Rights Network, who are presently working on conceptualization and measurement issues, in order to ensure an accurate count of people with disabilities (National Disability Rights Network 2019).

We also look forward to increased scholarly and legal dialogue surrounding recent controversies related to voter identification laws, many of which have been criticized for unduly targeting and disaffecting minority groups. While our results suggest little problems with voter identification among people with disabilities, we should add the caveat that this group has low overall rates of voting and registering to begin with. If and when those with disabilities reach voter turnout rates commensurate with people without disabilities, political behaviourists may in fact start to see disproportionate effects emerge. This is particularly true if one considers that anticipation of problems with administrative hurdles may increase perceptions of intimidation and discrimination among those requiring special assistance. One proactive suggestion in this area could be for disability service organizations to help prospective voters with outreach efforts- such as voter registration drives- as well as regular email or text alerts noting registration cutoff dates, identification requirements, specific accommodations at polling locations, and so forth (Schriner and Shields 1998). Relatedly, others have highlighted the important role of caregivers and families in facilitating the self-advocacy of people with disabilities (Agran, MacLean, and Andren 2016).

Administrative hurdles and electoral rules undoubtedly shape patterns of voter behaviour in any context. One of most disturbing discoveries presented here is that election administration also effects on one's psychological state. Electoral systems which impose or magnify perceptions of intimidation at the polls among any group of persons should garner both serious attention and pointed remedies. As a next step, May (2017) has proposed national legislation that incentivizes states to provide education to election administrators about the voting rights of people with disabilities. We agree and believe that poll workers may benefit from more specialized training, specifically with regard to accommodations for those with cognitive, physical, or emotional limitations. Such administrative efforts may serve to reduce the "chilling effect" of perceived hostile voting conditions (Belt 2016). Of course, we have demonstrated that poll workers may represent just one link in a long chain of systemic issues that plague political incorporation for those with disabilities. More nuanced understandings and classifications of disabilities, as well as longer lifespans worldwide, suggest the ubiquity of disability status as a topic of intensifying salience. As such, public discourse regarding the political experiences of these individuals and especially administrative actions designed to alleviate disenfranchisement, must follow suit.

Notes

1. For a review of the history of legislation about disability and voting, see Powell 2017.
2. See the National Academies of Science report on "Evolving Concepts of Disability" (2007).
3. As of January 2019, sixteen states have same day registration on Election Day. North Carolina allows for same day registration during their period of early voting, but not on Election Day itself.
4. A commonality among researchers in this field is the struggle to locate both quality measures of disability and quality measures of political outcomes within the same dataset. Other datasets do offer better measurement of disability using questions about disability types. The General Social Survey last did so in 2006 and the Current Population Survey does so regularly in their November Voting and Registration Supplement. We choose the CCES for our analyses here because of the breadth of political questions in the survey. Although offering current data, the CPS does not include, for example, measures of partisanship, ideology, political interest, political knowledge, campaign activity, or online engagement, some of which are standard predictors of voting behavior and all of which are central to our analysis as either dependent or independent variables.
5. Age squared was included in order to control for non-linear effects of age on our dependent variables (see Donovan, Tolbert, and Smith 2009).
6. Defined as Alabama, Arkansas, Florida, Georgia, Louisiana, Mississippi, North Carolina, South Carolina, Texas, and Virginia (see Powell and Johnson 2019).

7. Recall, CCES question wording does not differentiate between absentee ballots mailed voluntarily (i.e., by request) and those ballots mailed within vote by mail only states (e.g., Colorado, Washington).
8. See the NCLS report on Online Voter Registration (2018).

Disclosure statement

No potential conflict of interest was reported by the authors.

References

Agran, Martin, William E. MacLean, Jr., and Katherine Anne Kitchen Andren. 2016. "My Voice Counts, Too: Voting Participation Among Individuals with Intellectual Disability." *Intellectual and Developmental Disabilities* 54 (4): 285–294.

Alvarez, R. Michael, Delia Bailey, and Jonathan N. Katz. 2008. "The Effect of Voter Identification Laws on Turnout." California Institute of Technology Social Science Working Paper 1267R. January. https://papers.ssrn.com/sol3/papers.cfm?abstract_id=1084598.

Americans with Disabilities Act. 1990. "What is the Definition of Disability Under the ADA?" Accessed February 20, 2019. https://adata.org/faq/what-definition-disability-under-ada.

Barreto, Matt A., Stephen Nuño, Gabriel R. Sanchez, and Hannah L. Walker. 2018. "The Racial Implications of Voter Identification Laws in America." *American Politics Research*. doi:10.1177/1532673X18810012.

Bartels, Larry M. 2000. "Partisanship and Voting Behavior." *American Journal of Political Science* 44 (1): 35–50.

Belt, Rabia. 2016. "Contemporary Voting Rights Controversies Through the Lens of Disability." *Stanford Law Review* 68: 1491–1550.

Brault, Matthew W. 2012. "Americans with Disabilities: 2010." *U.S. Department of Commerce, Economics and Statistics Administration, U.S. Census Bureau.*

Broadway, Molly. 2018. "Curbside Voting and Other Options for People with Disabilities Who Can't Stand in Line." Accessed February 20, 2019. https://www.disabilityrightstx.org/2018/10/24/curbside-voting/.

Bureau of Labor Statistics. 2018. "Persons with a Disability: Labor Force Characteristics Summary." Accessed February 20, 2019. https://www.bls.gov/news.release/disabl.nr0.htm.

Campbell, Angus, Philip E. Converse, Warren E. Miller, and Donald E. Stokes. 1960. *The American Voter*. New York: John Wiley & Sons.

Carmon, Irin. 2016. "Donald Trump's Worst Offense? Mocking Disabled Reporter, Poll Finds." August 11. Accessed January 30, 2019. https://www.nbcnews.com/politics/2016-election/trump-s-worst-offense-mocking-disabled-reporter-poll-finds-n627736.

Carpini, Michael X. Delli, and Scott Keeter. 1996. *What Americans Know About Politics and Why it Matters*. New Haven: Yale University Press.

Centers for Disease Control and Prevention. 2017. "Disability and Health Overview." Accessed February 20, 2019. https://www.cdc.gov/ncbddd/disabilityandhealth/disability.html.

Chen, Margaret, and Jennifer S. Rosenberg. 2009. "Expanding Democracy: Voter Registration Around the World." June 10. *Brennan Center for Justice.* Accessed February 26, 2019. https://www.brennancenter.org/publication/expanding-democracy-voter-registration-around-world.

Curry, Allison E., Benjamin E. Yerys, Patty Huang, and Kristi B. Metzger. 2017. "Longitudinal Study of Driver Licensing Rates among Adolescents and Young Adults with Autism Spectrum Disorder." *Autism* 22 (4): 479–488.

Dalton, Russell J. 2017. *The Participation Gap: Social Status and Political Inequality.* Oxford: Oxford University Press.

Donovan, Todd, Caroline J. Tolbert, and Daniel A. Smith. 2009. "Political Engagement, Mobilization, and Direct Democracy." *Public Opinion Quarterly* 73 (1): 98–118.

Dunlop, Dorothy D., Susan L. Hughes, and Larry M. Manheim. 1997. "Disability in Activities of Daily -Living: Patterns of Change and a Hierarchy of Disabilities." *American Journal of Public Health* 87 (3): 378–383.

Erikson, Robert S., and Lorraine C. Minnite. 2009. "Modeling Problems in the Voter Identification-Voter Turnout Debate." *Election Law Journal* 8 (2): 85–101.

Fahmy, Dalia. 2018. "Americans are Far More Religious than Adults in Other Wealthy Nations." *Pew Research Center.* Accessed February 20, 2019. http://www.pewresearch.org/fact-tank/2018/07/31/americans-are-far-more-religious-than-adults-in-other-wealthy-nations/.

Fowler, James H. 2006. "Habitual Voting and Behavioral Turnout." *Journal of Politics* 68 (2): 335–344.

Friedman, Carli. 2018. "'Every Vote Matters': Experiences of People with Intellectual and Developmental Disabilities in the 2016 General Election." *Review of Disability Studies: An International Journal* 14 (1): 1–13.

Friedman, Carli, and Aleska L. Owen. 2017. "Defining Disability: Understandings of and Attitudes Towards Ableism and Disability." *Disability Studies Quarterly* 37 (1). http://dsq-sds.org/article/view/5061/4545.

Georgia Secretary of State. 2018. "Voters with Disabilities." Accessed February 20, 2019. http://sos.ga.gov/index.php/elections/voters_with_disabilities.

Green, Donald, Bradley Palmquist, and Eric Schickler. 2004. *Partisan Hearts and Minds: Political Parties and the Social Identities of Voters.* New Haven: Yale University Press.

Haelle, Tara. 2018. "Hospitalized or Disabled? You Can Still Vote – And Receive Federally Protected Help." November 5. Accessed January 23, 2019. https://www.forbes.com/sites/tarahaelle/2018/11/05/hospitalized-or-disabled-you-can-still-vote-and-receive-federally-protected-help/#39b2a9f7756c.

Hajnal, Zoltan, Nazita Lajevardi, and Lindsay Nielson. 2017. "Voter Identification Laws and the Suppression of Minority Votes." *Journal of Politics* 79 (2): 363–379.

Hall, Thad, and R. Michael Alvarez. 2012. "Defining the Barriers to Political Participation for Individuals with Disabilities." *The Information Technology and Innovation Foundation Accessible Voting Technology Initiative.* Working Paper #1.

Hershey, Marjorie Randon. 2009. "What We Know About Voter-ID Laws, Registration, and Turnout." *Perspectives on Politics* 42 (1): 87–91.

Highton, Benjamin. 1997. "Easy Registration and Voter Turnout." *Journal of Politics* 59 (2): 565–575.

Huddy, Leonie, Lilliana Mason, and Lene Aarøe. 2015. "Expressive Partisanship: Campaign Involvement, Political Emotion, and Partisan Identity." *American Political Science Review* 109 (1): 1–17.

Igielnik, Ruth. 2016. "A Political Profile of Disabled Americans." *Pew Research Center.* Accessed February 5, 2019. http://www.pewresearch.org/fact-tank/2016/09/22/a-political-profile-of-disabled-americans/.

Knack, Stephen. 1995. "Does 'Motor Voter' Work? Evidence from State-Level Data." *Journal of Politics* 57 (3): 796–811.

Kraus, L., E. Lauer, R. Coleman, and A. Houtenville. 2018. *2017 Disability Statistics Annual Report.* Durham, NH: University of New Hampshire.

Layman, Geoffrey C. 1997. "Religion and Political Behavior in the United States." *Public Opinion Quarterly* 61 (2): 288–316.

Lewis-Beck, Michael S., William G. Jacoby, Helmut Norpoth, and Herbert F. Weisberg. 2008. *The American Voter Revisited*. Ann Arbor: University of Michigan Press.

Marshall, Shawn, Malcolm Man-Son-Hing, Frank Molnar, Lynn Hunt, and Hillel Finestone. 2005. "An Exploratory Study on the Predictive Elements of Passing On-the-Road Tests for Disabled Persons." *Traffic Injury Prevention* 6 (3): 235–239.

Mattila, Mikko, and Achillefs Papageorgio. 2016. "Disability, Perceived Discrimination and Political Participation." *International Political Science Review* 38 (5): 505–519.

May, Hillary. 2017. "The Last Frontier of Disenfranchisement: A Fundamental Right for Individuals with Cognitive Disabilities." *William and Mary Law Review* 59 (2): 692–730.

Miller, Peter, and Sierra Powell. 2016. "Overcoming Voting Obstacles: Convenience Voting by People with Disabilities." *American Politics Research* 44 (1): 28–55.

Muhlhausen, David B., and Keri Weber Sikich. 2007. "New Analysis Shows Voter Identification Laws Do Not Reduce Turnout." The Heritage Center for Data Analysis. CDA07-04. September 10.

Naifeh, Stuart. 2015. "Driving the Vote: Are States Complying with the Motor Voter Requirements of the National Voter Registration Act?" *Demos*. Accessed February 27, 2019. https://www.demos.org/publication/driving-vote-are-states-complying-motor-voter-requirements-national-voter-registration-a.

National Academies of Science. 2007. "Evolving Concepts of Disability." In *Improving the Social Security Disability Decision Process*, edited by John D. Stobo, Michael McGeary, and David K. Barnes, 18–29. Washington, DC: National Academies Press.

National Conference of State Legislatures. 2018. "Online Voter Registration." Accessed June 19, 2019. http://www.ncsl.org/research/elections-and-campaigns/electronic-or-online-voter-registration.aspx.

National Conference of State Legislatures. 2019a. "Same Day Voter Registration." Accessed February 14, 2019. http://www.ncsl.org/research/elections-and-campaigns/same-day-registration.aspx.

National Conference of State Legislatures. 2019b. "Voter Identification Requirements Voter ID Laws" http://www.ncsl.org/research/elections-and-campaigns/voter-id.aspx.

National Conference of State Legislatures Website. 2019c. "Automatic Voter Registration." Accessed February 27, 2019. http://www.ncsl.org/research/elections-and-campaigns/automatic-voter-registration.aspx.

National Disability Rights Network Website. 2019. "Census 2020: Count Everyone, Include Everyone." Accessed June 18, 2019. https://www.ndrn.org/issues/census-2020/.

Norris, Pippa. 2004. "The Evolution of Election Campaigns: Eroding Political Engagement?" Paper presented at the conference on Political Communications in the 21st Century, St Margaret's College, University of Otago, New Zealand.

Powell, Sierra. 2017. "Voting." In *Disability and U.S. Politics: Participation, Policy, and Controversy*, edited by Dana Lee Baker, 95–114. New York: Praeger Publishers.

Powell, Sierra, and April A. Johnson. 2019. "Patterns and Mechanisms of Political Participation among People with Disabilities." *Journal of Health, Politics, Policy, and Law* 44 (3): 381–422.

Predit, Robert. 2009. "Baby Boomers May Prove More Disabled than their Elders." *ABC News*. Accessed February 20, 2019. https://abcnews.go.com/Health/Healthday/baby-boomers-prove-disabled-elders/story?id=9079220.

Priestley, Mark, Martha Stickings, Ema Loja, Stefanos Grammenos, Anna Lawson, Lisa Waddington, and Bjarney Fridriksdottir. 2016. "The Political Participation of Disabled People in Europe: Rights, Accessibility, and Activism." *Electoral Studies* 42: 1–9.

Reher, Stefanie. 2018. "Mind This Gap, Too: Political Orientations of People with Disabilities in Europe." *Political Behavior*. Advance Online Publication. doi:10.1007/s11109-018-09520-x.

Roberts, David. 2018. "The Simple Voting Reform That Works Wherever It's Tried." *Vox*. Accessed June 11, 2019. https://www.vox.com/policy-and-politics/2018/5/23/17383400/vote-by-mail-home-california-alaska-nebraska.

Root, Danielle, and Liz Kennedy. 2018. "Increasing Voter Participation in America." *Center for American Progress*. Accessed February 27, 2019. https://www.americanprogress.org/issues/democracy/reports/2018/07/11/453319/increasing-voter-participation-america/.

Rosenstone, Steven J., and Raymond E. Wolfinger. 1978. "The Effect of Registration Laws on Voter Turnout." *American Political Science Review* 72 (1): 22–45.

Ross, Martha, and Nicole Bateman. 2018. "Disability Rates Among Working-Age Adults are Shaped by Race, Place, and Education." *Brookings*. Accessed February 20, 2019. https://www.brookings.edu/blog/the-avenue/2018/05/15/disability-rates-among-working-age-adults-are-shaped-by-race-place-and-education/.

Schlozman, Kay Lehman, Sidney Verba, and Henry E. Brady. 2012. *The Unheavenly Chorus: Unequal Political Voice and the Broken Promise of American Democracy*. Princeton: Princeton University Press.

Schriner, Kay, and Todd G. Shields. 1998. "Empowerment of the Political Kind: The Role of Disability Service Organizations in Encouraging People with Disabilities to Vote." *Journal of Rehabilitation* 64 (2): 33–37.

Schur, Lisa, and Meera Adya. 2013. "Sidelined or Mainstreamed? Political Participation and Attitudes of People with Disabilities in the United States." *Social Science Quarterly* 94 (3): 811–839.

Schur, Lisa, Meera Adya, and Douglas Kruse. 2013. "Disability, Voter Turnout, and Voting Difficulties in the 2012 Elections." U.S. Election Assistance Commission Report. Accessed February 15, 2019. https://www.eac.gov/assets/1/1/Disability%20and%20voting%20survey%20report%20for%202012%20elections.pdf.

Schur, Lisa, Mason Ameri, and Meera Adya. 2017. "Disability, Voter Turnout, and Polling Place Accessibility." *Social Science Quarterly* 98 (5): 1374–1390.

Schur, Lisa, and Douglas Kruse. 2000. "What Determines Voter Turnout? Lessons from Citizens with Disabilities." *Social Science Quarterly* 81 (2): 571–587.

Schur, Lisa, Todd Shields, Douglas Kruse, and Kay Schriner. 2002. "Enabling Democracy: Disability and Voter Turnout." *Political Research Quarterly* 55 (1): 167–190.

Schur, Lisa, Todd Shields, and Kay Schriner. 2003. "Can I Make a Difference? Efficacy, Employment, and Disability." *Political Psychology* 24 (1): 119–149.

Schur, Lisa, Todd Shields, and Kay Schriner. 2005. "Generational Cohorts, Group Membership, and Political Participation by People with Disabilities." *Political Research Quarterly* 58 (3): 487–496.

Self Advocates Becoming Empowered. 2017. "Voters with Disabilities Election Report." Accessed February 28, 2019. https://www.sabeusa.org/wp-content/uploads/2017/03/2016-Voter-Survey-Final-Report-28229.pdf.

Van Hees, Suzanne G.M., Hennie R. Boeije, and Iris de Putter. 2019. "Voting Barriers and Solutions: The Experiences of People with Disabilities During the Dutch National Election in 2017." *Disability and Society*. Advance Online Publication. doi:10.1080/09687599.2019.1566052.

Verba, Sidney, Kay Lehman Schlozman, and Henry E. Brady. 1995. *Voice and Equality: Civic Voluntarism in American Politics*. Cambridge: Harvard University Press.

Wald, Kenneth D., and Allison Calhoun-Brown. 2014. *Religion and Politics in The United States*. 7th ed. Lanham: Rowman & Littlefield.

Wass, Hanna, Mikko Mattila, Lauri Rapeli, and Peter Söderlund. 2017. "Voting While Ailing? The Effect of Voter Facilitation Instruments on Health-Related Differences in Turnout." *Journal of Elections, Public Opinion, and Political Parties* 27 (4): 503–522.

World Health Organization. 2019. "Disabilities." Accessed February 20, 2019. https://www.who.int/topics/disabilities/en/.

Migrant populations and external voting: the politics of suffrage expansion in Central America

Kevin Pallister

ABSTRACT

Recent decades have seen an enormous expansion in the number of countries allowing their nonresident citizens to vote from abroad, and an emerging literature has sought to identify the factors that lead countries to adopt such external voting policies. This article contributes to this literature by examining the heretofore neglected cases of El Salvador and Guatemala, both of which have large expatriate populations and yet were slow to adopt external voting. I show that the eventual adoption of external voting in these cases was influenced by persistent emigrant lobbying for enfranchisement, the diffusion of an international norm of external voting, and partisan calculations. I also find that two factors largely overlooked in previous research – resource constraints and crowded electoral reform agendas – help account for long delays in policy change. Differences in the reform process across the two countries reflect the varying impact of norm diffusion across countries and differences in the countries' political party systems.

The last several decades have seen an enormous expansion in the political rights extended to migrants living outside their country of origin. This has coincided with, and been a response to, the growth of international migration. By 2015, an estimated 244 million people comprising 3.3% of the world's population were living outside their country of origin (United Nations Population Fund n.d.). Increasing migration raises significant questions about citizenship, rights, and political representation that have historically been tied to the territorial nation-state.

As greater numbers of people live outside their country of origin, more countries have reformed their laws to allow external voting (also known as out-of-country voting), which permits

> qualified individuals, independently of their professional status, to take part from outside the national territory in referenda or in supra-national, national, or subnational elections held in a country of which they hold citizenship but where they permanently or temporarily do not reside. (Lafleur 2015, 843)

Some 56 countries adopted external voting in the 1990s and 2000s (Lafleur 2013, 25), and by 2018 approximately 139 countries allowed at least some of their citizens to vote from abroad.[1] Allowing citizens to vote from abroad appears to have become an international norm, although countries vary significantly in which offices external voters may elect, what restrictions on the suffrage apply (such as a maximum number of years that a citizen may live abroad and retain the right to vote), and what voting methods are used.

In this article I present comparative case studies of the adoption of external voting in El Salvador and Guatemala. I show, first, that emigrant lobbying for enfranchisement was prominent in both cases, although it took many years for lobbying to come to fruition – even when the home country was heavily dependent on migrant remittances. Second, partisan interests were not always relevant to discussions of external voting, especially in Guatemala where political parties are ephemeral and lack clear social bases of support. Third, the diffusion of an international norm of external voting played a role in both cases, although direct international pressure for the adoption of external voting was inconsistent across the two countries. Finally, reform was delayed in both countries by a factor that has received scant attention in the literature on external voting: crowded electoral reform agendas that made external voting a second-order concern. I show that the higher priority given to electoral reforms such as modernizing voter registries and decentralizing polling places delayed the adoption of external voting past the point when consensus on its desirability was well-established.

Why adopt external voting?

The number of countries allowing external voting has grown despite the logistical and financial challenges that it poses.[2] Effective implementation requires setting up enough voting sites to provide reasonable access to the diaspora, adopting measures to prevent fraud when postal voting is employed, and providing voter identification and registration services to migrants who in some cases immigrated into their country of residence illegally. All of these can be expensive and administratively demanding.

The adoption of external voting may also present political challenges. The prospect of citizens who no longer live in the country providing pivotal swing votes may not be widely accepted in the home country. Moreover, if migrants left their country for political reasons, such as fleeing persecution, then the diaspora may be distinct from the electorate at home in their political views and partisan identifications. Incumbents therefore may not favour emigrant enfranchisement for purely partisan reasons, especially where the external vote may prove pivotal to the outcome – as has been the case in elections in Italy, Cape Verde, Romania, and Tunisia (Brand 2014; Turcu and Urbatsch 2015, 412).

Yet in most cases the effects of voting from abroad have been limited. Turnout is often very low, as many migrants may lack interest in the politics of their home country and procedural hurdles to registering and voting may be high (Hutcheson and Arrighi 2015; Navarro Fierro, Morales, and Gratschew 2007, 32–33). Despite the administrative costs and political opposition that external voting may engender, the practice has spread widely in recent decades. This trend has prompted a growing number of studies that investigate why countries adopt external voting.

The extension of suffrage to excluded groups has often resulted from pressure from excluded groups themselves, from the initiative of political elites seeking partisan advantage, and from the spread of international norms. The literature on external voting has generally focused on these same factors to explain of the extension of suffrage to citizens living outside their country of citizenship, as well as focusing on several variables unique to the enfranchisement of migrants.

In many cases, organizations of migrants lobby their home governments demanding voting rights. Analyses have found that external voting was adopted in response to migrant pressure in the United States (Ellis 2007, 43) and some Latin American countries (Lafleur 2013; Navarro 2007, 231). Emigrant lobbying for enfranchisement may be more effective when migrants have some leverage over their home government, such as when migrants send significant remittances to their home country (Lafleur 2011). Nevertheless, in some cases external voting has been adopted in the absence of pressure from migrants to do so – for instance, in Brazil, Peru, and Honduras (Navarro 2007, 231). In other cases, pressure from migrant organizations has been unsuccessful in winning the right to vote from abroad, as was the case for Afghanistan's 2014 presidential election (Bekaj and Antara 2018, 74).

Partisan interests can also affect the adoption of voting abroad. Naturally, political parties and politicians may support or oppose external voting depending on whether they expect migrant voters to support them or the opposition. Such expectations can shape not only decisions over the adoption of external voting, but also the details of legislation, such as voter registration requirements and the method of voting from abroad (Lafleur 2011). The case study literature identifies several cases – such as Honduras, Senegal, and the United Kingdom – where the decision to adopt external voting is attributed to partisan calculations (Ellis 2007, 43–44; Navarro 2007, 231; Vengroff 2007). Scholars have considered whether left-wing or right-wing parties are more likely to champion voting rights for migrants. In Italy, the right advocated external voting in expectation of gaining votes from expat voters. More common, at least in Latin America, has been for left-wing parties to champion external voting. Some have hypothesized that leftist parties in power will be more likely to institute external voting, both because doing so is consistent with their image of inclusion, and because Latin American emigrants often fled right-wing regimes and are seen as left-leaning. In Chile, for example, left-wing parties supported external voting while conservative parties opposed it (Erlingsson and Tuman 2017, 300). One quantitative analysis has found that countries in Latin America and the Caribbean governed by a left-wing executive are more likely to adopt external voting than are other countries in the region (Erlingsson and Tuman 2017).

Others have argued that the adoption of voting abroad has been caused in part by the diffusion of an international norm. Although offering provisions for emigrants to vote from abroad is not a strong legal norm,[3] the practice has spread rapidly in a short period of time and is often endorsed by international organizations. Turcu and Urbatsch (2015, 414) note that diaspora enfranchisement can be a visible signal of a government's commitment to democracy. In addition, international pressure and socialization through international organizations may also contribute to the adoption of external voting, as when international election observation missions criticize countries for failing to provide external voting. Turcu and Urbatsch (2015) find evidence for diffusion of external voting from neighbouring countries, although other work finds no evidence of diffusion in the adoption of external voting in Latin America and the Caribbean (Erlingsson and Tuman 2017).

Several other factors more specific to emigration may help explain the adoption of external voting. First are the economic benefits that may flow from maintaining ties to diasporas, including economic remittances from migrants and business linkages that migrants can help facilitate. It is generally believed that extending political rights to emigrants helps maintain their psychological attachment to the homeland, and thereby encourages remittances and other economic ties (Leal, Lee, and McCann 2012, 540). Indeed, Leblang (2017) finds that migrants from countries that allow dual citizenship remit more money to their homeland than do migrants from countries that do not allow dual citizenship. It is plausible that the adoption of external voting also helps secure remittances. Qualitative work has found that "at the discursive level, emigrants and domestic actors have repeatedly used the impact of emigrants on the home country's economy as an argument to justify external voting" (Lafleur 2011, 496). Yet there has been little empirical testing of the hypothesis that securing remittances motivates the adoption of external voting, with one study finding a non-linear relationship: the adoption of external voting becomes more likely as remittances increase up to a point, but as remittances reach high levels the adoption of external voting becomes less likely (Erlingsson and Tuman 2017).

Second, economic development may facilitate the adoption of voting abroad, as the economic and bureaucratic resources needed to implement external voting are significant. Conducting voting abroad typically costs about five to ten times as much per registered voter as does in-country voting (Erben, Goldsmith, and Shujaat 2012, 1). Rhodes and Harutyunyan (2010) find that countries with higher levels of economic development are more likely to allow external voting.

Finally, processes of democratic transition may be likely times for the adoption of external voting. Although some authoritarian regimes such as Syria and Egypt have introduced external voting (Brand 2014), many countries with external voting adopted it after transitioning to democracy (Rhodes and Harutyunyan 2010, 476). Democratic transition opens a window of opportunity for suffrage reform, and enfranchising migrants holds symbolic value – especially where some citizens had fled into exile under the previous authoritarian regime.

Studies of external voting thus suggest that external voting is more likely to be adopted by countries: (1) whose expatriate citizens strongly lobby for their enfranchisement; (2) where the party in power believes external voters will support the party; (3) that are governed by a left-wing party; (4) that are open to the internalization of international norms (such as those that are surrounded by neighbours that have adopted external voting); (5) that receive significant remittances from citizens living abroad; (6) with high levels of economic development; and (7) that are undergoing democratic transition.

There is still much that is not known about how different variables interact in influencing the adoption of external voting, such as how emigrant communities mobilize international norms to frame the issue of external voting in their advocacy (see, e.g. Escobar 2017, 6) or how the size of the emigrant population might affect partisan interests through the political influence that migrants may enjoy over family members back home. In addition to a few large-n statistical analyses, the existing literature includes numerous individual and comparative case studies. Yet with a few exceptions, the case study literature has often been descriptive rather than focused on elucidating the causal mechanisms that are implicated in quantitative studies. Palop-García and Pedroza (2019, 416) point out the need for better process tracing in work on external voting in order to "follow how political actors negotiate, frame and battle for or against enfranchisement."

   This article seeks to make such a contribution by tracing the path that external voting has taken in two Central American countries: El Salvador and Guatemala. After years of debate, El Salvador adopted external voting in 2013 while Guatemala did so in 2016. I draw on news reports, archival sources, and secondary literature to apply existing theories of diaspora enfranchisement to the two cases.

   El Salvador and Guatemala are ideal cases to analyze the influence of emigrant lobbying, economic dependence, and international norms on the adoption of external voting. Both countries have large emigrant populations that would be expected to push for their enfranchisement, while the size of the expatriate population would also be predicted to provoke partisan and normative concerns about the external vote swaying election outcomes (see Hutcheson and Arrighi 2015). Both countries are also highly dependent on economic remittances, making them most-likely cases for remittances to contribute to the adoption of external voting. Both also have strong ties to the United States and various international democracy promoting actors (such as the Organization of American States and various international election observation organizations). At the same time, the two cases display differing levels of political party institutionalization and variation in the ideological orientation of governments, thus allowing for examination of how political party interests affect external voting adoption.

   The delayed adoption of external voting in both cases also poses a puzzle, considering that external voting rights are widely seen as lending electoral legitimacy and promoting national reconciliation in countries with a history of political conflict and large-scale emigration resulting from that conflict (Erlingsson and Tuman 2017, 296) – conditions applicable to both Guatemala and El Salvador. As many countries in Latin America and around the world adopted external voting, these cases lagged behind for reasons not fully accounted for in extant theories of expatriate enfranchisement.

El Salvador's slow road to migrant enfranchisement

The 2014 presidential election was the first time that Salvadoran citizens could vote from abroad. Estimates of Salvadoran citizens living abroad vary in the range of 1.8–3 million, or nearly one-third of the national population, with most Salvadorans abroad living in the United States.[4] The issue of allowing voting by Salvadorans abroad had been on the country's political agenda for two decades, but it wasn't until January 2013 that the Legislative Assembly passed a law authorizing external voting.

   Voting rights for Salvadoran migrants had been debated from the time the country undertook an overhaul of its electoral system leading up to the transitional 1994 elections. In subsequent years a number of electoral reforms were adopted, but proposals for external voting stalled. At least six bills related to voting abroad were introduced in the Legislative Assembly between 2000 and 2010, including bills introduced by deputies of the leftist FMLN and three other parties. Some of these bills would have allowed Salvadorans abroad to vote in legislative and municipal elections as well as presidential contests, and at least one would have allowed citizens abroad to nominate their own candidates to the Legislative Assembly (ISD 2012, 8; Villalta and Urbina 2009, 22–24).

   Of these bills, only a transitory measure was approved by the Legislative Assembly for the 2009 elections to allow Salvadorans who obtained an identity card abroad to vote for president in a special voting centre in San Salvador. This measure necessitated costly travel and potentially posed legal problems for undocumented Salvadorans leaving and reentering the United States (NDI 2009, 2; OAS 2009, 8). FMLN legislators abstained from voting on this measure, "citing the measure as discriminatory against voters who cannot afford to return for the election" (NDI 2009, 2; see also Meyer 2009). Only 39,463 Salvadorans living abroad had obtained their identity card out of country, and of these only about half of one percent returned to El Salvador to vote (EUEOM 2009b).

After the FMLN won the presidency for the first time in 2009, president Mauricio Funes made external voting a higher priority. He had publicly pledged to implement external voting before being elected, and he reiterated that promise after the election (Villalta and Urbina 2009, 27). This gave external voting greater prominence on the country's political agenda, forcing other parties to take a position on the issue.

The bill that ultimately instituted external voting had its origins in a commission established by President Funes that brought together officials from the Supreme Electoral Tribunal (TSE), the National Registry of Natural Persons, and other relevant state agencies. The result of this commission was a bill presented to the Legislative Assembly in July 2012. Although deputies from the conservative ARENA and GANA parties raised some questions about funding the project, they ultimately endorsed the bill, which received near unanimous approval in the Assembly (O'Reilly 2014; *Contrapunto*, Jan. 24, 2013). The law allowed voting from abroad via mail, for presidential elections only. Subsequently, a ruling by the Supreme Court in 2016 extended the right to vote to legislative and municipal elections.

A principal challenge in implementing external voting was the need to issue national identification cards to Salvadorans living abroad. The new law required voters abroad to travel to a consulate to obtain an ID card that listed their address abroad. The ID card cost the citizen $35 (Iaconangelo 2014). Delays in issuing ID cards and a limited budget for external voting hindered voter registration efforts (Moronta 2013b; *El Diario de Hoy*, April 18, 2013). Only 10,337 Salvadorans living abroad registered to vote for the 2014 election (IFES 2014, 3). Only 2,727 votes from abroad reached El Salvador for the first round of the election, and of those only 1,909 were valid (Iaconangelo 2014), with the rest being nullified, many because the forms were not filled out correctly. The results were favourable for the FMLN, whose candidate received over 63% of the second-round vote from abroad, compared to just over 50% of the vote domestically – though the external vote did not account for the full margin of victory (TSE 2014, 42, 44).

What led to El Salvador's introduction of external voting? Perhaps the most critical factor was the persistent pressure from migrant organizations. Organizations of Salvadorans living abroad actively advocated for the extension of voting rights to the diaspora. Salvadoran migrant groups like the Red Nacional Salvadoreña Americana (National Salvadoran American Network) held meetings with Salvadoran government officials to advocate for voting rights (Landolt 2003, 315; *El Diario de Hoy*, Oct. 2, 2011), while Salvadoreños en el Mundo (Salvadorans in the World [SEEM]) – an association of Salvadoran migrant NGOs – lobbied legislators, political parties, the TSE, and other agencies from 2003 onward to get external voting adopted (Villalta and Urbina 2009, 6).

Migrant groups enjoyed access to policymakers, as delegates of political parties and the Supreme Electoral Tribunal attended conventions of Salvadorans living abroad (*El Diario de Hoy*, Dec. 13, 2011). SEEM successfully lobbied a multiparty commission considering electoral reforms in 2007 to add external voting to its list of agenda items (Martel 2010, 73;

Villalta and Urbina 2009, 26). In 2012, SEEM and two domestic NGOs filed a case in the Constitutional Chamber of the Supreme Court of Justice challenging the constitutionality of not allowing Salvadorans to vote from abroad (ISD 2013; Moronta 2012).

Migrant organizations kept up the pressure as the external voting law was in the final stages of debate. In the days before the law's passage, Salvadorans living abroad submitted more than 1,000 signatures to the Legislative Assembly urging approval of the law (Moronta 2013a). Eleven NGOs of Salvadorans abroad issued an open letter to the Legislative Assembly calling for the bill to be approved (*El Diario de Hoy*, Jan. 13, 2013).

The access and leverage enjoyed by migrant groups was bolstered by the importance of remittances to the Salvadoran economy. Remittances from Salvadorans living abroad totalled an estimated $2.4 billion in 2000 and $4.2 billion in 2013, or nearly 17% of the country's gross domestic product (Cohn, Gonzalez-Barrera, and Cuddington 2013). The connection between remittances and voting rights was not lost on Salvadoran migrant activists, who frequently mentioned remittances when discussing the importance of extending voting rights in the media. Given the overwhelming importance of remittances to the Salvadoran economy, "lawmakers are hoping to keep Salvadoran's [sic] living abroad involved in the country's politics in the hope that this money will continue to generously flow home," as one news report noted (O'Reilly 2014).

Domestic civil society groups in El Salvador also supported the introduction of external voting, and in some cases worked with migrant NGOs. Numerous Salvadoran NGOs and the Salvadoran Chamber of Commerce called on El Salvador to facilitate voting abroad (Villalta and Urbina 2009, 24–25), and in 2009 a coalition of NGOs presented the Legislative Assembly with a proposal on behalf of Salvadoreños en el Mundo to introduce external voting (Martel 2010, 73). Several NGOs submitted a similar proposal again in 2012 (ISD 2013).

These efforts by Salvadoran citizens were reinforced by international actors. Voting abroad was recommended by a number of international election observation missions, most notably the 2009 and 2012 observer missions from the European Union (EUEOM 2009b; Mision de Expertos Electorales 2012, 25; see also Meyer 2009). The experiences of other countries in implementing voting from abroad were also taken into account. For instance, the government sponsored a forum where representatives from Mexico and Bolivia shared their experiences implementing external voting (*El Diario de Hoy*, Nov. 25, 2010). In a 2005 report, the United Nations Development Program (UNDP) also recommended implementing voting abroad (Villalta and Urbina 2009, 19), and in 2011 the UNDP spearheaded a technical study that concluded that postal voting was the best option to implement external voting (UNDP 2011).

Domestically, the TSE was supportive of voting abroad, especially in the late stages of debate when it appeared it would become a reality. For instance, the TSE encouraged the Legislative Assembly to pass the external voting bill quickly in 2013 so the electoral body would have sufficient time to implement it for the 2014 election (*El Diario de Hoy*, Jan. 5, 2013).

Some analysts have speculated that uncertainty about how external voting would impact the fortunes of El Salvador's political parties was an impediment to its adoption (Ribera 1997; Villalta and Urbina 2009, 4; *El Diario de Hoy*, June 15, 2007). On balance the leftist FMLN was more supportive of voting abroad than were other parties, perhaps because the organization had established transnational ties with the migrant community dating back to the 1980s (Landolt 2003, 306), while the ARENA party had "never developed any significant organized popular political support base in Salvadorian communities in the U.S." (COHA 2013). Illustrating this pattern, in 2013 a U.S.-based group of Salvadorans "published a strongly worded declaration in the Salvadoran newspaper, *La Prensa Gráfica*, [supporting] the presidential campaign of the leftist Farabundo Marti National Liberation (FMLN) party" (COHA 2013). While the FMLN may have anticipated strong support from external voters, uncertainty or reticence about the electoral effects of external voting on the part of other parties likely played a role in delaying its adoption.

Indeed, President Funes of the FMLN was a strong and persistent advocate of external voting, and his "lobbying efforts became so strong that other political parties had to adopt a clear position" (Bravo 2013, 13). This precipitated a long-recognized dynamic in the politics of suffrage extension: as the possible enfranchisement of an excluded group loomed on the horizon, even parties reluctant to enfranchise that group fear alienating a large number of citizens who may be on the brink of winning the right to vote. Seeking to avoid electoral retaliation by a newly enfranchised group (or even seeking to win their political loyalty), those parties ultimately endorse their enfranchisement.[5]

The implementation of external voting did indeed open a new front in electoral competition, leading the major parties to solicit support from voters abroad. Given the tight margin of victory in the 2009 presidential contest (fewer than 70,000 votes), the Salvadoran migrant vote could be decisive. This led to political parties campaigning in the U.S., with vice presidential candidates for ARENA and the FMLN visiting the U.S. to meet with groups of Salvadorans (COHA 2013; *El Diario de Hoy*, Feb. 3, March 23, Aug. 4, 2013). The enfranchisement of diaspora citizens became a campaign issue: in one campaign spot, the FMLN presented the external voting law as a promise fulfilled (*El Diario de Hoy*, Feb. 3, 2013). As in many other countries, however, the low turnout of Salvadorans abroad in the 2014 election minimized the impact of external voting on domestic electoral politics.

Aside from partisan interests, external voting was also delayed by a crowded electoral reform agenda. Voting abroad was just one of many electoral reforms considered from the mid-1990s onward, with other issues taking greater priority. After the 1994 transitional elections, El Salvador introduced a new national identity document and automatic voter registration to address serious deficiencies in the voter registry. The country also undertook the decentralization of polling places throughout the country to facilitate voter access and considered reforms related to political party regulations, campaign finance, allowing independent candidacies, and the adoption of gender quotas for political party lists. Some of these reforms addressed urgent concerns about electoral integrity and voter access, and required substantial resources and focus from the electoral commission. In this context, implementing external voting was considered a secondary matter to be addressed once other electoral reforms were in place.

Guatemala's torturous path to external voting

The road to voting rights for Guatemalan citizens abroad has been as torturous as in El Salvador. The issue of voting rights for the more than one million Guatemalan migrants[6] has been on the country's agenda since Guatemala made a transition to civilian rule in the 1980s, but not until 2016 did Congress finally approve external voting.

Consideration of external voting dates back to the mid-1980s, when a constituent assembly drafted a new constitution and electoral law. While debating the electoral law in 1985, an amendment to a bill was introduced that would have allowed Guatemalans abroad to vote in embassies and consulates for president and congressional deputies. The amendment generated extensive debate on the assembly floor, and that debate highlights how discussion of the issue evolved over the following three decades.[7]

Speaking on the floor of the constituent assembly, a few assembly members mentioned the importance of remittances from migrants for the nation's economy, and the priority that should be given to maintaining migrants' ties to the homeland. More common were normative and legalistic expressions of the idea that citizens have the right to vote regardless of their location or residence. One legislator also noted that the U.S., as a model democracy, allowed voting abroad, and suggested that Guatemala might improve its democratic image by doing likewise. Yet opponents of the amendment raised a number of objections. Some concerned specific provisions, such as the loose voter identification requirements specified in the amendment. Others concerned the logistical difficulties of implementing voting abroad, especially considering Guatemala's lack of resources. Some legislators claimed that citizens living abroad would not be well informed about the situation in the country, implying that they should not vote in national elections, while others strongly challenged this claim. Finally, some legislators suggested vaguely that voting abroad would facilitate election fraud. Ultimately the amendment was defeated, with only 17 of the 50 legislators present voting in favour. However, even some of the deputies who spoke against the amendment acknowledged that in the future voting from abroad would be more feasible.

The issue of external voting was not taken up again until the country undertook a series of electoral reforms in the 1990s and 2000s that proceeded through Congress at a glacial pace. The reform process began with the 1996 peace accords that ended the country's civil war. An ad hoc electoral reform commission convened the following year solicited proposals from civil society groups and other stakeholders. Of approximately two dozen proposals received, three – one from a political party, one from a civil society group, and one from the attorney general's office – included measures to allow voting from abroad (Acción Ciudadana et al. 2005; "Reformas Electorales..." n.d.). However, the bill to reform the electoral law produced by the commission in 1998 did not include provisions for external voting. According to Zapata (2003, 339), the political party representatives on the commission did not express opposition to external voting, but the Supreme Electoral Tribunal (which also had representatives on the commission) held that it lacked the resources and technical capacity to carry out voting abroad.

The commission's electoral reform bill, which included reforms in a number of areas including election administration and campaign finance, stalled in Congress for several years. Meanwhile, two standalone bills were introduced by deputies (in 2002 and 2004) that would have amended the electoral law to allow for external voting. These bills made no headway in Congress, but as discussions of wide-ranging reforms to the electoral law resumed in 2003, the political parties agreed to add an article to the reform bill that would allow Guatemalans residing abroad to vote (*Prensa Libre*, March 7, 2003). As negotiations proceeded, however, Congress made the fateful decision to dust off the original bill that had been pending in Congress for several years, and in 2004 it passed the wide-ranging reform to the electoral law that did not contain provisions for voting abroad. In passing the 2004 reform, Congress promised to pass follow-up reforms within 90 days. Voting abroad was one of the items on this second-generation reform agenda. But more than two years passed before Congress approved another set of reforms to the electoral law, as negotiations bogged down on issues like campaign finance, internal party democracy, and party list quotas for women and indigenous peoples (Pallister 2017, ch. 5). Ultimately the reforms approved in 2006 were limited to minor technical matters, while Congress continued to postpone substantive reforms, including external voting.

In the following years, sporadic efforts were made to adopt external voting. Between 2005 and 2013 at least eight bills were introduced in Congress that would have implemented voting abroad. Until 2012, however, all of these bills also included other electoral reforms, such as increasing public funding of political parties. None of these bills made it out of committee. A 2012 bill dealing only with voting abroad was approved by the electoral committee and passed on to the full Congress, where it was not put up for a vote. Meanwhile, in 2011, the country's Human Rights Ombudsman filed a case in the Supreme Court challenging the TSE's lack of mechanisms facilitating voting for Guatemalans abroad (*Prensa Libre*, Feb. 8, 2011); the court denied the suit a few weeks later.

But voting for migrants appeared to be in sight when the Supreme Electoral Tribunal proposed reforming the electoral law in 2012. The proposal included wide-ranging reforms, including voting abroad. Another broad electoral law reform bill that included voting abroad was presented by legislators from various political parties in 2013, and was approved in an initial reading. In July 2014, the Constitutional Court issued a ruling approving most of the amendments to the law, including the provision for voting abroad (Corte de Constitucionalidad 2014). It was then up to Congress to give the court-sanctioned portions of the bill final approval. But Congress failed to take action to pass the bill into law before the 2015 general election.

Finally, external voting was included in a package of electoral reforms passed by Congress in April 2016. The law was based on a 2015 bill introduced by the TSE, along with measures from the 2013 bill introduced in Congress and other amendments.[8] There was no public dissent from the introduction of external voting, though legislators disagreed about whether migrants should only vote in presidential contests or also in legislative elections as well.[9] Ultimately the new law allowed migrants to vote only in presidential elections. The new law requires that external voting be first implemented in the country's 2019 election; decisions about the procedures to be used for migrants to vote were left to the TSE.[10]

A number of factors both propelled the movement towards adopting external voting and impeded the measure's final approval. Advocacy by migrant organizations was a persistent source of political pressure. Organizations of Guatemalan migrants consistently advocated for voting rights since the mid-2000s, with advocacy efforts taking a number of forms, including meeting with government officials and the TSE, lobbying Congress, filing court cases, and issuing public statements which received significant coverage in the Guatemalan press.

In 2004, representatives of Guatemalans living in the U.S., organized in the Coalition of Guatemalan Organizations Resident in the United States (Conguate), met with President Óscar Berger and several cabinet members during their visit to Washington to advocate for their interests, among which were voting rights. As a result, Berger pledged to promote reforms to the electoral law to allow Guatemalans abroad to vote (*Prensa Libre*, May 2, 2004). This echoed an earlier pledge by President Portillo in 2001, who told migrant leaders in Washington, D.C. that he would send to Congress a bill to incorporate voting abroad into the pending electoral reforms (Zapata 2003, 324).

Migrant groups also publically advocated for voting rights – for instance, requesting in 2004 to participate in the next general elections (to be held in 2007) (*Prensa Libre*, Dec. 4, 2004). In early 2005, an organization of Guatemalans living in the U.S. sent a petition with the signatures of 2,000 Guatemalan migrants to Congress, the executive branch, and the TSE urging that migrants be allowed to vote and have their own representative in Congress. The proposal was supported by 28 migrant organizations, and migrant leaders threatened to file a lawsuit challenging the 2007 elections as unconstitutional if Guatemalans abroad were denied the vote (*Prensa Libre*, Feb. 18, 2005). The response to this proposal from some party leaders was tepid, but the chair of the electoral committee in Congress pledged to consider the proposal for inclusion in "second generation" electoral reforms. At least one TSE magistrate also offered some support for the measure after meeting with a migrant organization in Los Angeles (*Prensa Libre*, Feb. 19, 2005).

In subsequent years advocates turned to the courts and public opinion. In 2013, migrant leaders met with a judge on the Constitutional Court to discuss voting abroad, in anticipation of the Court reviewing a bill reforming the electoral law (*Prensa Libre*, Nov. 6, 2013). In 2015, citizen groups (both domestic and abroad) turned to public advertisements urging reform to make voting abroad a reality (*Emisoras Unidas*, Jan. 22, 2015). Meanwhile, leaders of the Association of Guatemalans Abroad met with magistrates of the TSE and leaders in Congress in 2015 to lobby for the reform, and threatened to file suit in the Inter-American Court of Human Rights for Guatemala's failure to provide voting for citizens abroad (*El Periódico*, Feb 4, 2015; *Emisoras Unidas*, Feb. 3, 2015). The same year, another migrant organization held a mock election in the United States in which over 66,000 Guatemalans reportedly participated by casting symbolic ballots for Guatemala's presidential election (*El Periódico*, Feb. 28, 2017).

The political clout of migrant organizations was bolstered by the importance of economic remittances to the country's economy. Remittances increased from $810 million in 2000 to $5.4 billion in 2013, or approximately 10% of the country's gross domestic product (Cohn, Gonzalez-Barrera, and Cuddington 2013). In their public statements, migrant leaders often invoked the issue of remittances when urging the adoption of external voting (*La Hora*, Feb. 3, 2015; *El Periódico*, Feb. 4, 2015). The issue is not lost on lawmakers: most of the bills in Congress seeking to implement voting abroad specifically mention remittances in their exposition of motives, and legislators frequently mentioned remittances in public statements and in Congressional floor debate.

The examples of other countries that have adopted external voting also played a role. As early as 1985, one constituent assembly member hoped that Guatemala would emulate the U.S. by adopting voting abroad. Likewise, the preamble to one bill introduced in Congress in 2012 noted that 115 countries "permit voting by their citizens residing abroad, such that by approving this law, our country would join the majority of democratic and modern states of the world."[11] Rulings by the Constitutional Court have also referred to the experiences of other countries in implementing external voting. There was little direct pressure from the international community to adopt external voting, however. International election observers were less insistent on recommending external voting for Guatemala than they were in the case of El Salvador. Of ten major international election observer missions from 1995 through 2015 for which reports are available, only two included the adoption of external voting as a recommendation for electoral reform.[12] Voting from abroad was also not among the recommendations for reform from domestic election observation groups.

Domestically, all major political actors expressed general support for external voting. There was a marked change of rhetoric over time, as explicit public opposition to voting rights for migrants disappeared. No major political actor in recent years has claimed that migrants should not vote because they are not sufficiently familiar with what is happening in the country. The external voting provision in the 2016 law was approved in Congress by a vote of 123–6, and the floor debate on the article included no opposition to the notion of migrants voting from abroad. Prior to the vote, Congressman Jean Paul Briere (a member of the electoral committee in Congress) likewise noted in an interview that no political parties in Congress opposed external voting (CB24 2015).

Yet while political parties publically expressed support for final approval of amendments to the electoral law in 2014 (*Prensa Libre*, July 12, 2014), the two largest parties in Congress, Partido Patriota and Líder, suggested that the reforms would "require more analysis" (*Prensa Libre*, July 15, 2014). As the electoral law reforms stalled, the 2015 election approached – which provided further justification for delaying the implementation of voting abroad. In February 2015 the chair of the migration committee in Congress stated that it would not be possible to prepare the logistics of external voting in time for the September election, and that funds had not been allocated for voting abroad in the year's budget. Another common justification for delaying implementation of the measure was the fact that most Guatemalans abroad lacked a national identity card needed to register and vote (*Emisoras Unidas*, Feb. 10, 2015).

These factors – the economic costs and the difficult logistics of implementation – were important impediments to final approval of external voting. The identification issue is particularly challenging given the fact that many Guatemalans abroad are undocumented. The economic costs of implementing external voting is another obstacle, and shows a potential limit to its diffusion: while the examples of other countries have played some role in pushing the measure forward, the experiences of neighbouring countries like Honduras and Mexico have shown disappointing results, perhaps showing Guatemalan officials that the meager turnout of migrant voters is not worth the cost.

Procedural and institutional factors also delayed reform. Amendments to the electoral law require a supermajority vote in Congress, necessitating significant consensus building. More importantly, voting abroad was often tied up with contentious election reforms such as campaign finance oversight and party list quotas. As legislators considered all of these reforms together, external voting was repeatedly postponed.

Discussion

Like many other countries, El Salvador and Guatemala considered adopting external voting in the 1990s and 2000s. The factors identified in previous research partly explain the passage of reform in the two countries. In both cases, emigrant lobbying put the issue of voting abroad on the political agenda, and in both cases migrant activists emphasized economic remittances as a justification for external voting. Yet emigrant advocacy was not sufficient to ensure passage of reform, even when remittances from migrants were essential to the home economy. Indeed, migrants lobbied for many years before external voting was adopted.

The diffusion of an international norm and emulation of other countries that have implemented voting abroad also played some role. International diffusion has sometimes taken the form of explicit recommendations from international election observers to implement voting abroad – although this was more the case in El Salvador than in Guatemala, illustrating how this international norm has played out differently in the two contexts. Also in El Salvador, officials met with their counterparts from other Latin American countries to discuss their experiences with voting abroad, and the United Nations Development Program drew on the experiences of other Latin American countries in recommending an implementation strategy for voting abroad.

In both cases, the normative debate over external voting receded over time. As one paper on external voting observes, "[f]or many, it will be unacceptable for a population no longer residing in the country to have such influence when they do not have to live with the results of the election on a daily basis" (Erben, Goldsmith, and Shujaat 2012, 2). Yet in El Salvador and Guatemala such sentiments are no longer voiced often by political elites. While this change in discourse may reflect normative change, it may also reflect partisan calculations. As Lafleur (2011, 487) observes in the case of Mexico, once external voting was on the agenda no political party was willing to openly oppose it, lest they face the wrath of newly enfranchised migrants if the measure were approved. This dynamic may help explain the nearly universal rhetorical support for external voting rights among political parties in El Salvador and Guatemala leading up to its final legislative approval.

Nevertheless, these Central American cases also show that partisan interests do not always drive the adoption of external voting. The literature suggests that governing parties expecting to benefit from external voting, and leftist parties in general, are likely to adopt voting abroad. The El Salvador case is consistent with this, as external voting was passed only after the presidency was won by the leftist FMLN, which enjoyed substantial support from Salvadorans living abroad. But in Guatemala, where political parties are weak and ephemeral, partisan interests were less relevant. While many Guatemalans fled violence during the country's period of right-wing military rule, since the late 1980s no party has been a clear successor of the military regime, and leftist parties hoping to win support from expats abroad have been much too weak domestically to pass legislation. Lacking clearly identifiable social bases, hardly any parties seemed poised to benefit or be disadvantaged by the extension of voting rights to Guatemalan migrants.

Finally, despite widespread support for extending voting rights to expatriates, reform was delayed by crowded electoral reform agendas and a lack of (or unwillingness to devote) resources to implement external voting. In both cases, lawmakers and administrators focused on other pressing concerns before approving external voting. Both El Salvador and Guatemala have histories of election fraud, and as they transitioned to democracy they faced daunting challenges in constructing capable electoral management bodies and secure and accessible voting procedures. Policymakers thus prioritized reforms that would institutionalize fair elections that would enjoy domestic legitimacy, at the expense of delaying the enfranchisement of citizens abroad. Both countries introduced new national identity cards, modernized their voter registries, and carried out costly decentralization of polling places throughout their national territories (Pallister 2017). They also debated contentious reforms related to campaign financing, gender quotas, and other issues.

The effect was to crowd out external voting, which as a costly policy requiring substantial technical capacity on the part of state agencies was considered a second-order priority to be put off to the future when other features of the electoral system were consolidated. This suggests that rather than democratization providing a window of opportunity for the enfranchisement of migrants, as has been suggested (e.g. Palop-García and Pedroza 2019, 405–406), the electoral reforms that countries undergo during prolonged transitions can actually delay external voting by crowding out the issue from the policy agenda.

Conclusion

This article has traced the process of external voting adoption El Salvador and Guatemala. In both cases, emigrant lobbying put the issue on the agenda during and after periods of democratic transition. These efforts were bolstered by a changing international normative environment that was reflected in domestic actors' discourse. Partisan interests were only relevant in one case, suggesting that the influence of this factor is limited to countries with political parties that have clearly distinguishable constituencies in the electorate. Where such parties are lacking, the principal impediment to external voting is not concern about the partisan consequences, but the fiscal costs and administrative challenges that voting abroad entails and the priority given to other electoral reforms. As more countries accumulate experience with voting abroad and potentially face disappointment over low turnout levels and high costs, these considerations are likely to grow more pertinent in the years ahead, and will merit greater consideration by scholars of voting rights.

Notes

1. This number is based on a review of data from International IDEA (2018). I exclude countries that have approved legislation permitting voting from abroad but appear to have not yet taken steps to implement it, as well as countries that only allow a limited set of citizens abroad (such as government employees) to cast ballots.
2. I use the terms external voting, out-of-country voting, and voting from abroad interchangeably. I also use the terms emigrants, expatriates, diaspora, and nonresident citizens interchangeably to refer to citizens residing temporarily or permanently outside of their country of origin.
3. Voting rights for migrants, and even for refugees, are largely outside the scope of international law, with the exception of the 1990 Convention on the Protection of the Rights of All Migrant Workers and Members of Their Families.
4. See various estimates in EUEOM 2009a, 4; UNDP 2011, 32; and O'Reilly 2014.
5. As Keyssar (2009, 33) puts it in his work on suffrage in the U.S., in a context of tight partisan competition, if "any party or faction – out of conviction or political self-interest – actively promoted a broader franchise, its adversaries experienced pressure to capitulate."
6. The number of Guatemalans living outside of the country is uncertain; estimates typically put the figure between 1 and 2 million.
7. All material on the constituent assembly debates is from *Diario de las Sesiones de la Asamblea Nacional Constituyente*, No. 111 (August 8, 1985) and No. 112 (August 13, 1985), accessed by the author at the Congressional Library in Guatemala City.

8. The TSE bill did not include a provision for voting abroad, but its introductory letter expressed TSE support for external voting.
9. Conflicting amendments on this point were introduced in Congress in 2015 and during floor debate on the final bill in 2016. In April 2015, one bill was introduced apart from broader electoral reforms to institute external voting, and it would have allowed migrants to vote for Congressional as well as presidential elections. The bill was not referred to committee until February 2016, and never came out of committee.
10. For the 2019 presidential election, the TSE only implemented external voting in four cities in the U.S., where the majority of Guatemalan migrants reside.
11. Iniciativa 4490, introduced by deputy Jorge Adolfo de Jesus García Silva.
12. The reports come from six missions from the Organization of American States (OAS), two missions from the European Union, one mission from the National Democratic Institute, and one mission from the Carter Center. The recommendations for external voting came from the 2007 European Union mission and the 2015 OAS mission.

Disclosure statement

No potential conflict of interest was reported by the author.

References

Acción Ciudadana, Comisión Específica de Asuntos Electorales del Congreso de la República, and the State University of New York. 2005. "Base de Datos de Propuestas de Reformas a la Ley Electoral y de Partidos Políticos." CD-ROM.
Bekaj, Armend, and Lina Antara. 2018. *Political Participation of Refugees: Bridging the Gaps*. Stockholm, Sweden: International Institute for Democracy and Electoral Assistance.
Brand, Laurie. 2014. "The Stakes and Symbolism of Voting from Abroad." *Washington Post Monkey Cage*, June 5. http://www.washingtonpost.com/blogs/monkey-cage/wp/2014/06/05/the-stakes-and-symbolism-of-voting-from-abroad/.
Bravo, Vanessa. 2013. "Communicating External Voting Rights to Diaspora Communities: Challenges and Opportunities in the Cases of El Salvador and Costa Rica." *Revista Internacional de Relaciones Públicas* 3 (5): 5–26.
CB24. 2015. "Casi un Millón de Guatemaltecos en EE.UU. Podrían Votar en las Siguientes Elecciones." September 6. https://www.youtube.com/watch?v=KB9UY2ldplE.
COHA (Council on Hemispheric Affairs). 2013. "The 2014 Presidential Elections in El Salvador and the Transnational Electorate." http://www.coha.org/the-2014-presidential-elections-in-el-salvador-and-the-transnational-electorate/comment-page-1/.
Cohn, D'Vera, Ana Gonzalez-Barrera, and Danielle Cuddington. 2013. "Remittances to Latin America Recover—but Not to Mexico." *Pew Research Center*, November 15. http://www.pewhispanic.org/2013/11/14/2-remittance-trends/.
Corte de Constitucionalidad. 2014. "Expediente 5352-2013." July 11.
Ellis, Andrew. 2007. "The History and Politics of External Voting." In International IDEA, *Voting from Abroad: The International IDEA Handbook*. International Institute for Democracy and Electoral Assistance and the Federal Electoral Institute of Mexico.
Erben, Peter, Ben Goldsmith, and Aysha Shujaat. 2012. "Out-of-Country Voting: A Brief Overview." IFES White Paper, International Foundation for Electoral Systems.

Erlingsson, Hafthor, and John P. Tuman. 2017. "External Voting Rights in Latin America and the Caribbean: The Influence of Remittances, Globalization, and Partisan Control." *Latin American Policy* 8 (2): 295–312.

Escobar, Cristina. 2017. "Migration and Franchise Expansion in Latin America." GLOBALCIT Observatory / European University Institute.

EUEOM (European Union Election Observation Mission). 2009a. "El Salvador Legislative, Municipal and PARLACEN Elections – 2009, Preliminary Statement." San Salvador, 20 January.

EUEOM (European Union Election Observation Mission). 2009b. El Salvador Final Report, General Elections 2009.

Hutcheson, Derek S., and Jean-Thomas Arrighi. 2015. ""Keeping Pandora's (Ballot) box Half-Shut": a Comparative Inquiry Into the Institutional Limits of External Voting in EU Member States." *Democratization* 22 (5): 884–905.

Iaconangelo, David. 2014. "El Salvadorans Living Abroad Cast Historic Ballots." *Latin Times*, February 6. http://www.latintimes.com/el-salvador-presidential-elections-2014-el-salvadorans-us-cast-historic-vote-after-winning-right.

IFES (International Foundation for Electoral Systems). 2014. "Elections in El Salvador: 2014 Presidential Elections: Frequently Asked Questions." January 29.

International IDEA. 2018. "Voting from Abroad Database." https://www.idea.int/data-tools/data/voting-abroad.

ISD (Inciativa Social para la Democracia). 2012. "Propuesta para el Ejercicio del Sufragio en el Exterior.".

ISD (Inciativa Social para la Democracia). 2013. "Ejercicio del Sufragio de Salvadoreños en el Exterior." May 13. http://www.isd.org.sv/isd/index.php/noticias/489-ejercicio-del-sufragio-de-salvadorenos-en-el-exterior.

Keyssar, Alexander. 2009. *The Right to Vote: The Contested History of Democracy in The United States.* New York: Basic Books.

Lafleur, Jean-Michel. 2011. "Why Do States Enfranchise Citizens Abroad? Comparative Insights From Mexico, Italy, and Belgium." *Global Networks* 11 (4): 481–501.

Lafleur, Jean-Michel. 2013. *Transnational Politics and the State: The External Voting Rights of Diasporas.* New York: Routledge.

Lafleur, Jean-Michel. 2015. "The Enfranchisement of Citizens Abroad: Variations and Explanations." *Democratization* 22 (5): 840–860.

Landolt, Patricia. 2003. "El Transnacionalismo Político y el Derecho al Voto en el Exterior: El Salvador y sus Migrantes en Estados Unidos." In *Votar en la Distancia: La Extensión de los Derechos Políticos a Migrantes, Experiencias Comparadas*, edited by Leticia Calderón Chelius, 301–323. Mexico City: Instituto Mora.

Leal, David L., Lee Byung-Jae, and James A. McCann. 2012. "Transnational Absentee Voting in the 2006 Mexican Presidential Election: The Roots of Participation." *Electoral Studies* 31: 540–549.

Leblang, David. 2017. "Harnessing the Diaspora: Dual Citizenship, Migrant Return Remittances." *Comparative Political Studies* 50 (1): 75–101.

Martel, Juan José. 2010. *Fundamentos para la Modernización del Sistema Político Electoral Salvadoreño: Una Propuesta desde la Sociedad Civil.* San Salvador: Friedrich Ebert Stiftung.

Meyer, Mareen. 2009. "Presidential Elections in El Salvador: Expectations for Change and the Challenges Ahead." Washington Office on Latin America, March 12.

Misión de Expertos Electorales de la Unión Europea en El Salvador. 2012. "Elecciones Legislativas y Municipales, 11 de Marzo 2012.".

Moronta, Gloria. 2012. "Polémica por el Voto Exterior." *Transparencia Activa*, December 20. http://www.transparenciaactiva.gob.sv/polemica-por-el-voto-exterior/.

Moronta, Gloria. 2013a. "Insisten en la Pronta Aprobación del Voto en el Exterior." *Transparencia Activa*, January 16. http://www.transparenciaactiva.gob.sv/insisten-en-la-pronta-aprobacion-del-voto-en-el-exterior/.

Moronta, Gloria. 2013b. "Aprueban 40 Millones de Dólares para Elecciones de 2014." *Transparencia Activa*, March 21. http://www.transparenciaactiva.gob.sv/aprueban-40-millones-de-dolares-para-elecciones-de-2014/.

Navarro, Carlos. 2007. "El Voto en el Extranjero." In *Tratado de Derecho Electoral Comparado de América Latina*, edited by Dieter Nohlen, Daniel Zovatto, Jesús Orozco, and José Thompson, 224–252. Stockholm: FCE, Instituto Interamericano de Derechos Humanos, Universidad de Heidelberg, International IDEA, Tribunal Electoral del Poder Judicial de la Federación, Instituto Federal Electoral.

Navarro Fierro, Carlos, Isabel Morales, and Maria Gratschew. 2007. "External Voting: A Comparative Overview." In International IDEA, *Voting from Abroad: The International IDEA Handbook*. International Institute for Democracy and Electoral Assistance and the Federal Electoral Institute of Mexico.

NDI (National Democratic Institute). 2009. "El Salvador Election Bulletin." February 19.

OAS (Organization of American States). 2009. "Informe de la Misión de Observación Electoral, Elección de Presidente y Vicepresidente del 15 de Marzo de 2009 en la República de El Salvador." December 7.

O'Reilly, Andrew. 2014. "El Salvador Allows Citizens Living Abroad to Vote in Presidential Elections." *Fox News Latino*, January 25. http://latino.foxnews.com/latino/politics/2013/01/25/el-salvador-allows-citizens-living-abroad-to-vote-in-presidential-elections/.

Pallister, Kevin. 2017. *Election Administration and the Politics of Voter Access*. London and New York: Routledge.

Palop-García, Pau, and Luicy Pedroza. 2019. "Passed, Regulated, or Applied? The Different Stages of Emigrant Enfranchisement in Latin America and the Caribbean." *Democratization* 26 (3): 401–421.

"Reformas Electorales en 1997 por Diversas Instituciones, Volume 1." Document #Ley 547, Supreme Electoral Tribunal Documentation Center, Guatemala City.

Rhodes, Sybil, and Arus Harutyunyan. 2010. "Extending Citizenship to Emigrants: Democratic Contestation and a New Global Norm." *International Political Science Review* 31 (4): 470–493.

Ribera, Ricardo. 1997. "Aritmética y Política: Propuestas de Reforma del Sistema Electoral." *Estudios Centroamericanos*, no. 579-580 (Jan-Feb.).

TSE (Tribunal Supremo Electoral). 2014. "Memoria Especial: Elecciones 2014".

Turcu, Anca, and R. Urbatsch. 2015. "Diffusion of Diaspora Enfranchisement Norms: A Multinational Study." *Comparative Political Studies* 48 (4): 407–437.

UNDP (United Nations Development Program). 2011. "Voto desde el Exterior: Estudio Técnico de Factibilidad para la Implementación del Voto de los Salvadoreños y las Salvadoreñas Residentes en el Exterior para las Elecciones Presidenciales de 2014".

United Nations Population Fund. n.d. "Migration." http://www.unfpa.org/migration.

Vengroff, Richard. 2007. "Senegal: A Significant External Electorate." In International IDEA, *Voting from Abroad: The International IDEA Handbook*. International Institute for Democracy and Electoral Assistance and the Federal Electoral Institute of Mexico.

Villalta, Ramón, and Jorge Urbina. 2009. "Sistematización: El Proceso del Voto de los Salvadoreños en el Exterior. Salvadoreños en el Mundo, Iniciativa Social Para La Democracia, and Friedrich Ebert Stiftung. http://isd.org.sv/isddocs/participacion-ciudadana-transparencia-municipal/SISTEMATIZACIONVOTOENELEXTERIOR.pdf.

Zapata, Patricia. 2003. "El Voto en el Exterior de los Guatemaltecos: Reivindicación de los Migrantes y Promesa Presidencial." In *Votar en la Distancia: La Extensión de los Derechos Políticos a Migrantes, Experiencias Comparadas*, edited by Leticia Calderón Chelius, 324–344. Mexico City: Instituto Mora.

Inclusive voting practices: lessons for theory, praxis, and the future research agenda

Toby S. James ⓘ and Holly Ann Garnett ⓘ

ABSTRACT

Inclusive voting practices have been defined in this special issue to refer to policy instruments which can reduce turnout inequality between groups and mitigate other inequalities within the electoral process. This concluding article reflects on the lessons learnt from the empirical studies about (a) how citizens come to be excluded at the ballot box; (b) which electoral processes are effective at bringing about greater inclusion; (c) what the wider effects of inclusive voting practices are; and (d) why such policies instruments not undertaken by the state. It argues that there are major lessons for the theorizing of democracy, as well as policy and practice in elections worldwide.

The twentieth century ended with a sense of triumphalism about the apparent success of liberal democracy, with the political system heralded as "the end of history" (Fukuyama 1989). Elections are at the heart of this system and democracy promotion was an ingredient of foreign policy and a key focus of the international community (Carothers 2003; James 2020, 160–196). Decades later, concerns have been raised about whether democratic backsliding is underway, and a fourth wave of autocratization has taken place (Mechkova, Lührmann, and Lindberg 2017). Triggers for this have included the behaviour of politicians who have been encouraging polarization, socio-economic inequalities and transformations in digital communication (Levitsky and Ziblatt 2018; Moore 2018; Runciman 2018). These have been so severe that some have argued that we are witnessing the end of representative democracy – the system in which citizen involvement is limited to taking part *just* at periodic elections (Tormey 2015). Solutions for democratic renewal have been broad ranging and often involved broader socio-economic reform or rewiring of political communication infrastructures.

The importance of elections for securing democracy has, therefore, come under pressure. But while well-run, periodic elections do not guarantee democracy, a polity cannot be a democracy *without* elections. Many proposals to augment democracy or redress significant problems may have great cause, but they should not overlook fundamental problems in the electoral process itself.

This special issue has focused on one such problem that has remained unresolved, even at liberal democracy's zenith. Radical conceptual and policy rethinking may, therefore, be required. The problem is relatively simple. Elections are decided by who votes. Many people do not participate at an election. As the introduction to this special issue demonstrated, those who vote are not the same as those who do not. It follows that the results of many elections, the structure of many governments and coalitions, the policies that are passed by legislatures, and the individuals who sit in legislatures to represent the people are all likely to be affected by the turnout gap. New challenges to democracy such as the use of digital communications and the role of dark money in elections, will need to be addressed and considered as well; but the problem that we sketch out cannot be overlooked.

To return to the research questions set out in the introduction, this special issue considered the questions:

- What are the different causal pathways for causing exclusion at the ballot box? Who tends to be excluded or negatively affected by voting processes?
- Which electoral processes are effective at ensuring inclusion? Which are not? What proactive state action and regulation is required?
- Beyond introducing political equality, what are the wider effects of inclusive voting practices?
- Given their importance, when and why are such policies instruments not undertaken by the state?

The remainder of this concluding article returns to these questions. Firstly, it sketches out the different pathways to turnout exclusion and inequality that were identified in the empirical articles that formed this special issue. Exclusion and inequality come in many forms throughout all societies, stemming from many complex economic, cultural and political relationships. We are more narrowly focused here on how this can be present in the electoral process itself since this system is supposed to be characterized by political equality. Secondly, the article identifies examples of inclusive voting suggested by the contributions to this special issue. Thirdly, the article draws together the evidence about the effects of these voting practices. Fourthly, the article considers the lessons for why such voting practices, given their normative basis, are (or are not) adopted.

Pathways for exclusion

The introduction set out a strategic-relational framework to conceptualize the different factors that may lead to citizens not voted. This rests on a distinctive theory of the relationship between structure, agency and political change which has not previously been used to explain non-participation. It holds a number of advantages over existing accounts that tend to be limited to logics of calculus, borrowing from rational choice theory. A number of pathways for exclusion were postulated in the introduction which include the effects of electoral laws, the availability of financial resources, cultural practices, the strategic behaviour of actors, and informational resources. Subsequent articles show how these are indeed important pathways for exclusion with empirical analysis.

What have we learned?

There has never been much doubt that the *electoral laws and institutions* can be a pathway for exclusion, but the articles in this special issue provided new insights. The franchise defines who has the right to even participate in an election, and who does not. History shows many examples of states excluding citizens from elections altogether on the basis of gender, ethnicity or the absence of property ownership. This pathway of exclusion continues today; however, as Victoria Shineman demonstrated in her article on felon disenfranchisement, with four million American citizens denied the right to vote due to laws that restrict voting based on a criminal record. The USA is clearly not alone. One study found that 29 out of 66 jurisdictions surveyed worldwide had voting restrictions on prisoners who are convicted and serving a prison sentence (Penal Reform International 2016). But, as Shineman demonstrates, disenfranchisement can extend after their sentence is served, and even if mechanisms are in place that could re-instate their voting rights

The effects of other electoral laws and institutions were also revealed too with new research. Guntermann, Dassonneville and Miller drew attention to how the level of compulsion involved in voting could affect turnout. James and Clark showed that the requirement to present identification before being able to vote in English local election pilots led many to not be able to cast a ballot. For some, this was because they didn't have the correct form of identification on election day. Others, however, protested about the requirement to provide identification by not casting a ballot. Voter identification requirements are common in many polities, but the research provides new evidence that it provides a pathway to exclusion – especially in countries where a single identification requirement is not issued by the state.

The differential effects of voter identification requirements, alongside voter registration and ballot submission methods, were explored by Johnson and Powell. Using survey data, they revealed that voters with disabilities experience greater barriers in American elections.

Electoral rules may directly affect how elections are run, but they also require humans to implement them (also see James 2020). The *technical, managerial and financial resources* available to electoral officials matter too. The implementation of electoral rules can, therefore, be another pathway to exclusion. Anthony and Kimball showed how this can happen in their case study of the implementation of new voter identification requirements in Missouri. They showed that identification was unevenly requested by electoral officials in two elections. Voters, therefore, had uneven and unequal experiences. Meanwhile King showed how voter experiences at polling stations were uneven across the 2008, 2012, 2014, and 2016 US elections. Compared to white, Hispanic, and Asian voters, African American voters were most likely to report waiting more than 30 minutes or experiencing a problem with the voting machine or their voter registration.

The *strategic actions* of other actors are an exclusionary pathway laid bare by Schneider and Carroll. Electoral violence had plagued many elections worldwide (Höglund 2009; Hafner-Burton, Hyde, and Jablonski 2013; Birch and Muchlinski 2018). It involves, as Schneider and Carroll freshly define it, "purposeful or calculated" acts to " … to discourage or prevent an individual or group from participating, or to alter an election process or outcome". But what is particularly important is that it can be gendered in nature. Drawing from fieldwork in Uganda they provided examples of (predominantly male) youth gangs being paid to intimidate eligible and entitled voters. This obviously violates the principles of equality set out in the introduction in the gravest way.

Their research is significant in that it provides evidence of how *cultural practices* can become exclusionary. Electoral violence does not require explicit threats or acts of harassment. It is often the "unsaid" practices that can be exclusionary throughout the electoral cycle. Exclusionary cultural practices were also recorded by James and Clark who noted how "men shouting at women" was sometimes a feature of behaviour inside polling stations at English local elections. The reasons for King's finding that wait times and other problems are unevenly distributed by ethnicity would require further investigation, but if these differences are the result of uneven resource distribution then this suggests systematic racism in American election administration.

The role and importance of informational and educational resources, which was flagged as a potential pathway in the introduction, was less clear from the specific studies published here.

Inclusive voting practices

This special issue defined inclusive voting practices as *policy instruments which can reduce the voter turnout inequality between groups and mitigate other inequalities within the electoral process.* The introduction was clear that such policy instruments may have different effects in different contexts as actors respond to divergent meanings and culturally diverse settings. The articles do point to some broader generations about likely inclusive voting practices, however. These would seem to include the *enfranchisement of those citizen*s who are principally affected by public policy decisions within a policy. Shineman's study focused on disenfranchised felons, but many states also have franchise laws based on arbitrary historical factors rather than a rationale democratic theory. The voting rights of citizens who are barred from voting because they are "underage", living abroad on Election Day or not considered a citizen in legal terms (eg, because of nationality) should also be considered. The idea that people who are "principally affected" should have the right to vote is not new.

Compulsory voting would appear to be an inclusive voting practice based on the discussion provided by Dossenveille et al. More relaxed voter identification requirements, at least in polities where a single state issued form of national identification does not exist, would also appear to be important to avoid the unnecessary prevention of voting, based on the findings from James and Clark, and Anthony and Kimball, in this special issue.

Better *resourced electoral management bodies* would appear to be one take-away point from King's study, on the basis that differences in wait times may result from uneven investment. The study of voter ID in Missouri points to the need for better investment in *poll worker training*. Such training is not purely about improving knowledge of "facts" about the electoral process, but training about democratic values and behaviours.

Mechanisms for identifying electoral violence, which should prominently include gendered electoral violence is a further important lesson from Schneider and Carroll. The independent and external *observation of elections* has been the prominent, albeit imperfect, tool commonly used by the international community. Clearly this should continue, but the gendered nature of electoral irregularities that come from broader societal relations should be more explicitly noted.

The wider effects of inclusive voting practices

The introduction to this special issue set out the normative case for inclusive voting practices, which included anchoring it in democratic theory. A strategically selective environment in which individual or groups of citizens may be more or less likely to vote as a result of factors outside of their control required states to undertake interventionist policy instruments in order to bring about political equality in the electoral process. The crucial effect of an inclusive voting practice is, therefore, by definition, that it alleviates political inequality.

The studies show the wider effects of inclusive voting practices, however, which strengthens the case for their adoption. Victoria Shineman looked at the effects of restoring voting rights to previously disenfranchized citizens on political efficacy. King provided evidence that voter confidence could be negatively affected by the absence of inclusive and robust practices. Schneider and Carroll identify the nature of representation can be affected.

This is not an exhaustive summary of all possible inclusive voting practices, not least because the studies included in this volume are finite. The article authors will also have their own views about what policies should follow from their work, which may differ from ours. However, it is important that a leap is made from research to praxis if the ambition/work of this volume is to be realized.

Why are inclusive voting practices (not) adopted?

Explaining why political institutions change has been a common focus of enquiry within political science. Although it was slow to take off, there is now a wide body of work on why electoral systems (Dunleavy and Margetts 1995; Blais 2008; Renwick 2010) and even other electoral institutions, such as electoral administration (James 2012; Pallister 2017) change. The introduction to this special issue set out a strategic-relational approach in which different paths to change were more likely than others. This is a new approach which emphasizes that making changes will take place in a context more conducive for some outcomes than others.

For example, Pallister provides new evidence of the forces behind the adoption of inclusive voting practices that allow non-resident citizen to vote from abroad. This was based on cases of El Salvador and Guatemala. He finds that lobbying from an emigrant community was crucial for enfranchisement alongside the diffusion of international norms. Partisan calculations, the availability of resources and the policy agenda were also important factors. This research helps remind us that those looking to promote inclusive voting practices are involved in an active politics struggle where strategic agency is important. Skills, strategy and agency will shape whether inclusive voting practices are adopted.

Conclusion: conceptual and policy consequences, and a call to action

Democracies worldwide remain plagued by turnout gaps. There are highly uneven levels of participation which have profound consequences for policies and politics within each state. To address this and bring about the realization of democratic ideals states should identify differential levels of turnout and other forms of exclusion in the policy process and consider the reforms necessary to fix this. This has been the main argument of this special issue.

There are a number of conceptual and policy consequences of these ideas. Not least, evaluating whether a state is a democracy may need to include an assessment of whether the state takes proactive measures to rectify the consequences of the strategically selective environment on which actors find themselves. This means that it should be a feature of the concepts, datasets and reports from organizations such as VDEM and Freedom House that provide these assessments (Freedom House 2019; V-Dem 2019). The classification of constitutional systems had been a common focus of politics scientists and the electoral system in place has usually been used to decide into which category a country should be placed (Lijphart 1999; Gerring, Thacker, and Moreno 2005). Given that countries will vary according to whether they have repressive, laissez faire or interventionist procedures for promoting inclusive voting, it would make sense for this to be featured here too. There are also consequences for practice since whether inclusive voting practices are in place could be featured and normatively supported in reports by international electoral assistance agencies and overseas observers. It should feature in the "best practice tools" on electoral observation such as the Carter Center (2014)'s *Election Observations and Standards* manual. It should be featured in textbooks and undergraduate lectures that define what a democracy is and differentiate between electoral systems.

Each article in this special issue has brought forward research about what could be an inclusive voting practice, but much further research is needed. The context-specific nature of inclusive voting practices as a policy instrument means that cross-national studies are important, but regional, national and local contexts need to be explored in detail to see how interventions interact in different environments. Research needs to follow up on the introduction of such interventions to see what effects they have in the long term. Research also needs to have a broader geographical reach. It has hereto continued to be dominated by an analysis of American elections because of the strength of the US research community and the state-level variation in practice that provides some quasi-experimental conditions. But scholars should reach out further, not just to the established democracies of Western Europe and Australia, but the new and consolidating democracies and electoral autocracies of Asia, Africa and beyond. The move towards the use of biometrics in electoral registration and as a required form of voter identification, for example, may pose a major threat to inclusivity. Such innovations have been more widespread outside of Western Europe and North America (Cheeseman, Lynch, and Willis 2018). The research agenda on inclusive voting practices should, therefore, be global.

Disclosure statement

No potential conflict of interest was reported by the authors.

ORCID

Toby S. James ⓘ http://orcid.org/0000-0002-5826-5461
Holly Ann Garnett ⓘ http://orcid.org/0000-0002-2119-4399

References

Birch, Sarah, and David Muchlinski. 2018. "Electoral Violence Prevention: What Works?" *Democratization* 25 (3): 385–403. doi:10.1080/13510347.2017.1365841.
Blais, André. 2008. *To Keep or To Change First Past the Post? The Politics of Electoral Reform.* Oxford: Oxford University Press.
Carothers, Thomas. 2003. *Aiding Democracy Abroad.* Washington, DC: Brookings Institution Press.
Carter Center. 2014. *Election Observations and Standards: A Carter Centre Assessment Manual.* Atlanta: Carter Center.
Cheeseman, Nic, Gabrielle Lynch, and Justin Willis. 2018. "Digital Dilemmas: The Unintended Consequences of Election Technology." *Democratization*, 1–22.
Dunleavy, Patrick, and Helen Margetts. 1995. "Understanding the Dynamics of Electoral Reform." *International Political Science Review* 16 (1): 9–29. doi:10.1177/019251219501600102
Freedom House. 2019. *Freedom in the World 2019.* Washington, DC: Freedom House.
Fukuyama, Francis. 1989. "The End of History?" *The National Interest* 16: 3–18.
Gerring, John, Strom C. Thacker, and Carola Moreno. 2005. "Centripetal Democratic Governance: A Theory and Global Inquiry." *The American Political Science Review* 99 (4): 567–581. doi:10.1017/S0003055405051889
Hafner-Burton, Emilie M., Susan D. Hyde, and Ryan S. Jablonski. 2013. "When Do Governments Resort to Election Violence?" *British Journal of Political Science* 44 (1): 149–179. doi:10.1017/S0007123412000671
Höglund, Kristine. 2009. "Electoral Violence in Conflict-ridden Societies: Concepts, Causes, and Consequences." *Terrorism and Political Violence* 21 (3): 412–427. doi:10.1080/09546550902950290
James, Toby S. 2012. *Elite Statecraft and Election Administration: Bending the Rules of the Game.* Basingstoke: Palgrave Macmillan.
James, Toby S. 2020. *Comparative Electoral Management: Performance, Networks and Instruments.* New York: Routledge.
Levitsky, Steven, and Daniel Ziblatt. 2018. *How Democracies Die.* New York: Penguin.
Lijphart, Arend. 1999. *Patterns of Democracy.* London: Yale University Press.
Mechkova, Valeriya, Anna Lührmann, and Staffan I Lindberg. 2017. "How Much Democratic Backsliding?" *Journal of Democracy* 28 (4): 162–169. doi:10.1353/jod.2017.0075
Moore, Martin. 2018. *Democracy Hacked: How Technology Is Destabilising Global Politics.* Oneworld.
Pallister, Kevin. 2017. *Election Administration and the Politics of Voter Access.* Routledge.
Penal Reform International. 2016. *The Right of Prisoners to Vote: A Global Overview.* London: Penal Reform International.
Renwick, Alan. 2010. *The Politics of Electoral Reform: Changing the Rules of Democracy.* Cambridge: Cambridge University Press.
Runciman, David. 2018. *How Democracy Ends.* Basic Books.
Tormey, Simon. 2015. *The End of Representative Politics.* John Wiley & Sons.
V-Dem. 2019. *Democracy Facing Global Challenges: V-Dem Annual Democracy Report 2019.* Gothenburg: V-Dem.

Index

Note: **Bold** page numbers indicate tables, *italic* numbers indicate figures.

accessible voting practices: polling stations
  for disabled people 80, **88**, 88–89; *see also*
  disabilities, people with
Achakzai, Sitara, assassination of 68
administrative irregularities at polling locations
  80, 85–86, **86**
Africa, voter registration in 2
age of voters, voter turnout and 2–3
agency and structure relationship 7
Alvarez, R. Michael 127
Atkeson, Lonna Rae 82, 125
Avery, James M. 127

ballot secrecy 90
Bangladeshi-origin communities 91, **91**
Bardall, Gabrielle 64
Beetham, David 5, 10, 11
Berelson, Bernard 40
Birch, Sarah 62, 64
Blais, André 41
Bodet, Marc André 41
Bosia, Michael 71
Brady, Henry E. 140
Bullock III, Charles S. 81–82
bureaucratic hurdles for citizens 80, 86–88, **87**

Campbell, Angus 140
classical democratic theory 21
Cloward, R. A. 6
Coleman, Stephen 79
compulsory voting: alternative indicators of
  representation 41; analysis of data 43–45;
  arguments for re. inequality 39–40; data
  sources 43; equality under 42–43; high-income
  groups as better represented 46–49, *47, 48, 49*;
  high turnout, equality under 42–43, 54; high
  turnout, rich/poor gap with 52, **53**; hypotheses
  42, 43; ideological congruence 41, 43, 44, 46,
  47; as inclusive voting practice 179; income,
  voter turnout and 39–40; income inequalities in
  representation 41–42, 44–49, *47, 48, 49*; party

preferences 41, 43, 44, 46, *48*; quality of the vote
  43; as reducing inequalities in representation
  53–54; results of study 45–53, *47, 48, 49, 50,*
  51, 53; rich/poor gap in countries with *50,*
  50–52, **51**
confidence of voters: demographics and 127–128;
  early voting and 122; electoral irregularities
  and 118–119, 120–121, 124–127, **125, 126**;
  local, state and national 125–127; measures
  of 121; racial/ethnic groups 125, 127; trust in
  government, comparison with 120–121
Consolidated Appropriations Act of 2018 128
Converse, Philip E. 41
cultural context/practices: as exclusionary 8;
  strategic-relational framework 8; for voting,
  importance of 6–7; *see also* gendered electoral
  violence

Dahl, R. 5, 10, 11
deliberative theory 21
democracy: classical democratic theory 21;
  classification of countries as, inclusive voting
  practices and 181; concern over backsliding of
  176; defining 10; elections and 176; electoral
  irregularities and 118–119; external voting and
  transition to 162
demographics, voter confidence and 127–128
diaspora enfranchisement *see* migrant
  communities, enfranchisement of
disabilities, people with: administrative difficulties
  150–151, **151**; barriers for 138; control variables
  145–146; convenience voting measures 139,
  141–142, 149–150, **150**; data sources and
  measures 143–146; democracy and political
  participation by 137; dependent variables
  144–145; detachment from the political system
  141, 142; disability status 143–144; distance
  from the political system 141; Europe 139;
  expanding population of 138; future research
  153–154; hypotheses 140–142; intimidation
  at polls, perception of 151, 154; legislation